SCOTTISH TRUSTS
A DRAFTING GUIDE

AUSTRALIA
Law Book Co.
Sydney

CANADA and USA
Carswell
Toronto

HONG KONG
Sweet & Maxwell Asia

NEW ZEALAND
Brookers
Wellington

SINGAPORE and MALAYSIA
Sweet & Maxwell Asia
Singapore and Kuala Lumpur

SCOTTISH TRUSTS
A DRAFTING GUIDE

By

H. Reynold Galbraith
*Solicitor (Dual Qualified in Scotland and in
England & Wales), B.L. (Glasgow), MA (Kent),
SSC, Partner, Donaldson Alexander Russell &
Haddow, Solicitors, Glasgow.
Former Diploma Tutor in Wills, Trusts, Executries
and Tax at the University of Glasgow and Glasgow
Graduate School of Law*

THOMSON

™

W. GREEN

Published in 2006 by
W. Green & Son Ltd
21 Alva Street
Edinburgh EH2 4PS

www.wgreen.thomson.com

Typeset by LBJ Typesetting Ltd, Kingsclere
Printed and bound in Great Britain by
MPG Books, Bodmin, Cornwall.

No natural forests were destroyed to make this product;
only farmed timber was used and replanted

A CIP catalogue record for this book is available from
the British Library.

ISBN-10 0-414-01599-1
ISBN-13 978-0-414-01599-9

PREFACE

"Trust drafting is a professional skill. Trust drafting of deeds requires trust law, succession law, a considerable amount of tax law (and time and energy to keep up to date), some property law, and a dash of insolvency and family law)"[1]

This modest textbook attempts to provide help for the trust drafter engaged in drafting trust deeds in Scotland. There are a number of excellent works in England but there appears to be a dearth of books specifically devoted to trust drafting in Scotland. This text is therefore a diffident attempt to redress the balance of advantage, which our English counterparts have enjoyed for some years.

It is hoped that it will be of assistance particularly to solicitors and others who are involved with drafting trust deeds. It may be most useful to the practitioner who does not do much in the way of drafting trusts yet will also serve as a reminder for those with greater experience. It is appreciated that an involvement in the drafting of trust deeds is not the sole province of the legal profession in Scotland whether solicitor, paralegal or more rarely advocate, but extends to insurance companies, bank trustee departments and to the growing number of firms of financial advisors. The period in the run-up to finalisation of this book has seen a quite spectacular and often bizarre attempt by Her Majesty's Revenue and Customs ("HMRC") to "modernise" trust tax law. Some of this, at date of publication, may not have been passed. In spite of, or despite this, the section on tax treatment of trusts and the problem solving sections may also be of assistance to Chartered Accountants both in Scotland and in the rest of the UK.

It is also hoped this volume will be of use to students generally and particularly those on post qualifying diploma courses.

While it is not meant to be a textbook on trust law, it is nevertheless the most recent textbook on trusts and may therefore be of interest to the general reader for a ready short treatment of the law of trusts in Scotland.

It does not deal with NHS trusts or unit trust investment trusts. These have separate legislation. Similarly, it will not deal with such esoteric subjects as transcontinental trusts, sham trusts and the like.

In addition, it is hoped that the treatment of tax and trusts (which is a particular interest of the writer and sometimes threatens to engulf writings on trusts) has been dealt with in a simple and easily comprehensible manner.

The more astute reader will realise that some of the chapters follow courses which the author has had the privilege of writing for continuing professional development; indeed the genesis of the present volume stems from a course on trust drafting run for Central Law Training (Scotland) Limited who have been a source of support and encouragement to the author over the years.

Chapter One introduces trusts, their history and deals with preliminary matters such as capacity, domicile and terminology.

---

[1] James Kessler Q.C.; *Drafting Trusts and Will Drafting : A Modern Approach* (6th edn).

Chapter Two deals with alternatives to trusts. It may seem slightly incongruous or indeed inappropriate that a textbook on trust drafting should do so, but no apology is made for this, particularly having regard to the high professional costs sometimes involved in setting up and indeed running trusts. At a time when trusts and in particular trust tax law is facing cataclysmic changes, it would certainly do no harm to review possible alternatives.

Chapter Two also attempts to identify problem clients, how they can be helped, and which trust would be appropriate to them.

Chapter Three deals with different types of trusts and outlines their uses, together with the tax treatment of trusts and in particular inheritance tax, capital gains tax and income tax. Particulars are given of stamp duty since these may easily be involved in trust dispositions where, e.g., a trust may sell a half *pro indiviso* share in the matrimonial home to the surviving spouse. In this case, stamp duty could be a factor.

This aspect, i.e. tax treatment, is particularly fraught not least because of the matters which will be raised following on the introduction of the Her Majesty's Revenue and Customs' attempt to "align" tax treatment of trusts. It is a source of some worry that a view seems to come from Whitehall that trusts are exclusively for the super rich. The super rich will use trusts prepared by their clever lackeys, the lawyers, and other professional advisors to unjustly deprive the Revenue of tax. While this view has a certain validity it is extremely restrictive. Many families are well below this category and seek, legitimately, to pass on the benefit of the upsurge in value of, e.g., their house to the next generation.

It will be attempted to include the recent fairly extensive trust tax provisions of the Finance Act 2006; this has not been an easy task given that certain of the old regime of trust taxation still remains or is affected by transitional provisions. While there has been a plethora of comment following on the infamous "Budget 2006" proposals it remains to be seen how exactly these new provisions will work in practice in detail. It is clear that trusters and testators will shy away from, say, accumulation and maintenance trusts, but will they opt instead for a discretionary trust, a bereaved minor trust or a bare trust to provide for their under-age progeny?

Chapter Four deals with general principles regarding trust drafting and certain problems and pitfalls, which may arise including pre-owned assets trust.

Chapter Five attempts to set the scene for trust drafting of individual trusts by dealing with the powers and duties of trustees and the use of statutory and non-statutory provisions. The Charities and Trustee Investment (Scotland) Act 2005 will be reviewed particularly as regards its impact on the Trusts (Scotland) Act 1921.

Chapter Six deals with particular types of trust deed, problem solving and continues the provisions which were dealt with or introduced in Chapter Three. Drafts have been included to deal with particular problems. These are by no means exhaustive but suggestions are given where they may be adapted as appropriate. Further drafts have been provided in Appendix I.

Having set up the trust, Chapter Seven deals briefly with running the trust and provides certain types of draft minutes of meetings, deeds of assumption and so forth, including ending the trust with a discharge, **which should always be obtained.**

Although not strictly relevant, the question of post death planning or deeds of variation is considered at Chapter Eight. No apology is given for this strict lack of relevance since it is an extremely important and valuable tool for practitioners. The question of use of deeds of variation is considered in particular with a view to introducing discretionary and other trusts. The use of discretionary trusts to deal with the question of children of the deceased or others who are not fully *capax* is also addressed.

Chapter Nine draws certain trust threads together and also makes some predictions as to the future of trusts which are now the subject of ongoing reports by the Scottish Law Commission previously referred to.

CURRENT INTEREST

The writing of this text comes at a time when there is great controversy about trusts and in particular the modernisation of trusts tax by HMRC. It must have been difficult to imagine the public outcry over a subject, which is fairly arcane, and, to put it mildly, boring to the general public. *The Daily Mail* in a leading article "Brown's u-turn over tax on thrift," by Benedict Brogan,[2] referred to the stealth tax (inheritance tax); other tabloid newspapers took this up as well, one going to the extent of issuing its readers with a car sticker enjoining the government to abolish inheritance tax!

TRUST DRAFTING

The author is greatly indebted to James Kessler Q.C. both for his excellent textbook "*Drafting Trusts and Will Trusts,*" and for the online trusts discussion forum.

A WORD ABOUT STYLES

This is a matter which has caused much soul searching. Attempts to trace ownership of styles have largely failed. The author freely admits he has drawn on styles culled from textbooks, the Law Society Diploma materials in which he was involved on the periphery, his own firm's, and others. He is reminded of an anecdote told to him by one of his principals. This older solicitor recalled the days when solicitors went out of the office for their coffee to one of the many coffee houses in Glasgow and concerned the use of umbrellas. The older solicitor's view, which seemed to be common, was that if you contributed one umbrella at the start of the season to the favoured coffee house umbrella stand, you were entitled to take one from the stand when you

---

[2] June 8, 2006.

needed one. The author respectfully considers that he has contributed styles to the profession over the years at seminars and therefore feels that he is entitled. . . !

TERMINOLOGY

I shall attempt to use Scottish terminology. English and other readers will appreciate, e.g. that a truster is a settlor, a liferent trust is an interest in possession trust; a fiar is a remainderman and so on. I have been tempted to use the expression "appoint" or "powers of appoint-ment" meaning to transfer or give trustees authority to transfer, or select and transfer on the theory that it is a lost cause! However, I have preferred the more usual and Scottish meaning wherever possible. It is a source of concern that English terminology should be used in Scotland including by the Scottish Executive! Probably this trend has been hastened by the passing of "English" Finance Acts!!! I am reminded of a possibly apocryphal anecdote that children in the UK, when asked to say how they would summon the emergency services by telephone, indicated that they would dial "911" (the US emergency call number) rather than "999"!

It is also a matter of concern that the idea should give general credence to the fallacy that English and Scots Law and Practice as regards trusts are similar. This is a dangerous assumption and should be guarded against especially by those involved in trust drafting who do not have a background in Scots Law. It would seem from recent pronouncements of Her Majesty's Treasury that they take the view that the law and practice are similar.

On that topic, it was interesting to note that the Finance (No.2) Bill 2006 recently introduced proposed changes in the inheritance tax treat-ment of trusts to be considered in Committee. The provisions to "align" will trusts created major problems in relatively straightforward family wills (and even for the intestate estate). HMRC seemed anxious that existing flexible wills should no longer have the benefit of the spouse exemption; that new wills setting up liferent and fee trusts (residue on a life interest trust for the surviving spouse) with the fairly usual "power to advance" capital will not qualify for the spouse exemption; and the existing standard practice of combining a nil-rate band trust with a liferent trust of residue for the surviving spouse will result in tax charges on the nil-rate band trust being calculated by reference to the value of the residuary "estate".

Many existing family wills have been drafted to give the surviving spouse a liferent in residue, often with the fairly standard power to the trustees to transfer funds to other beneficiaries. There are a number of reasons why this was a relatively standard procedure, notably when the testator has been married more than once and has children from earlier marriages. All such wills have been drafted on the basis that the spouse exemption will be available on the testator's death. However, these should now be examined carefully because such a trust may **not satisfy the requirements** for an immediate post-death interest ("IPDI") and so spouse relief will not be available in the event of the testator dying without having altered his will. It is difficult to quantify the horror which drafters and those involved in trust advice felt when reading the proposals in the original Bill. The other view, which seemed to come across, was a misunderstanding by HMRC that trusts actually had validity outside tax planning. It would be naïve to suggest that this was not often the rationale for trusts. However, it ignored the vast range of uses to which trusts are routinely put. Some of these are dealt with at Chapters Two, Three and Six.

The lack of knowledge, which seemed to stem from ignorance of the age of consent in England and Wales, i.e. 18, and Scotland, i.e. 16,[3] beggars belief.

CIVIL PARTNERSHIP ACT

On the topic of terminology, with the passing of the Civil Partnership Act as amended by the Family Law (Scotland) Act 2006, it is necessary to deal with not only surviving spouses but also surviving civil partners. While this text will not go into the matter in full detail and with a view to avoiding cumbersome clauses, the expression "surviving spouse" will, unless the context so stipulates, mean either surviving spouse or civil partner. In certain cases it may be relevant to include "co-habitee".

I have been, and expect to be, criticised for the fragmented nature of the book and for including matters which do not at first glance seem relevant to the topic. It could and has been argued that matters such as post death planning and pre-owned assets tax should not necessarily find a place in a textbook on trust drafting. However, I accept and welcome this criticism. My defence is that I intend the text to be of assistance to practitioners; one of the problems facing practitioners is to be able to find articles or matters of interest quickly and this has been the rationale for inclusion. In addition, deeds of variation are a fruitful source of setting up trusts. As I explain, a claim for professional negligence may (and rightly) fall on a practitioner who fails to bring to the attention of a surviving spouse, executors, trustees or indeed the truster or testator the utility of a mini-discretionary trust as an IHT saving vehicle. It goes without saying that trust practitioners ignore at their peril the possible impact for clients of the pre-owned assets tax.

THANKS

I would like to take this opportunity to thank all my colleagues at Central Law Trading and on the Post Qualifying Diploma. In particular, I would like to thank Loudon Downs, Beth Hamilton, Elspeth Talbot and John Kerrigan for their support and assistance over the years. I would particularly like to thank John Kerrigan for, firstly, his excellent text on *"Drafting for Succession"* and, secondly, for being instrumental in rescuing my manuscript from what could have been oblivion!

I would also like to thank Lorna Harper, Rhona Cameron and Alastair Galbraith for their help in typing, proof reading the text and compiling tables.

---

[3] Age of Legal Capacity (Scotland) Act 1991.

All mistakes in the text and in the law, which it is attempted to be as at July 31, 2006, are mine.

Rennie Galbraith
Glasgow July 30, 2006.

TABLE OF CONTENTS

Preface vii

Abbreviations xvii

Table of Cases xix

Table of Statutes xxi

Chapters

1. Introduction and trusts generally
   1–01 Introduction 1
   1–02 Definitions 5
   1–03 Domicile 6
   1–04 A firm can act as trustee 7
   1–05 Beneficiaries 7
   1–06 Legal requirements 9
   1–07 Notarial execution 9
   1–08 Classification of trusts 10
   1–09 Constitution of trusts 11
   1–10 Setting up a trust 11
   1–11 Can an attorney set up a trust? 11

2. The use of trusts and their alternatives
   2–01 Introduction 13
   2–03 Outright gifts 16
   2–04 Payments to parents or guardians 16
   2–05 National Savings products 16
   2–06 Powers of attorney 17
   2–07 Nominees 17
   2–08 Insurance products 18
   2–09 Charities 18
   2–11 *Negotiorum gestor* 19

3. Types of trust and tax consequences
   3–01 Introduction 20
   3–03 Inheritance tax 21
   3–07 Capital gains tax 26
   3–08 Other changes to trust tax law 26
   3–09 Potentially exempt transfers 27
   3–10 Treatment of new trusts after March 22, 2006 28
   3–13 Common aspects of trust taxation 28
   3–65 A word about stamp duty 54
   3–66 Joint property 54

4. Trust drafting generally
   4–01 Introduction 59
   4–02 Negligence 60
   4–13 Avoiding claims of negligence 66
   4–20 Making deeds user friendly 69
   4–28 Aims of clients 72

4–29	Selection of trustees (14/28)	72
4–30	Restrictions	73
4–45	The auctor principle	78
4–46	The pre-owned assets tax	79
4–53	Flexibility	84
4–54	Spouses, civil partners, cohabitants and others?	85

5. Conditions and powers of trustees

5–01	Introduction	87
5–02	Trusts (Scotland) Act 1921	89
5–04	Trusts (Scotland) Act 1961	93
5–05	Trustee Investments Act 1961	93
5–06	The Trustee Act 2000	96
5–07	Policy statement	97
5–08	General powers	99
5–51	Additional powers	115
5–52	Format of trust deed	118

6. Particular types of trust deeds and problem solving

6–01	How do we choose which type of trust to utilise?	120
6–02	Discretionary trusts	121
6–26	Accumulation and maintenance trusts	133
6–61	Liferent trusts	144
6–95	Disablement trusts	156
6–99	Charitable trusts	158
6–104	Offshore trusts	161
6–105	Bare trusts	161
6–116	Pilot trusts	168

7. Trust administration

7–01	Running the trusts	171
7–02	Minutes of meetings	171

8. Current trends in post death planning or deeds of variation

8–01	Introduction	175
8–02	Variations and disclaimers generally	177
8–03	Variations and discharges/discharge/disclaimers contrasted	178
8–04	Inheritance tax	179
8–05	Capital gains tax	182
8–08	Other taxes	183
8–10	Suggested use of deeds of variations/discharges/discharge/disclaimers	183
8–16	Destinations	186
8–17	Gift with reservation	186
8–18	Charities	186
8–19	Revaluation relief for quoted shares	187
8–20	Discretionary trusts	187
8–21	Using variations to clarify wills and trusts	187
8–26	Miscellaneous	195
8–30	Other relevant statutory provisions	195

8–31	Alimentary liferents	196
8–32	Postponed vesting and contingent rights	196
8–33	Legal rights	196

9. The future and conclusion

9–01	Child trust fund	201
9–02	Charities & Trustees Investment (Scotland) Act 2005	202
9–04	What are the Scottish Law Commission doing about trusts?	203
9–05	The future—trusts being set by attorneys	205
9–06	Finally	206

Appendix I: Styles

A.1	Checklist/questionnaire	211
A.2	Letter of engagement	215
A.3	Deed of trust	218
A.4	Backletter	219
A.5	Deed of variation	220
A.6	Deed of variation incorporating discharge of destination	227
A.7	Style of disposition incorporating sale of one-half share of house by trustees to surviving spouse	231
A.8	Style of standard security over one-half pro-indiviso share by surviving spouse	235
A.9	Old fashioned trust disposition	236
A.10	Deed of assumption	239
A.11	Discharge by beneficiary	240
A.12	Discretionary trust	241
A.13	Deed of assumption and conveyance	246
A.14	Deed of assumption and conveyance incorporating Resignation	247

Bibliography	249
Useful Web Sites	250
INDEX	251
CD User License and Instructions	259

TABLE OF ABBREVIATIONS

The Journal of the Law Society of Scotland	The Journal
Inheritance Tax Act	IHTA
Taxation of Chargeable Gains Act	TCGA
Income and Corporation Taxes Act	ICTA
Potentially Exempt Transfers	PETs
Pre-owned Assets Tax	POT
Capital Gains Tax	CGT
Finance Act	FA
Inheritance Tax	IHT
The Law Society of Scotland	The Society
Nil Rate Band	NRB
Stamp Duty Land Tax	SDLT

TABLE OF CASES

Allan's Trustees v Lord Advocate; sub nom. Allan's Trustees v Inland Revenue Commissioners, 1971 S.C. (H.L.) 45; 1971 S.L.T. 62.. 1–04, 6–46

Allen v Revenue and Customs Commissioners [2005] S.T.C. (S.C.D.) 614; 8 I.T.L. Rep. 108.. 1–03

Blackwood v Robertson, 1984 S.L.T. (Sh. Ct.) 68..................... 4–09

Carey's Trustees v Rose, 1957 S.C. 252; 1957 S.L.T. 309.............. 4–41

Collie and Buyers, 1981 S.L.T. 191................................ 8–32

Douglas-Hamilton v Hamilton's Trustees; sub nom. Douglas-Hamilton v Duke of Northumberland, 1961 S.C. 205; 1961 S.L.T. 305........ 8–31

Dundee General Hospitals Board of Management v Bell's Trustees; sub nom. Dundee General Hospitals v Walker [1952] 1 All E.R. 896; 1952 S.C. (H.L.) 78... 1–03

Holmes v Bank of Scotland; sub nom. Davidson v Bank of Scotland, 2002 S.L.T. 544; 2002 S.C.L.R. 481.............................. 4–11

Hunter v Hanley, 1955 S.C. 200; 1955 S.L.T. 213.................... 4–02

Inland Revenue Commissioners v Clark's Trustee, 1939 S.C. 11; 1939 S.L.T. 2.. 1–05

Judge (Walden's Personal Representative) v Revenue and Customs Commissioners [2005] S.T.C. (S.C.D.) 863; [2005] W.T.L.R. 1311... 6–62

Lanthier v Philpos, unreported.................................... 4–02

MacArthur (Inspector of Taxes) v Greycoat Estates Mayfair Ltd [1996] S.T.C. 1; 67 T.C. 598... 4–24

McIver's Trustees v Inland Revenue Commissioners; sub nom. McIver v Inland Revenue Commissioners; McIver's Trustees v Lord Advocate [1973] S.T.C. 398; 1973 S.C. 189........................... 4–43

Mair v Wood, 1948 S.C. 83; 1948 S.L.T. 326........................ 4–09

Ross Harper & Murphy v Banks, 2000 S.C. 500; 2000 S.L.T. 699........ 4–09

Russell v Inland Revenue Commissioners [1988] 1 W.L.R. 834; [1988] 2 All E.R. 405; [1988] S.T.C. 195............................... 8–28

Sarris v Clark, 1995 S.L.T. 44; 1993 S.C.L.R. 927................... 4–45

Soutter's Executry v Inland Revenue Commissioners [2002] S.T.C. (S.C.D.) 385; [2002] W.T.L.R. 1207.............................. 8–12

T, Applicant, 2005 S.L.T. (Sh Ct) 97; 2005 G.W.D. 26–501........ 1–11, 9–05

White v Jones [1995] 2 A.C. 207; [1995] 2 W.L.R. 187................. 4–11

TABLE OF STATUTES

*[References in **bold** are to reproduced legislation.]*

1921   Trusts (Scotland) Act (11 &
     12 Geo. 5 c.58) ... 5–01–5–03,
               5–05, 9–02, 9–04
     s.4 .... **5–03**
     s.4(f) 1–05
     s.4A **5–03**
     s.4B **5–03**
     s.4C **5–03**
     s.21 1–09
1961   Trusts (Scotland) Act
     (c.57) 5–01, 5–02, 5–04,
            5–05, 8–27, 8–31, 8–32
     s.5 .... 4–37, 4–41, 4–43
1961   Trustee Investments Act (9
     & 10 Eliz. 2
     c.62) 5–01, 5–02, 5–05
     Pt III 5–05
     Pt IV 5–05
     s.6(1) 5–07
     Sch.1, Pt I 5–05
     Sch.1, Pt II 5–05
     Sch.15 5–05
1964   Succession (Scotland) Act
     (c.41) 1–07
     s.2 1–07
     s.9 1–07
     s.21A 1–06
     Sch.3 1–07
1966   Law Reform (Miscellaneous
     Provisions) (Scotland)
     Act (c.19)
     s.6 4–37
1983   Mental Health Act (c.20) 3–54
1984   Inheritance Tax Act (c.51) .. 4–48,
               6–26, 8–20
     Pt III c.II 3–06
     Pt III c.III 3–06
     s.3(3) 8–33
     s.3A 3–34
     s.14 8–08
     s.27 .... 6–08, 6–16
     s.49 3–42
     s.49A 3–42
     s.52(1) 3–36
     s.60 8–20
     s.62 .... 3–17, **3–43**, **3–63**
     s.65 4–43
     s.71 ..... 3–06, 3–30, **3–31**, 4–37,
             6–26, 6–26A, 6–28
     s.80 3–43
     s.83 8–20
     s.89 .... **3–52**, 3–55
     s.89(1) 3–54
     s.89(3) 3–54

1984   Inheritance Tax Act—*cont.*
     s.89(4) 3–06, 3–54
     s.93 8–30
     s.142 .... 3–17, 4–19, 8–01, 8–02,
         8–04, 8–06, 8–07, 8–12,
        8–19, 8–23, 8–25, 8–30, 8–33
     s.142(1) 4–51, 8–33
     s.142(2) 8–04, 8–33
     s.142(2A) 8–04
     s.142(5) 8–30
     s.142(6) 8–04
     s.144 .... **3–17**, 8–13, 8–22
     s.179 8–19
1986   Finance Act (c.41)
     s.103 .... 6–03, 8–12
1986   Financial Services Act (c.60)   5–05
1988   Income and Corporation
     Taxes Act (c.1) 4–47
     s.147A 3–39
     s.505 .... 6–08, 6–16, 8–08
     ss.660–662 .... 4–34, 8–08
     ss.660–694 4–31
     s.660A ... 4–46, 4–47, 4–50, 8–08
     s.660B 3–39
     s.663(4) 4–32
     ss.663–670 4–32
     s.670 4–32
     ss.671–682 4–33
     s.673 .... 4–33, 4–43
     s.674 4–33
     s.674A 4–33
     s.677 4–33
     s.678 4–33
     s.683 4–33
     s.686 .... 3–39, 6–62
     s.695(3) 8–31
     s.696(5) 8–31
     s.698 .... **8–24**
     s.698(1A) 8–31
     s.698(1B) 8–31
     s.698(2) 8–31
1991   Age of Legal Capacity
     (Scotland) Act (c.50) ... 1–03,
                  1–05
     s.2(2) 1–03
     s.3 1–03
     s.4 .... 1–03, 1–05
1992   Social Security
     Contributions and
     Benefits Act (c.4)
     s.64 3–54
     s.71 3–54

1992 Social Security Contributions
and Benefits (Northern
Ireland) Act (c.7)
s.64 3–54
1992 Taxation of Chargeable
Gains Act (c.12)
s.17 3–19
s.18 3–19
s.62 .... 4–19, 8–01, 8–02,
8–04–8–07, **8–23**, 8–25
s.62(6) ... 8–01, 8–04, 8–05, 8–33
s.62(6)(a) 8–23
s.62(7) 8–33
s.64 8–23
s.72 3–07
s.73 3–07
s.76(1) 8–30
s.77 8–07
s.86 8–07
s.87 8–07
s.165 .... 3–19, 3–37, 3–38
s.260 .... 3–06, 3–09, 3–19, 3–37
s.260(2)(a) 3–07, 3–46
s.260(2)(d) 3–07, 3–38
s.260(7) 3–06
s.286(3) 3–19
Sch.1 para.1 .... 3–55, **3–56**
Sch.1 para.2 3–20
1995 Requirements of Writing
(Scotland) Act (c.7) 1–06
s.1 1–09
s.1(2)(c) 1–06
s.2 1–09
s.3 1–06
s.4 1–06
2000 Financial Services and
Markets Act (c.8) 4–10
2000 Trustee Act (c.29) 1–01, 5–01,
5–06
s.1 5–06
s.4 5–06
s.4(3) 5–07
s.5 5–06
s.14 5–06
s.15 5–06
s.20 5–06
s.22 5–06

2003 Finance Act (c.14)
Sch.3 para.1 3–65
2004 Finance Act (c.12) 3–08
s.84 4–46
Sch.15 4–46
Sch.15 para.3 4–46
Sch.15 para.6 4–46
Sch.15 para.8 .... 4–46, 4–47
Sch.15 para.11(2) 4–50
Sch.15 para.13 4–52
Sch.15 para.21 4–46
2004 Civil Partnership Act (c.33) .. 3–04,
9–03
s.131 .... 4–53, **4–54**
2005 Income Tax (Trading and
Other Income) Act (c.5) .....
4–46
2006 Finance Act 2006 (c.25) ....
3–03–3–05,
9–03
s.156 .... **3–06**

Acts of the Scottish Parliament

2000 Adults with Incapacity
(Scotland) Act (asp 4) ... 2–06
s.1(2) 1–11
s.53 1–11
2005 Charities and Trustee
Investment (Scotland)
Act (asp 10) 1–01,
5–01–5–03, 5–05, 5–23, 5–35,
6–99, 6–101, 9–01
Pt 1 9–01
Pt 1 c.2 9–03
Pt 3 .... 9–01, 9–02
92(2) 5–05, 9–02
ss.92–94 9–02
ss.92–95 5–05
s.122 9–03
2006 Family Law (Scotland) Act
(asp 2) 3–04, 3–06, 3–68
s.3 4–54
s.25 4–54
s.29 4–54

Chapter One

INTRODUCTION AND TRUSTS GENERALLY

In Scots law, a trust is created when property is vested in a person or body (the trustees) who hold the titles to the property but hold it for the use or the benefit of others, known as the beneficiaries. A person who gives property to another on trust is termed a truster.[1]

INTRODUCTION

The origins of trusts in Scotland go back many hundreds of years. The **1–01** Institutional Writers refer to them. Throughout their history and particularly in the last three centuries they have shown a propensity or propensities for flexibility and resilience combined with a certain stubbornness. These propensities have manifested themselves in dealing with and solving problems.

The modern genesis of the trust stems from medieval times. It was utilised by a landowner who went off to the Crusades. Due to the vagaries of feudal conveyancing and the inability of female and under age relatives to hold, contract and deal with property, the landowner would appoint someone as a "trustee" to hold his land and property when he went to war.

In more recent times it was traditionally utilised as a protection for the property of an *incapax*, those with problems of addiction or for charities, as well as dealing with the relationships of married couples, pensions, unit trusts and the keeping together or conservation of family wealth. In the previous two centuries *mortis causa* trust deeds were utilised almost exclusively for the bulk of wills. Indeed, most were titled "Trust Disposition and Settlements." This was helped greatly by the introduction of estate duty, the precursor of inheritance tax ("IHT"). The husband would leave his estate to his wife in liferent and to his children in fee. This was extremely common in those days. However, in recent times this type of trust has not proved quite so popular, in particular since the introduction of capital transfer tax, now known as IHT which generally requires the aggregation of the liferented funds with the deceased's liferentor's estate for IHT purposes. This aspect of modern tax and trust development will be considered in more detail later on.

In more recent times, trusts have been used for securing and retaining tax advantages. Recent legislation has tended to progressively erode this, which has in turn led to quite spectacular developments to overcome and

---

[1] In England and Wales and in tax legislation also known as a settlor. Jones and Mackintosh, *Revenue Law in Scotland.*

counteract central government's attempts to clamp down. Indeed, the government in some respects has refused to "play this game". The most striking example of this is the introduction of pre-owned assets tax legislation, which outlaws a broad range of certain activities and then gives exceptions. Recent changes to trust tax law have continued this trend with a vengeance!

The flexibility of trusts can be seen not only in their use for private trusts with which this volume will be concerned, but also in their uses for investment vehicles (i.e. investment trusts). Major hospitals are administered as trusts as are many of our charities. Although fenced in with national health legislation the basic vehicle of the trust is retained.

Glasgow City Council recently announced its intention to transfer its "cultural" functions into a special charitable trust[2] to be formed.

The life insurance industry routinely uses trusts in conjunction with life insurance products. The trusts written by life insurance companies in the UK alone each year will run into many thousands.

Trusts can often crop where least expected. "Stroke of the pen trusts"[3] are considered by some commentators as "trusts which are not established in traditional deeds of trust and are often inserted to protect individuals from the effect of insolvency. These may appear in, for example, deeds of conditions regulating housing developments where property agents hold funds on trust for residents, commercial contracts or trust clauses in dispositions."[4]

Paradoxically, the Government has recognised the value of trusts. They have recently[5] introduced a childrens' trust, namely "The Child Trust Fund". This is a savings and investment account for children. Children born on or after September 1, 2002 are eligible if child benefit has been awarded for them and they live in the UK. The Government will make a payment[6] to the parents, which is to be invested in a trust for the child. Thereafter the initial balance can be added to by parents, relatives and others and the sums accrued or invested will be held in trust for the child reaching the age of 18!

In or around 1981 some of the staff in the Keeper of Her Majesty's Registers Office took part in industrial action. The result of this was that it became difficult if not impossible to record deeds in, inter alia, the Register of Sasines. Potentially, the conveyancing aspects of this were disastrous. The original seller would continue to be infeft and his title could be undermined before the purchaser's title could be registered or recorded.

At this time of crisis, the legal profession turned again to trusts and it became standard practice for the infeft seller to grant a deed of trust in which he narrated that he was heritably vest in the subjects, giving details of his recorded title. He then narrated that he had sold the subjects to the purchaser, but because of industrial action it was not possible for this to be recorded. He therefore confirmed and declared that in so far as he

---

[2] *Glasgow Herald*, Saturday, September 9, 2006.
[3] *Investing in the Future*, Alan W. Eccles, S.L.T. 2006, 5, 23–27.
[4] Alan W Eccles, S.L.T. 2006, 5.
[5] *Glasgow Herald*, January 15, 2005.
[6] Presently £200.00.

remained infeft in the said subjects, he did so in trust only for the said purchaser.

This deed was placed with the title deeds until the matter could be resolved and the deed recorded in the usual manner.

This was an excellent example of the flexibility of trusts, and indeed its successor has found its way into modern conveyancing, and of course missives now provide for the inclusion therein and dispositions routinely contain a clause such as, "and I hereby confirm and declare that in so much as I remain infeft in the subjects hereby disponed, despite the delivery of this Disposition, I hold the same in trust for the purchaser and his successors and subject to their directions until registration of the subjects in the Land Register of Scotland is effected without exclusion of indemnity".

It is fair to say, however, that in Scotland the use of trusts has lagged well behind the use made by our English and Welsh counterparts. The reasons for this stem partly from our reluctance to use discretionary trusts. In England, trusts are used much more generally. Indeed, their system of conveyancing utilises trusts and thus English drafters are more comfortable with the concept and use. There are other reasons why this should be the case but at the root of it is probably our lack of familiarity.

In recent years, trust drafters in Scotland have lagged well beyond those south of the border. As stated, one reason for this may be the historical reason and stems from the fact that the trusts form a fundamental vehicle which is used by English and Welsh conveyancers. Until recently this was not the case with Scottish conveyancing but lately there has been controversy over the use of trust clauses in disposition. A recent article in the *Journal of The Law Society of Scotland* ("The Journal") June 1, 2004, p.12, deals with this and with the case of *Burnett's Trustees v Grainger* 2004 S.L.T. 513.

It is also generally acknowledged that trust law in Scotland has failed abysmally to keep pace with the modern way of life, investment and even the way shares are held. This can cause real problems with, e.g. arranging to hold shares in the name of nominees or under the crest system.

The present Government has been aware of this for over a decade and requested the Scottish Law Commission to carry out a review of trusts. Trustees' powers to invest were reviewed in the report "Trustees' Powers and Duties"[7]; The English Law Commission also carried out their own review and one of the results of this was the Trustee Act 2000. This will be looked at later on as a possible "blueprint" for Scotland but broadly it increases powers of investment for trustees in England and Wales quite spectacularly. The first result in Scotland has been the Charities and Trustee Investment (Scotland) Act 2005, which is helpful and will be considered in more detail later on. It does not go quite as far as the Trustee Act in England and Wales but, of course, its main thrust is as regards charities. Further trust discussion papers are to follow.

As mentioned earlier, trusts in Scotland developed in a different way from those in England. In England and Wales, therefore, trusts developed from certain peculiarities in the English system of land

---

[7] Issued jointly with the (English) Law Commission 1999. Scot. Law Com. 172.

tenure. Most commentators agree that the concept of trust in Scotland owes much to the influence of English trust law although the concept of trust or a similar concept to it is to be found in Roman law.

The influence of English law and practice of trust is still extremely prevalent today and certainly at a more than superficial level. The reasons for this do not reflect well on the Scottish legal profession, those responsible for teaching the profession or those responsible for Scottish legislation. English terminology abounds and, as a result principally of English legislation which refers to "settlors" rather than "trusters", and trusts with interest in possession rather than liferent trusts, the vast bank and array of taxation law tends to use English terminology. Indeed, the trust law relating to charities is almost a complete transplant of English law to the law of charities in Scotland and thus will form a monument to the stupidity and ignorance of Scots law and powers for the Scottish Parliament.

There also appears to be a reluctance to teach trust law at University level. In Scotland, this is verging on a national disgrace. Law graduates and those emerging from the diploma will be lucky to have more than a basic grounding in trusts. Those emerging (successfully) from the diploma will have almost no chance of drafting even a simple trust deed although excellent styles are given in the materials. In Scotland only a handful of practitioners are comfortable with trusts. As stated above, it was not always thus, and in the not so distant past liferent trusts were very common.

There are many constraints, economic and otherwise, on universities and those also engaged in the teaching of legal practitioners, but it seems bizarre that in many cases parties involved in trusts will probably go as their first port of call to a chartered accountant or other professional rather than a solicitor! One of the main rationales for this book is to assist practitioners in these matters.

In addition, it is also fair to say that trust legislation in Scotland has failed to keep up with the speed of modern commercial and social practices.

It should be noted that trusts in Scotland have a different position in law from their English counterparts. A trust generally arises where a property is transferred by one person, the truster, to another, the trustees, to be held for the benefit of the truster or some third party known as the beneficiaries. The property transferred becomes the trustees' absolute property **subject to the conditions of the trust and his or her fiduciary duty**. There are of course many types of trusts. The fiduciary solution appears not only in trusts but also in partnerships, curatories, guardianships, executries and bankruptcy as well as in public trusts where the purposes are charitable works or educational pursuits.

In England and Wales, a truster or settlor creates a trust by transferring assets to the trustees to hold on terms for persons either specified by names or otherwise who are known as the beneficiaries. The trustees are treated as a distinct legal entity from the beneficiaries and the truster, apart from bare trusts or where specific anti-avoidance legislation comes into play.

Academics have great fun with definitions, but for the rest of us this can **1–02**
lead to madness. An holistic approach will be taken to these, that is to
say, concentrating on the uses and features; thus a trust is the legal
relationship created *inter vivos* or on death by a person, the truster, when
assets have been placed under the control of a trustee or trustees for the
benefit of a beneficiary or for a specified purpose. This definition may be
useful but it is not comprehensive. It identifies the persons involved in
the trust, the truster, the trustee and the beneficiary. However, this
identification is not enough in itself, since without further particulars or
further matters a trust is not properly constituted. The truster requires to
alienate or deliver property to constitute the assets of the trust. Most
definitions of trust will focus on these three different concepts.

While we take trusts, to a certain extent, for granted they are alien to
other jurisdictions. Mainly for this reason the Hague Convention specifically dealt with trusts and provided a useful definition which was
enshrined in the Recognition of Trusts Act 1987 as follows:

> "For the purposes of this Convention, the term "trust" refers to the
> legal relationship created—inter vivos or on death—by a person, the
> *settlor* (author's emphasis), when assets have been placed under the
> control of a trustee for the benefit of a beneficiary or for a specified
> purpose.
> A trust has the following characteristics—
>
> (a) the assets constitute a separate fund and are not a part of the
>   trustee's own estate;
> (b) title to the trust assets stands in the name of the trustee or in
>   the name of another person on behalf of the trustee;
> (c) the trustee has the power and the duty, in respect of which he is
>   accountable, to manage, employ or dispose of the assets in
>   accordance with the terms of the trust and the special duties
>   imposed upon him by law.
>
> The reservation by the settlor of certain rights and powers, and the
> fact that the trustee may himself have rights as a beneficiary, are not
> necessarily inconsistent with the existence of a trust."

It should be noted that, for certain tax purposes, such as IHT, every time
new property, assets or funds are conveyed to the trust this may
represent a new "trust" for these tax purposes.

There are other types of relationships, which are similar to this such as
Negotiorum Gestor which is known to the law of Scotland, but generally
speaking, the foregoing relationship covers most of these three. It may,
of course, be the case that one or the other parties may occupy one or
more of these capacities. For example, a truster may also be a trustee or
indeed one of several trustees. He may also be the sole or one of the
class of beneficiaries. The other aspect of the trust as stated is the
conveyance of property and also the question of trust purposes. The
truster must stipulate the purpose of the trust, which may well include
terms upon which the beneficiaries will take any benefit. It would, of
course, be a logical absurdity for the truster to be exactly the same
person as the trustee and the beneficiary.

More recently there may be a classification for us to become familiar with, namely a trust which has "relevant property" and is subject to what might be described as the "discretionary trust" regime, and trusts which do not, such as trusts for the disabled.

DOMICILE

1–03 Domicile will not, generally speaking, be an issue with trusts whether as regards the truster, trustees or beneficiaries. However, it may be relevant in connection with a trust which is set up under a will. Most of those approaching solicitors with a view to making trust deeds or wills will in the past have been domiciled and resident in Scotland. However, we do live in an increasingly nomadic society, and questions of domicile have become more common. The full scope of this aspect of the law is outwith the range of this textbook but a question such as "where do you regard as your home?" will generally provide the complete clue as to domicile.

In a recent case, *Allen & Another v Revenue & Customs* [2005] (STC) (STD) 614, the matter came to light in the context of inheritance tax where vast quantities of tax can hinge on the matter. Broadly speaking, the deceased, a widow, was born in the UK and her childhood was spent there and in the US. She married and, with her husband, lived around the world in connection with his employment with an international company. They bought a house in Spain and lived there until the husband died. Regrettably, the widow by then had become very ill and was obliged to live with her half sister in the UK. Her house in Spain was kept ready for her return. She had in the meantime also bought a house in the UK, which was to be made available for her care. The revenue were unable to establish a UK domicile. The deceased, Mrs Johnson, had regarded the Spanish residence as her domicile of choice at the date of death.

The other essential aspect of a trust is that it forms a separate entity from the truster, the beneficiaries or indeed the trustees. Thus, first, the truster needs to alienate or deliver property (to constitute the assets of the trust) to trustees, and in order to do so he must have capacity. Accordingly an *incapax* cannot create a trust. In terms of the Age of Legal Capacity (Scotland) Act 1991, a person of the age of 12 years and over has testamentary capacity, and therefore can create a testamentary trust (s.2(2)). A person of 16 years and over can create an *inter vivos* trust but, if under the age of 18 years at the date of the transaction, can apply to the court (provided he does so before the age of 21 years) to have the transaction set aside as a prejudicial transaction being a transaction which an adult, exercising reasonable prudence, would not have entered into (s.3). A solicitor, if dealing with a client under 18 who wishes to set up *inter vivos* trust, must tread carefully. A firm can create a trust.

Secondly, dealing with the trustees; the trustee's duty is described as fiduciary. "A fiduciary duty is one which must be discharged with a good conscience and, regardless of personal interests and prejudices, for the benefit of another" per Lord Normand in *Board of Management for Dundee General Hospitals v Bell's Trustees* 1952 S.C. (HL) 78 at 88.

Anyone who has legal capacity to hold and deal with property may act as a trustee. Accordingly, an *incapax* cannot. Again, in terms of the Age of Legal Capacity (Scotland) Act 1991, a person of 16 years or over could act as trustee. Obviously, consideration would require to be given to the transactions into which a trustee between the ages of 16 and 18 years was entering. The reason for this is that such transactions could be set aside by a court on application by the trustee before attaining 21 years if these should be prejudicial transactions (one which an adult exercising reasonable prudence would not enter into in the circumstances existing at the time and which has caused, or is likely to cause the applicant substantial prejudice). It may be appropriate to have any such transactions ratified by the court in advance (s.4).

A FIRM CAN ACT AS TRUSTEE

An increasingly popular trustee in professional firms is the use of the **1–04** trustee company. The trustee company would probably be formed by the partners of the firm of solicitors advising the truster. All partners of the firm require to be directors of the company and only they can be such directors and secretary. The company holds assets nominally only and accordingly makes no profits and does not require to make any companies' returns. It has limited liability and yet to execute deeds etc. requires the signature of any two directors view partners of the firm. Once constituted, the nominee company tends to be used as trustee in several trusts and executries. Accordingly, a system requires to be developed to distinguish the assets held by the company in trust A from the assets held in trust B. We see "Account Designation" referred to on stock transfer forms which can be utilised for this purpose.

The truster can be a trustee but it is important that the alienation or delivery of the property constituting the assets of the trust is clearly recorded and demonstrated.

Often, as regards trusts set up particularly in wills, a truster or testator will wish a professional person such as a solicitor to act as one of the trustees. This will be beneficial to the truster in that he secures the services of someone who is familiar with his affairs. It may be beneficial to the solicitor in that the business of running the trust may be retained. However, with new regulations and so forth, there may be **quite justifiable** reluctance from professionals to act as trustees. Nevertheless, there may be instances where, e.g. the trustees are elderly and there is no one else. It is not advisable to set up any trust with the trusters appointing only themselves as trustees. To validly set up a trust there must be delivery and it will be apparent that proof of "delivery" between trusters and trustees who happen to be the same people would be difficult. Clients would therefore always be advised to appoint an additional trustee to themselves where they are the trusters of a trust. Lord Reid said in *Allan's Trustees v Inland Revenue*, 1971 S.L.T. 62: "I think that we can now accept the position as a reasonable development of the law, that a person can make himself a Trustee of his own property provided that he also does something equal to delivery or transfer of the Trust Fund."

BENEFICIARIES

A beneficiary can be a trustee but if he is a sole trustee and sole **1–05** beneficiary then the trust purposes are extinguished. It is inadvisable to include as trustees any beneficiaries from the class of beneficiaries in a discretionary trust. The resulting conflicts would prejudice the smooth running of the trust. However, this may be unavoidable in "mini-discretionary trusts" set up under wills where wife and children are represented as trustees.

From the tax point of view, the appointment of the truster or his spouse as trustee and, in the discretionary trust, the truster or trustee being included as a beneficiary might **well result in the income of the trust being regarded for tax purposes as the truster's own**. Similarly, if the trust assets include shareholdings in a family company, then the truster should again avoid acting as trustee.

Acceptance of the office of trustee is required to make the appointment of the trustee effective. Acceptance may, however, be expressed or implied. Similarly, declinature may be expressed or implied. Further trustees may be assumed.

Although *delectus personae* (the fact that the truster has chosen that particular person to be a trustee because of the faith he has in him and his specific qualities) and *delegatus non potest delegare* (those to whom power is delegated do not have power to delegate) apply in that trustees must perform duties personally and have individual responsibility for their actions as trustees, there is some laxity in interpretation. The decision of the majority of trustees prevails unless some or all trustees *sine qua non* (without whose agreement a decision cannot be carried— effectively a power of veto) and there may be a quorum set for decisions. The powers of the trust often include a power to appoint factors and law agents and to pay them suitable remuneration (Trusts (Scotland) Act 1921, s.4(f)). The selection of agents is usually up to the trustees' discretion.

Due to the fiduciary nature of their role trustees cannot be *auctor in rem suam* (an actor in his own cause) as this may allow a conflict to arise between personal interests and the interests of the trust. To act in their own interests when privy to the dealings of the trust could lead not only to a conflict of interest, but also deprive other parties of an equality of opportunity since the trustees are privy to knowledge of the trust. The trustee who acts as solicitor to the trust is not entitled to payment of anything other than outlays, nor can he employ his firm for remuneration **unless there is an express provision in the trust or the beneficiaries all agree** (beneficiaries not of full capacity!).

Any person can be a beneficiary. The beneficiary does not require to (and often will not) be capax. Beneficiaries can be as yet unborn, can belong to a prescribed class or can be required to be selected from a prescribed class. A witness to a trust deed can be a beneficiary though this should be avoided since it would appear to lay the deed open to challenge on the grounds of force or fear.

The beneficiary is entitled to take action against the trustees to ensure he benefits from the trust. This action could take the form of:

    a. a right by personal action, declarator or accounting to compel the trustees to administer the trust according to its terms;
    b. a right to interdict the trustees from breach of trust;
    c. a right to recover damages from the trustees for breach of trust;
    d. a right to petition the court to change the administration of the trust by replacing the trustees either with new trustees or with a Judicial Factor. *Inland Revenue v Clark's Trs* 1939 S.C. 11.

If the beneficiary has a vested right and then should die, the right would transfer according to the laws of succession.

It is possible for the beneficiaries to terminate the trust if all the interests in the trust have vested in the beneficiaries who are of full age and *sui juris* with the consent of all, although it must be noted that this cannot be done if any of the beneficiaries has an alimentary provision. Again, the Age of Legal Capacity (Scotland) Act 1991 would appear to give beneficiaries of 16 years and over full capacity, but the usual caveat regarding beneficiaries between 16 and 18 years being entitled to apply to the court before attaining 21 years to have the court aside the transaction as a prejudicial transaction applies. One method of clearing the path would be to apply for judicial ratification (s.4).

LEGAL REQUIREMENTS

There has never been a requirement for *inter vivos* trusts (in Scotland) to **1–06** be in writing. The absence of writing, however, always raises difficulties for probation. The Requirements of Writing (Scotland) Act 1995 reaffirms that *mortis causa* trusts must be in writing (s.1(2)(c)). This deals with wills executed after August 1, 1995. Wills must be attested under s.3. They must be signed by the grantor on every page (not necessarily at the foot but this is preferable). It must be attested by one witness who should sign on the last page. If the will is subscribed but not attested the Act has a specified procedure, which forms a new s.21A of the Succession (Scotland) Act 1964. In terms of that section a will which is not attested must be set up under procedure as laid out in s.4. This makes provision for application to be made to the court either by way of summary application or in the course of other proceedings, such as for confirmation, to conclude that a document was subscribed by the grantor of it. The court will endorse the will to the effect that it has been signed by the grantor.

NOTARIAL EXECUTION

The Requirements of Writing (Scotland) Act 1995 sets out the rules for **1–07** notarial execution in s.9 and in Sch.3. Notarial execution no longer needs to be witnessed but attestation will only be competent when one witness signs. The docquet is no longer necessary. A particular form of testing clause will deal with this. It should be noted that the grantor may dispense with the reading aloud of the deed. A new requirement relates to the interest of the notary. Formerly, if he stood to gain from the deed the whole deed was invalid; now only the part under which the notary would stand to gain is invalid. Notarial execution should proceed as follows:

1. The grantor, notary and witness convene.
2. A declaration is made that the grantor is blind or is unable to write.
3. The document is read aloud by the notary, unless the grantor says that he does not wish the notary to do so.

4. Authority is given by the grantor to the notary to subscribe.
5. The notary subscribes the document; for wills he must subscribe every page. In every case he must sign in the presence of the witness.
6. The witness, who must be present throughout, signs immediately after the notary.
7. The testing clause is added to contain a statement that the deed was read (or not) and the grantor gave authority for the notary to sign. The notary and the witness should be designed in the testing clause which should also include the date and place of signing.

As regards *inter vivos* trusts there is no requirement for it to be written unless the truster is the sole trustee. If it is written then it must be subscribed by the granter (s.2). Obviously, it is preferable that it be in writing.

Delivery of the trust assets is essential and hence it is preferable to have more than the truster as trustee in order to illustrate that the property has been alienated by the truster. The debate as to what constitutes delivery is a lengthy one but, reduced to its simplest terms, any formal recording of the title to the assets in the names of the trustees should prove sufficient.

The requirement for the trust to be irrevocable ties in with the delivery of the assets in that once these have been alienated by the truster he has no claim to have them returned as that would revoke the trust. Since we are, on the whole, considering the creation of a trust then it is important to express in the drafting that the trust is irrevocable.

CLASSIFICATION OF TRUSTS

1–08 There are many classifications of trusts. Some of these are considerably ancient. The first classification is between private and public trusts. The main difference is that the public trust is for the benefit of the general public or a section of the general public whereas the private one is for a specified person or class. Generally speaking it will be the private trust which we are considering here. It may of course be that a trust which has been set up for individuals may finally become public when this private grouping dies out or becomes no longer relevant and the funds go to public cause. There are certain differences, but in the main, these are beyond the scope of this text.

The next main category is trusts with an interest in possession and those without an interest in possession. Generally speaking, the former comprise discretionary trusts and the latter liferent and fee trusts, and so forth. The accumulation and maintenance trust would also fall under discretionary trusts. This is the main classification for our purposes.

Another distinction would be those trusts set up by *mortis causa* deed and those by *inter vivos* deed. While this type of distinction will be referred to, it need not concern us at this juncture. These distinctions, while important to the theoretician, will merely be noted but not dealt with in any sustained manner. The emphasis, if possible, will be on practical problems and the practical solution of these by trusts.

Perhaps the most significant classification of trusts in future will be whether they give rise to an immediate post-death interest, where tax concessions are available or not when they will fall into a regime broadly equivalent to a discretionary trust regime. These latter will be known as "relevant property trusts".

CONSTITUTION OF THE TRUST

The final matter, which should be considered at this juncture, is the **1–09** question of the constitution of the trust. This in itself could give rise to what Scobie in her text *The Scottish Law of Trusts* refers to as being voluntary or involuntary constitution of trusts. Generally though, voluntary trusts are constituted in writing by a person who has the necessary legal capacity; thus children under the age of 16 years or persons of unsound mind cannot create trusts. A person of 17 or 18 years of age may create a trust but subject always to the possibility of reduction. The trust deed will attain the definition of the trust and the purposes for it and may also provide for the transfer and conveyance of property by the truster to the trustees.

We are concerned principally here with those types of trusts which arise out of voluntary deeds in writing which are within the definition of the Trusts (Scotland) Act 1921, s.21. Under the Requirements of Writing (Scotland) Act 1995, s.1, a written document complying in all respects with s.2 of the Act is required for the constitution of a trust.

SETTING UP A TRUST

Trusts are generally set up by deed of trust. This can be by *inter vivos* **1–10** deed or by will. An extension of this is by deed of variation and an example of this is shown in the appendix and elsewhere.

CAN AN ATTORNEY SET UP A TRUST?

This is a difficult question although, on balance, it is suggested that an **1–11** attorney can. Obviously it is necessary for specific powers to be included in the power. In recent years, grantors of power of attorneys are including or attempting to include what can be regarded as tax planning powers, e.g. to make tax efficient gifts. Although these are being challenged by the HMRC, it is likely the trend will and should continue. The following style can be used, perhaps as an adjunct of the gifts section:

"I hereby authorise my Attorney to set up and form Deeds of trust . . ."

A case which is of interest in this connection is *T, Applicant* 2005 S.L.T. (Sh Ct) 97.[8] Here a son who held a power of attorney for his parent, a woman aged 81 who was suffering from dementia and lacked capacity for independent living, sought an intervention order under the

---

[8] There is an extremely helpful article on this by Alan Eccles and Lisa Miller at 2006 S.L.T. (News) 1.

Adults with Incapacity (Scotland) Act 2000, s.53 authorising his mother's solicitor to execute a codicil to her will benefiting the son. This will left the house to the son, and the residue of her estate to the widow of another son. T's mother had further specified that T should be her principal beneficiary. Although T now had power to sell his mother's home, which lay empty, the wording of the testamentary provision meant that the net proceeds of the sale would fall into the residue of the estate to the benefit of his sister-in-law. The application was referred to the Public Guardian who suggested that intervention would not benefit the applicant in terms of s.1(2) of the Act.

The court held, granting the order, that: (1) the court had to have clear information on which it could act, and sufficient information had been given about the stated intentions of T's mother to satisfy the court that she would remedy the problem in the manner proposed if it was within her power to do so; refusal of the order would result in denial of justice to T and also in a positive injustice. (2) The Office of the Public Guardian had placed an unduly restrictive meaning on the word "benefit"; although the intervention would not be to the direct benefit of T's mother, she had already authorised the selling of the house and potential investment of the proceeds in the power of attorney, and the money at least would be available to be used for her benefit in her remaining years whereas at present there were effectively no such assets. Leaving to one side any criticism of the existing, it does seem as if courts in the future will be able to authorise not only wills but also trusts.

The Sheriff commenting on the effect of the case stated:

> "It may be that this case has no effect other than under reference to its own particular circumstances, and as an illustration of the kind of thing which may be authorised under the provisions of s.53 of the Act and the terms of an intervention order. **However, there may well be a point of more general importance which arises, and that is whether the existence of the kind of power which the court has authorised in this case imposes a duty on practitioners to advise on the terms of testamentary provisions made by their clients, in circumstances where they learn that a client has lost capacity to order his or her affairs further, and if necessary, to seek the permission of the court to make alterations to those provisions in accordance with known intentions, and in order to ensure that they are carried out as far as possible. It is obvious that there will be cases where there is opposition to such a proposed step, and dispute as to an adult's previously stated intentions.** That has not happened here, and I am satisfied, for the reasons already stated, that the order sought should be granted in this case."

It is suggested that this dictum could apply to attorneys setting up trusts whether *inter vivos* or *mortis causa*.

Chapter Two

THE USES OF TRUSTS AND THEIR ALTERNATIVES

"Do not ignore the obvious in favour of the subtle."[1]

INTRODUCTION

Nowadays, even more so than in the past, alienation of ownership assets **2–01** while still utilising the same is of paramount importance to trusters. The control of property and the protection of it and tax planning are still the focus of most trusts.

It may seem unusual to consider alternatives to trusts in a textbook on trust drafting. However, given the high cost of setting up and running trusts, it is as well to consider these if only to ensure that there is not a much cheaper and just as efficient alternative. Often the cost, which may seem high to the lay client, may be more than "offset" by the potential savings. £114,000 (2006/2007) can be saved (or lost) if full use of the nil rate band is lost. As will be seen later, even if the utmost economy is exercised in setting up and running a trust there will nevertheless be, at time of writing, many hundreds of pounds involved in drafting the trust deed and carrying out the formalities of settling it with the Inland HMRC.[2] The annual tax returns, under the self-assessment regime, which potentially involve a SA 900[3] (12 pages). If there are capital gains then a further nine pages is added. These, coupled with the guide and calculation notes, add up to a formidable number of pages. The point, as will be seen later on with regard to changes in the law for tax for discretionary trusts, is that people are pushed into the hands of professional advisors; nowadays even more so than in the past.

In addition practitioners can, as with other specialists, become too single minded where they may see a problem and quickly identify a trust as the answer without really considering alternatives. The old adage of allowing the tax tail to wag the trust dog is all too familiar. It used to be the case that a solicitor in Scotland had a general and wide training and practice. This is no longer the case and we live in an era of "specialists". There are many advantages to this but one major setback is that we may miss an obvious solution.

For these and other reasons, a brief note has been inserted as a reminder that trusts are not the universal panacea to a client's problems.

---

[1] Advice to Mediaeval History Students.

[2] On April 18, 2005 the Inland Revenue and Her Majesty's Customs and Excise amalgamated to form "Her Majesty's Revenue and Customs" ("HMRC"). The expression HMRC will be used throughout.

[3] 2004/2005.

There are a number of alternatives to setting up a trust. In this chapter these will be considered along with a brief look at the more common different types of trusts, where they should and, perhaps more importantly, should not be used with particular reference to particular problems and different types of beneficiary; in short to examine situations where trusts are not a complete waste of time and, more importantly, clients' money. Reference will be made to particular types of beneficiary. These areas may overlap to a greater or lesser extent and clients may indeed fall into more than one heading:

1. **Beneficiary not of full capacity**. It may be that provision has to be made for a beneficiary who is not of full mental or physical capacity. There are special trusts available for this type of beneficiary.
2. **Closely allied to this is a former spouse** or partner or co-habitee who is mentally incapable. This is closely allied to the previous category. Unfortunately with the passage of time one or other partners in the marriage may become mentally incapable. This is a situation which is regrettably becoming more and more familiar to practitioners. Some thought might be given at an early stage for assets to be transferred into a trust rather than have the horrendous expense and time delay of a guardianship order or intervention order. It would be available to the trustees under the discretionary trust to make payments in the event of the spouse requiring to be taken into care.
3. **Underage beneficiary**. Assets generally require to be kept out of the control of the truster's children or grandchildren. A trust is the ideal method of holding capital and/or revenue until beneficiaries attain full capacity.
4. **Foreign beneficiary**. It may not be legally possible for a foreign beneficiary to have assets transferred to him or her in their own country. A trust may provide the appropriate vehicle short or long term to hold these assets, either indefinitely or until the political situation in their country crystallises.
5. **Second spouse/partner**. A truster may wish to make provision for a second spouse or civil partner and also safeguard the inheritance of his children from a previous marriage.
6. **Beneficiary in receipt of public funds**. A trust may be a legitimate means of removing assets from a taxpayer's estate for the means of qualifying for benefit from public funds.
7. **"Comfortably off" couples**. The main problem for what can be described as "comfortably off couples" stems from the conflict between divesting a spouse of assets and leaving them with sufficient to live on. The first hurdle will be in determining what constitutes a "comfortably off" couple. Any definition is arbitrary, but for our purposes "comfortably off" couples would be those where the joint assets, including a house, could be around £500,000 to £600,000. The limit should be increased depending on the area in which the house was located.

   They may be concerned to avoid IHT on the second death but do not have sufficient assets excluding their home. A mini discretionary trust with power to the trustees to accept loans may provide the way forward.

8. **Clients with "high net worth"**. This group will be concerned mainly with tax planning.
9. **Clients with problems of addiction**. This could be anything from gambling addictions to problems with drink or drugs, but it may be that this does not fully explain the client's predicament; some people are simply not good at handling money.
10. **Clients who wish control of a family company to be restricted**. Trusts are increasingly being used to ensure that succession to, e.g. shares in a family company, passes to the persons whom the truster envisages.
11. **Legal rights**. Closely allied to this could be the use of a trust to avoid legal rights. Thus, moveable property, which might form the basis of legal rights of *legitim* might be placed in a discretionary trust to which the truster may have a right to benefit. Problems associated with this from a tax point of view are rather complex and will be referred to elsewhere in the text but it is worth noting here that these may over balance the advantages in particular cases.
12. **Clients who have suffered personal injury**. They may not have recovered fully but have received a large settlement, which they may wish to place in trust in the event that they have a relapse in later life.
13. **Recently divorced clients**. A person entering into marriage, perhaps for a second or third time, who has suffered the trauma of a financial settlement, may wish to dispose of assets into a trust.
14. **Financially vulnerable clients**. These need not be insolvent clients and indeed transferring assets into a trust while insolvent would not be effective anyway in the short term. These may be people in business or the professions who may face large personal claims. It is settled that placing assets in a properly constituted trust will protect them from personal liability.
15. **Employment benefits**. It may be, although the scope of this is outwith this text, that a firm's pension scheme could be set up under the vehicle of a trust.
16. **The undecided testator**. Occasionally it will occur that a testator is unable to make up his mind on the question of the ultimate destination of his assets. It may be that his beneficiaries at the time of considering drafting a will are in a state of rapid change, e.g. termination of marriages, new children, financial difficulties. In this event the testator may wish to leave his entire assets in his will in a discretionary trust. This may also be appropriate for younger testators who do not know what the future will hold. This matter is dealt with in some more detail at a later stage.

Approximately 30 years ago, in fact until the capital taxes legislation in 1984, most family wills would leave the estate in liferent to the spouse, usually the wife, and in fee to the children. This type of will was bolstered by the Estate Duty (Death Duty) Regime. Even moderate sized firms would "run" many hundreds of these types of trusts. However, like bowler hats and large lunches, these virtually vanished overnight.

The trust or some type of trust, however, does linger on in wills, e.g. for young beneficiaries where money is to be held in trust or otherwise. Often these sums are small. In addition, trusts are often used for parties who are *incapax*.

<h2 style="text-align:center">ALTERNATIVES TO TRUSTS</h2>

2–02   There are often a number of alternatives to parties using trusts, e.g:

- outright gifts;
- payments to parents or guardians;
- National Savings products;
- powers of attorney;
- use of nominees;
- insurance products;
- charities;
- *negotiorum gestor*.

<h2 style="text-align:center">OUTRIGHT GIFTS</h2>

2–03   Often clients will consider giving instructions to set up a trust for a child or children who may at this stage be well above the age of full legal capacity.[4] While it is helpful, and the financial advantages are obvious to the solicitor managing the trust, some thought might be given to an outright gift. In some older firms there are certainly scores, possibly hundreds, of extremely small trusts, which have been set up for this particular purpose. The solicitor's only involvement is often restricted to the trust tax return. The dividends are often mandated directly to the beneficiary. Looking through many of them it does seem that the matter could quite easily have been dealt with by making an outright gift to the child or beneficiary.

<h2 style="text-align:center">PAYMENTS TO PARENTS OR GUARDIANS</h2>

2–04   Most wills contain a power to the executors to pay over sums due to the parents or guardians of underage beneficiaries. Even if the will does not, on intestacy some method or vehicle should be explored for paying out, if only the income to the guardian under indemnity if necessary, so that full use can be made of the beneficiary's aggregated income entitlement in claiming income tax relief.

<h2 style="text-align:center">NATIONAL SAVINGS PRODUCTS</h2>

2–05   Investing in the maximum holding of index linked (£15,000) and/or fixed interest (£15,000) National Savings certificates are an extremely useful way of holding money for a beneficiary who is not yet of legal capacity. If

---

[4] Age of Legal Capacity (Scotland) Act 1991 c.50.

the child is particularly young, the funds can be turned over or rolled over into up-to-date issues. These do not require any tax return whatsoever and, while the rate of return is modest, they are extremely useful for this purpose. There are instances of premium savings bonds being utilised but, short of express instructions for this, caution would be indicated along with a reluctance to proceed along this line. The current regulations can be found on the National Savings website (*www.nsandi.com*).

At time of writing, there are two issues available of fixed interest certificates, the two year (33rd) issue yielding 3.20 per cent and the five year (83rd issue) yielding the same.

There are two issues of index linked certificates. The index linked issue presently offers a five-year (41st issue) and a two-year certificate (13th issue). The returns are linked to the index of retail prices plus 1.05 per cent for the two year and plus 1.10 per cent for the five year and as regards the two year for index linked plus 0.50 per cent. These are all tax-free products and up to £15,000 can be invested in each making a total of £60,000, which should be enough for most "small bequests". Up to £30,000 can be invested in premium bonds.

POWERS OF ATTORNEY

These have recently come into prominence as a result of the Adults with **2–06**
Incapacity (Scotland) Act 2000. The former procedure for this had been extremely simple but a considerably more complicated regimen has now been imposed. This would certainly cover many situations short of capacity and is an extremely cost effective solution, even with the additional safeguards, as compared to setting up a trust or attempting the costly time consuming and frequently unnecessary minefield of a setting up of a guardianship or intervention order.

NOMINEES

Some firms routinely use a form of trust in local authority house **2–07**
purchase situations where, in effect, the tenant/purchaser is being financed, usually by his/her children. A trust is set up along the lines of the style in the Appendix. It might be speculated if this was a correct usage or even an effective method of dealing with this type of case. It may raise more difficulties than it solves. It can only be speculated as to how the parties dealt with the trust income sections on their self-assessment forms! Perhaps in most or in many of these cases, a simple back letter would suffice whereby the tenant/purchaser narrates that he is holding the property as nominee of the "actual purchaser". A style is shown in the Appendix. Obviously, this is a matter merely between the tenant and the local authority seller. Disclosure must be made to the local authority. There may be difficulties about disclosure to a Building Society where, e.g. a loan is being obtained, but this should not preclude obtaining the loan. Obviously, this is not 100 per cent fireproof if, e.g. a widower tenant was to remarry there may be difficulties but the documentation can be set up in advance to overcome these problems. It

may be helpful if the tenant/purchaser inserts a provision in his will leaving his interest in the house to the "actual purchaser". Often, shares are routinely held in the name of nominees companies for stockbrokers but this can be applied to individuals as well.

INSURANCE PRODUCTS

2–08 There are numerous life insurance products on the market which can be utilised to provide funds to meet the eventual liability arising on death and/or to provide capital to meet IHT, which may become payable as a consequence of a future lifetime gift which is not a PEP. These products are generally life insurance policies of one description or another. They can be held on a trust for the policyholders' beneficiaries from the outset, e.g. the children. Normally, by the time parties get round to thinking about this they are fairly old from the point of view of ordinary endowment policies, which are not enjoying the best of popularity at present.

There are numerous types of insurance to cover the problem, such as the seven-year decreasing term, seven-year level term assurance, all of life assurance or term and last survivor term (convertible). The last of these does tend to produce a fairly cost effective type of solution. Basically, parties identify the sum involved (e.g. £100,000) which they wish to cover. The insurance company agrees to cover the last survivor of husband and wife for a period of, say, 10 years. The policy is written in trust for the beneficiaries above mentioned. After 10 years, a certain amount of capital has been built up through the payment of the premiums, and at that point the life assurance company will take a view as to whether to continue it. Obviously, if parties survive the 10 years they stand to lose all or to face difficulty insuring for a further term but, on the other hand, they have proved their ability to survive; the company may continue to insure them for a further 10 years or lesser period utilising the capital which has built up as part payment of future premiums.

Obviously, the premiums paid are regarded as gifts and in most cases these will be under the £3,000 annual allowance.

It is perhaps not strictly correct to call the foregoing an alternative to trust because a trust deed is produced. However it is seen as an adjunct to the life insurance (or assurance) product.

CHARITIES

2–09 Some charities will accept legacies or gifts from testator/donors who wish to make provision for beneficiaries who are not of full capacity. The charity will accept the donation and will "informally" agree to care for the legatee or beneficiary. I have not come across any difficulties in this type of arrangement.

At the other end of the scale, some charities will actually run an informal trust for the beneficiary. MENCAP will provide a standard trust deed into which as little as £5 can be lodged initially with the trustees being The National Trustees for the Mentally Handicapped (established by MENCAP). They will provide for income for the beneficiary as the primary beneficiary during his lifetime with charities directly involved in the particular beneficiary's illness being included thereafter for any named persons and in default from MENCAP itself.

Mencap Trust Company Limited

Mencap Trust Company Limited is a company that manages discre- **2–10** tionary trusts set up for people with a learning disability. It is run from Mencap's national centre.

Some people choose to appoint a company rather than an individual to act as the trustee of their trust. This is because they do not know anyone who can act as trustee, or because they do not want to place this responsibility on them. In addition, a trust company has expertise and experience in running trusts.

If a client is minded to consider it, Mencap Trust Company Limited can act as the trustee of an individual trust which the client sets up with the company. The company will work with the beneficiary's family and carers to ensure that they make the best decisions for them throughout their lives.

To set up a trust the following steps are necessary:

- Set up a discretionary trust with Mencap Trust Company Ltd under its standard form of trust with an initial amount of £5. This is basically a "Pilot Trust". The charges for setting up the trust are £293.75 (£250 plus VAT). The company will send all the paperwork needed to be completed.
- The client bequeaths to the trust a further sum of money under the terms of his will.
- On the client's death, the money will be paid to the trustees and the trust will be activated.

Mencap Trust Company Ltd is a not-for-profit organisation and the company will generally only act where there is at least £10,000 in the trust fund.

Negotiorum Gestor

In this connection, reference is made to Adrian Ward's excellent book **2–11** *The Power to Act*. In the book, he cites the example of neighbours who have just left for holiday abroad when you notice that one of their windows has been broken. You arrange for it to be repaired. In law, you are acting as a *negotiorum gestor* or one who intervenes to act without authorisation where it is reasonable to expect that authorisation will be given if it could be sought. Ward argues that it would be possible to apply this in a situation where the person is unable to manage his or her affairs temporarily to permanently because of absence or physical or indeed mental disability. Difficulty may occur in persuading banks to reimburse funds but it could be of use in emergencies.

Chapter Three

TYPES OF TRUSTS AND TAX CONSEQUENCES

"May you live in interesting times!"[1]

INTRODUCTION

3–01 In drafting trust deeds, as with many other deeds, it is of paramount importance to have a firm grasp of the taxation implications of trusts. This pervades the setting up of the trust, its administration and its ultimate termination whether this be from the trust being wound up, by distribution to a beneficiary or otherwise. Obviously, the drafter is concerned principally with income tax, capital gains tax ("CGT") and inheritance tax ("IHT"), but other taxes such as stamp duty land tax, value added tax **and more recently** pre-owned assets tax should not be overlooked.

There have been precious few instances where drafters (and trusters) have been helped but one is by the announcement that the IHT nil rate band is to be increased over the next few years as follows:

Tax year beginning	£
April 5, 2006	285,000
April 5, 2007	300,000
April 5, 2008	312,000
April 5, 2009	325,000

Crumbs of comfort

3–02 There have been few other consolations. The only other was the somewhat derisory one in the Finance Act 2005 where an exception was made for smaller trusts on the first £500, increased to £1,000 in the Finance Act 2006, of discretionary trust income, the tax rates are as follows:

> Rent and trading income–22%
> Savings income, e.g. bank interest–20%
> Dividends and distributions–10%

---

[1] Ancient Chinese Curse.

For Trust income over £1000:

> Rent and trading income–40%
> Savings income, e.g. bank interest–40%
> Dividends and distributions–32.5%

INHERITANCE TAX

Broadly speaking, inheritance tax is a tax which is payable on a **3–03** taxpayer's fortune at date of death and on assets which are given away during lifetime. Assets include property, possessions, money and investments. It applies if the taxable value of the taxpayer's fortune is above £285,000.[2] There are exemptions which allow a taxpayer to pass on amounts *inter vivos* or *mortis causa* without any inheritance tax being due. Thus, if the taxpayer's fortune is left to a spouse or civil partner and both are domiciled in the UK there is no inheritance tax to pay, even if the taxpayer's fortune is above the £285,000 threshold. In addition most gifts or transfers made more than seven years before death are exempt.

> **Danger Warning!!!**
> **The proposals in the Finance Act 2006 affect the inheritance tax treatment of transfers into most types of trust.**

Gifts

There are other types of gifts, such as wedding gifts and gifts in **3–04** anticipation of a civil partnership up to £5,000 (depending on the relationship between the giver and the recipient), gifts to charity, and £3,000 given away each year which are also exempt. The sustained treatment of these is outwith the scope of this text.

On the topic of civil partnerships it should be noted that a civil partnership is a new legal relationship or institution, which two people of the same-sex can form by signing a registration document. This is created by the Civil Partnership Act 2004 as modified by the Family Law (Scotland) Act 2006; the effects of this for tax purposes are substantially similar to marriage. It also provides same-sex couples who form a civil partnership with uniformity of treatment in an extensive range of legal matters with those different sex couples entering into a civil marriage.

Inheritance tax is payable on the value of transfers above £285,000 into a discretionary trust. However, proposals in the Finance Act 2006 affect, sometimes quite radically, the inheritance tax treatment of transfers into most other types of trust.

Budget 2006

In the Budget of 2006[3] The Chancellor of the Exchequer[4] introduced **3–05** yet another "attack" on trusts taxation. At the time of writing, the Royal Assent has been granted to the Finance (No.2) Bill 2006 as the Finance Act 2006.

---

[2] For 2006–07.
[3] Wednesday March 22, 2006.
[4] The Right Honourable Gordon Brown, strongly tipped by the press as the next Prime Minister.

In the House of Lords,[5] **Lord McKenzie of Luton**, speaking on July 17, 2006 for the Government, stated the Government's position as follows:

"The Government want to see a continuation of a fair and targeted inheritance tax system and are committed to providing certainty for families in this area. The Bill proposes increases in the inheritance tax threshold to £312,000 for transfers of value on or after 6 April 2008, and to £325,000 for transfers of value on or after 6 April 2009. The increased tax-free threshold of £285,000 for 2006–07 means that the number of taxpaying estates will be about 37,000 in the current tax year. Despite concerns about the numbers of people affected by inheritance tax, it remains the case that only around 6 per cent of the estates of those who die in 2006-07 will pay any inheritance tax.

The Budget announced new rules for two types of trust—known as 'accumulation and maintenance' and 'interest in possession'—that are currently exempt from the inheritance tax charges that already apply to other types of trust. It has become clear that some wealthy individuals are using these types of trust primarily as a way to shelter their wealth from inheritance tax. The Government believe that it is unfair for people to gain a tax advantage by using trusts in this manner.

It has been said that there should be no difference between the inheritance tax due on setting up a trust and giving assets away. I disagree. People who set up trusts continue to control how the money is used. That is not the same as an outright gift and there is no reason why they should be taxed in the same way. Therefore, we have taken action to ensure that the exemptions from IHT trust charges apply only where trusts are set up to cater for certain prescribed circumstances—that is, broadly, where they provide for the disabled or are set up on death, including for spouses and bereaved minor children. In all other cases, the normal charges for trusts will apply, preventing them being used to shelter wealth from inheritance tax.

There has been a lot of speculation in the media about this measure and the Economic Affairs Committee raised several concerns. For the avoidance of doubt, I can confirm a number of things. Where someone dies without having made a will, their bereaved spouse or civil partner will continue to get spouse relief, and spouse relief will continue to be due when an 'interest in possession' trust is set up under a will giving a life interest to a bereaved spouse or civil partner.

Where a trust is set up by a parent on their death for a bereaved minor, the trust charges will begin to accrue only from the child's 18th birthday. People will still be able to set up trusts that run on past a child's 18th birthday if they wish to do so. Most trusts that come within the new rules will not have any inheritance tax to pay. Inheritance tax will be due only from trusts that have amounts in

---

[5] On July 17, 2006.

excess of the threshold of £285,000, rising to £325,000 by 2009. This allowance can be in addition to the inheritance tax threshold that applies to a person's estate when they die. I reject statements that these changes will affect millions of people.

I read with interest the Economic Affairs Committee report's comments on the absence of consultation. The Government always consider the benefits of undertaking consultation and try to make as much room as possible for advance preparation ahead of changes to the tax regime. However, this will not always be possible—for example, in cases like this, where there is a significant risk of large-scale forestalling.

The Government recognise that trusts have an important role to play in helping people to manage their affairs, but we believe that the tax system for trusts should not provide artificial incentives for setting them up. Over the past few years, we have made a number of changes to close loopholes in the inheritance tax regime and the tax regime for trusts to ensure that people pay their fair share of tax. Alongside this work, we have also undertaken a programme of modernisation of the tax system for trusts, making changes to protect vulnerable people while ensuring that trusts are not used to achieve an unfair tax advantage."

This statement summarises HM Government's view on trusts. There is, perhaps, much to disagree with in this statement but it is reproduced in full as it appears to reflect the official view on trusts tax.

At the end of the day, it is probably worth stating that practitioners must advise and draft deeds to reflect the law as it stands, however much they disagree with it!

This text attempts to identify the proposed changes. In addition, since there is a state of transition it is necessary to deal with the old "regime" and the new.

It was, and is, extremely common for parents and grandparents to include accumulation and maintenance trust provisions in their wills in order that an estate inherited by issue is held in trust until they are 25 or older. Many, if not most, wills in Scotland will offer this as a standard provision where issue is involved.

Trusters who have set up, or have an interest in, accumulation and maintenance trusts and/or liferent trusts not meeting the new inheritance tax criteria about their terms and the circumstances in which they are created, will be affected. These trusts previously received special treatment, but if they do not qualify under the new rules, will now come within the mainstream IHT regime for trusts of "relevant property". Generally, relevant property trusts are trusts in which no person has a liferent or interest in possession. The changes apply to existing accumulation and maintenance trusts and liferent trusts, subject to the transitional rules, and apply on and after March 22, 2006 to new trusts, additions of new assets to existing trusts and, subject to transitional provisions, to other IHT relevant events in relation to existing trusts. Transitional rules provide for a period of adjustment for certain existing trusts up to April 6, 2008, and for continuing exclusion from the "relevant property" charges if they satisfy conditions for ongoing protection.

Finance Act 2006

3–06   The new provisions are introduced by FA 2006, s.156[6] which provides:

Rules for trusts etc.

156.—(1) Schedule 20 contains—

(a) amendments of provisions of IHTA 1984 relating to settled property,
(b) amendments of provisions relating to property that, for purposes of that Act, is property subject to a reservation, and
(c) related amendments of provisions relating to chargeable gains.

(2) Those amendments have effect as mentioned in that Schedule.

Schedule 20 amends the relevant sections of the IHTA 1984.

To summarise, new provisions incorporated in the Inheritance Tax Act 1984 provide a specific regime for "relevant property" trusts, i.e. discretionary trusts:

- an immediate "entry" tax charge of 20 per cent on lifetime transfers which exceed the IHT threshold into "relevant property" trusts;
- a "periodic" tax charge of up to 6 per cent on the value of trust assets over the IHT threshold once every 10 years; and
- an "exit" charge proportionate to the periodic charge when funds are taken out of a trust between 10-year anniversaries.

Prior to the passing of the Finance Act 2006 there were special rules for accumulation and maintenance trusts (s.71 IHTA) and liferent trusts. Lifetime transfers into these trusts were exempt from IHT if the truster survived seven years, and the trusts are not subject to the periodic or exit charges. **In future this is only to apply to: (1) trusts created on death by a parent for an underage child who will be fully entitled to the assets in the trust at age 18; (2) trusts created on death for the benefit of one liferent in order of time whose interest cannot be replaced** (more than one such trust may be created on death as long as the trust capital vests absolutely when the life interest comes to an end); or **(3) trusts which are created either in the truster's lifetime or on death for a disabled person** (see s.89(4) IHTA).

The broad effect is that the IHT treatment for discretionary trusts, i.e. "relevant property trusts" will be the "default" treatment for other trusts unless exempted. A precedent for this type of treatment can be found in the introduction of the pre-owned assets tax where, instead of detailing situations where tax was to be due it was provided that tax was to be due on all instances where a taxpayer continued to enjoy the use of an asset he once owned, unless exceptions were stipulated.

Accordingly, most other trusts will fall into what is described as the mainstream IHT rules for "relevant property" trusts. Where a trust is

---

[6] (c.25).

created for a child on the death of a parent, for instance, as a result of a clause in their will, IHT is payable at 40 per cent and will continue to be charged at 40 per cent unless the estate is below the IHT limit. If the age when the funds are to be released is 18 then nothing else will change. However, if the parents decide that the children cannot be trusted with an inheritance while still a teenager, then IHT will be applied where it was previously exempt.

It is likely that most testators will still elect to have the later age limit not withstanding the adverse tax position. Accordingly, in the case of trusts created on and after March 22, 2006, lifetime transfers into trusts will not qualify for special treatment **unless they are set up for a disabled person**. All other transfers will be immediately chargeable.

Trusts not qualifying for special treatment both *inter vivos* and *mortis causa* will be liable to the usual periodic and exit charges applying to "relevant property" trusts. Where existing accumulation and maintenance trusts provide that the assets in trust will go to a beneficiary absolutely at 18 or where the terms on which they are held are modified before April 6, 2008 to provide this, the current IHT treatment will continue. For the others which do not, **the trust assets will become "relevant property" from April 6, 2008** and the periodic and exit charges will apply. Ten-yearly anniversaries will arise by reference to the original date of settlement. These are based on three-monthly charges or fortieths. For the first 10 years after April 6, 2008, the rate of charge will reflect the fact that the property has not been "relevant property" throughout a full 10-year period. Thus, if the first 10-yearly anniversary falls in late October 2008, it will be one twentieth (two fortieths) of the normal charge.

For current liferent trusts the existing rules will run on until the interest in the trust property at March 22, 2006 comes to an end. If a beneficiary then takes absolute ownership, this will be regarded as a transfer by the person with the interest in the property—either a transfer on death or a "potentially exempt transfer" if they are still living—and will receive the same IHT treatment as now. The trust will have no further IHT consequences.

If the liferent interest comes to an end and the property remains on trust, this will be treated as **the creation of new trust property**.

- If it comes to an end during the lifetime of the person beneficially entitled to it, this will be a transfer creating "relevant property" (unless the new trusts are for charitable purposes) and will therefore be immediately chargeable.
- If the interest comes to an end on death, it will form part of the person's IHT estate as pre March 22, 2006 and the trust property will then become "relevant property" (unless the charity exemption applies).

In both cases, the periodic and exit charges will apply.

However, any new liferent trust which arises when a liferent trust created before March 22, 2006 comes to an end before April 6, 2008— whether on death or otherwise—will be treated as if it was in existence on March 22, 2006.

Where an individual is beneficially entitled to an interest in trust property, and continues to be treated for IHT purposes as owning the property, a termination of the interest in the individual's lifetime on or after March 22, 2006 will be treated as a gift for purposes under the IHT "gift with reservation" rules. Accordingly, if they retain the use of the trust property after their interest in it ends, it will remain chargeable in their hands in the same way as if they had formerly owned it outright.

Quite separate from the problems arising on death, it is worth noting that in certain circumstances it is possible to have to pay both capital gains tax and inheritance tax if assets are transferred *inter vivos* to a trust after April 5, 2006.

Suppose on August 17, 2006 George conveys property into a trust for his children who are all adult. He claims holdover relief on the basis that the gift into the trust is a chargeable transfer (TCGA 1992, s.260) and pays inheritance tax.

Four years later, his wife has a child who can now benefit from the trust! Accordingly, George must pay capital gains tax on the gain because it has become "settlor" interested. He cannot set off his inheritance tax liability against his capital gains tax bill. Moreover, he pays capital gains tax on the *untapered gain*. There is minimal relief under s.260(7) where the trustees later dispose of the asset.

CAPITAL GAINS TAX

3–07 Changes to the IHT treatment of trusts will have an impact for CGT:

- transfers into and out of trusts which now come within the "relevant property" rules, i.e. the discretionary trust regime will automatically be eligible for hold-over relief under s.260(2)(a) Taxation of Chargeable Gains Act 1992 ("TCGA");
- hold-over relief under s.260(2)(d) TCGA will be restricted to trusts which meet the new IHT rules for trusts for under age children;
- the special rules in ss.72 and 73 TCGA relating to the death of a person entitled to a liferent trust will be restricted to assets which are subject to a liferent trust which meets the new IHT criteria.

As previously stated, it seems that the media has only just discovered inheritance tax. We are regularly bombarded with articles about this unfair tax; that it is only supposed to be payable by "rich people". Indeed, one major popular newspaper issued free a car sticker with the legend "ABOLISH INHERITANCE TAX".

While the view may be taken that articles such as these insult the intelligence of most readers they should be seen as raising awareness on the tax and the possibilities of mitigating it, including the use of *mortis causa* and *inter vivos* trusts.

Over the past few decades, it is fair to say that the tax context under which trusts operate has changed continually. This makes it difficult for the drafter as well as trusters, beneficiaries, trustees and their advisors, but that does not mean trusts should be abandoned!

OTHER CHANGES TO TRUST TAX LAW

3–08 Certain recent changes to trust tax law have had a striking effect on drafters and those charged with running trusts. The restriction of repayment of tax credits on dividend income of UK companies has reduced the "tax pools" available to trustees when making distributions from discretionary trusts. In addition, there has been the withdrawal of the principal private residence relief from the sale of private dwelling-houses by trustees/beneficiaries where holdover relief had been claimed beforehand. Until very recently, perhaps the most striking reform was the introduction in the Finance Act 2004 of the rate of tax applicable to trusts of 40 per cent for discretionary and accumulation and mainte-nance trusts.

New trusts created for the benefit of disabled people will be able to avoid the new rules.

POTENTIALLY EXEMPT TRANSFERS

In addition, drastic changes are made in regard to potentially exempt **3–09** transfers ("PETs") as they affect trusts. Most experts believed that the IHT treatment of discretionary trusts was a "special" regime, designed to prevent assets being held on a long-term basis outside the inheritance tax regime; now it appears that apart from certain disability trusts this will be the default mode. The principle up until now was that a liferentor of trust property was for IHT purposes treated as the owner of the trust property he liferented. A charge arose on the liferentor's death. If the interest terminates in his lifetime, and outside the seven-year period up to the beneficiary's death, then there is no charge to inheritance tax.

Inter vivos liferent trusts created after March 22, 2006 **will now incur an inheritance tax entry charge exactly as if a discretionary trust had been created under the previous regime**. As stated, there will also be 10-yearly charges on the trusts assets and exit charges. An immediate inheritance tax charge will be a substantial disincentive to trusters who wish to provide for other family members. More outright gifts as PETs will probably be made.

Capital gains tax holdover relief under TCGA 1992, s.260 will be available on setting up new trusts, but that is a small consolation on the one hand and incentive on the other.

Existing accumulation and maintenance trusts will enjoy their current regime, but only if they **provide for absolute entitlement at the age of 18**. Very few do! This may create further work for the legal profession.

Existing liferent trusts are not affected by this change in treatment and the current rules will therefore continue to apply so long as the existing interests continue. Please watch out for existing trusts since there are proposals for the CGT uplift to market value on death to be abolished and accordingly both **inheritance and capital gains tax will apply**.

To recap, as regards *inter vivos* trusts, i.e. those created by trusters during their lifetime, and containing money put aside for the benefit of, say, grandchildren, until Budget Day 2006, IHT was avoided, at least at the standard 40 per cent rate. However, now, when new lifetime trusts are created, a new 20 per cent tax will be levied immediately on the amount over the IHT threshold whether the age at which the funds are paid out is 18 years of age or over. Thereafter, as time passes by, the periodic charge, up to a maximum of six per cent, and the exit charges will also be enforced. Again, the only exception will be trusts for the benefit of disabled people.

These changes virtually equate accumulation and maintenance trusts and liferent trusts with the regime for discretionary trusts. For IHT purposes, the legislation is very new at the time of writing but the foregoing is likely.

It seems likely that the "reform" of the tax regime for trusts will continue relentlessly or even remorselessly. The HMRC's trust modernisation consultation document of August 2004 may presage further changes in the Finance Acts to follow. As regards income tax and capital gains tax, the trust modernisation proposals went largely ahead as planned. Other proposals such as income streaming provisions, abolition of tax pools and a reduced rate of capital gains tax on estates appear to have been placed on the "back burner".

TREATMENT OF NEW TRUSTS AFTER MARCH 22, 2006

Summary

3–10   It seems fairly clear that subject to few exceptions, new trusts made on or after March 22, 2006 by way of *inter vivos* transfer will be regarded as "relevant property". In shorthand this means that the same IHT rules which apply to discretionary trusts will apply to that trust whether or not it is a liferent.

Accordingly any "transfers on death" will be subject to the relevant property regime unless it is a liferent for a surviving spouse and a qualifying "immediate post-death interest".

Surviving spouse's liferent

3–11   Any liferent which arises on death and which is held by the deceased's surviving spouse will be generally exempt from the relevant property regime. If the spouse's interest ends during their lifetime the "transfer of value" will become a PET provided another party becomes absolutely entitled to the assets or if they pass to a disabled trust. In all other cases it is likely that a chargeable lifetime transfer will arise.

Immediate post-death interest

3–12   Apart from the surviving spouse's liferent, any other new trusts created by death will be treated as relevant property unless on the end of the liferent another person becomes absolutely entitled or it is contained in a trust for a bereaved minor or a disabled trust comes into existence or the property goes to charity.

If there is any possibility however remote that it does not fall into this category, e.g. if there is a power to advance to the spouse then the liferent trust arising on trust will be relevant property.

COMMON ASPECTS OF TRUST TAXATION

3–13   There are certain aspects of tax which are common to all trusts, others which are common to one or more and yet others which are specific to one particular type of trust. It will be attempted to deal with all those which are common to all trusts first. As regards those matters which are common to two or more trusts *these will generally be dealt with as for the first type* of trust and thereafter referred to in the second or subsequent trust type. It will be attempted to deal with certain aspects of IHT and CGT under the following headings:

- When the trust commenced
- During the trust
- At termination of the trust

However, personal income tax will not be covered under these headings since this comes under the banner of personal or corporation tax which is outwith the scope of this text.

Turning to the question of the main categories of the trusts and a brief summary of each including a brief note of the tax consequences of each. These are summarised under the following heads:

1. Discretionary trusts
2. Accumulation and maintenance trusts
3. Liferent trusts

    (These are the big three and probably lead the Scottish Trust league table.)

4. Trusts for disabled persons
5. Charitable trusts
6. Offshore trusts
7. Bare trusts
8. Pilot trusts
9. Trusts for a bereaved minor

DISCRETIONARY TRUSTS

If the Scottish Trusts First Eleven had fielded a football team prior to **3–14** March 22, 2006 it would probably do so with a 4:2:4 formation at which time the forward line would consist of discretionary trusts, accumulation and maintenance trusts, liferent trusts and charitable trusts. However, it would be to discretionary trusts where the Scottish Trusts FA would look for the goals and the golden boot award!

These are trusts without an "interest in possession". No individual has the right to demand payment. Trustees are given discretion as to whom they should pay out and what amounts and at which times they pay out. Potential trusters who wished to obtain the benefit of retirement relief before it expired on April 6, 2003 may have transferred qualifying shares or assets to a chargeable trust.

IHT—discretionary trust

When trust commenced

If it is created *inter vivos* then it is a chargeable transfer and if the **3–15** truster bears the IHT, grossing up may apply. The rate is the lifetime rate of IHT, namely one half of 40 per cent, i.e. 20 per cent. This is levied over the value of the transfer over the nil rate band applicable at the time. Moreover, if we fail to advise a client of the advantages of say a mini discretionary trust in their will or *inter vivos* trust, then we could face a claim for negligence. The basic loss which may accrue on failure to utilise the nil rate band (NRB) (40 per cent of the current NRB) is easy to calculate.

Tax year beginning	£	Basic loss(£) @ **40%**
April 5, 2006	285,000	114,000
April 5, 2007	300,000	120,000
April 5, 2008	312,000	124,800
April 5, 2009	325,000	130,000

The high net worth client with a family should be advised as soon as possible about discretionary trusts with a view to utilising the seven-year relief. The comfortably-off couple with, say, total joint assets of between £400,000 to £600,000 depending on the area in which their house is situated, could be advised to have a bequest of a mini discretionary trust legacy of the nil rate band in their wills. In fact it is suggested that there will be few occasions when wills are drawn up without advice being given about possible NRB saving.

During trust

3–16 The 10-year charge is imposed on the relevant property in which no qualifying interest in possession exists. The rate is at 30 per cent of the lifetime rate of transfer, i.e. up to a maximum of 6 per cent (30 per cent of one-half of 40 per cent). There will be a proportion of the 10-year charge if property leaves the trust before a 10-year interval. While the 10-year or exit charge remains low, it is suggested that this type of trust with its obvious flexibility is the one to opt for as regards disabled beneficiaries, for comfortably off couples and also wealthy clients.

While the tax regime is harsh as outlined below, the advantages far outweigh the disadvantages. Every 10 years there will be the 10-year exit charge. It should be noted that previous chargeable transfers, i.e. in the seven years preceding, must be taken into account.

Example

On January 1, 1995, Mrs Campbell made an *inter vivos* discretionary trust and on that day transferred assets to the value of £90,000 into the trust. She had made chargeable transfers in the seven years before amounting to £170,000.

On December 31, 2004 the value of the trust stood at £500,000.

The 10-year charge is calculated at December 31, 2004

Step one	Add the chargeable transfers to the value at 31/12/2004	£170,000 + £500,000	£670,000
Step two	Calculate 20 per cent of this figure after deduction of NRB (£263,000)	20 per cent of (£670,000– £263,000)	£81,400
Step three	Calculate effective rate	(£81,400/ £500,000) 100 × 30 per cent	4.884 per cent
Step four	Tax due	4.884 per cent of relevant property, i.e. £500,000	£24,420

There will be a proportion of the 10-year charge if property leaves the trust before a 10-year interval. The rate is at 30 per cent of the lifetime rate of transfer, i.e. up to 6 per cent (30 per cent of one-half of 40 per cent).

There is scope for transferring assets to the next generation as follows:

John Tyler sets up under his will a discretionary trust of £285,000, when the NRB is £285,000 on May 5, 2006. On May 3, 2016 the value of the trust fund is £920,000 when the funds of the trust are removed. The calculation is based on full quarters or three month periods, of which there are 39 here. The effective rate is based on the earlier rate which the funds suffered. However, since there is no effective rate there is no exit charge.

IHTA 1984, s.144—discretionary trust

The IHTA 1984, s.144 provides: 3–17

144.—(1) Subsection (2) below applies where property comprised in a person's estate immediately before his death is settled by his will and, within the period of two years after his death and before any interest in possession has subsisted in the property, there occurs—

(a) an event on which tax would (apart from subsection (2) below) be chargeable under any provision, other than section 64 or 79, of Chapter III of Part III of this Act, or

(b) an event on which tax would be so chargeable but for section 75 or 76 above or paragraph 16(1) of Schedule 4 to this Act.

(1A) Where the testator dies on or after 22nd March 2006, subsection (1) above shall have effect as if the reference to any interest in possession were a reference to any interest in possession that is—

(a) an immediate post-death interest, or

(b) a disabled person's interest.

(2) Where this subsection applies by virtue of an event within paragraph (a) of subsection (1), tax shall not be charged under the provision in question on that event; and in every case in which this subsection applies in relation to an event, this Act shall have effect as if the will had provided that on the testator's death the property should be held as it is held after the event.

As previously stated, where a testator is uncertain as to whom he wishes to ultimately benefit, he may wish to postpone the choice and can do so taking advantage of IHTA 1984, s.144[7] which allows distributions to be made within two years of his death without any charge to additional inheritance tax out of assets transferred on discretionary trust by the will. Obviously, the terms of the will and the trust deed set up should be extremely wide to cover all exigences including charities. He may leave a letter to his trustees or leave this to their good sense.

The advantage of this is that some testators **object to the fact that their wills can be varied after death** under s.142. Under a s.144 discretionary trust, as the beneficiaries merely have a faint hope of benefiting, a s.142 variation is not competent and "rewriting" the will cannot take place. Section 142 often suffers from the problem of dealing with under age beneficiaries. Liferents, e.g. can only be made in favour of persons alive at the time of death. However, the discretionary trust and s.144 overcomes this.

Often this can be combined with a "mini discretionary trust" of the nil rate band.

Danger Warning!!!

It should also be pointed out that this may fall foul of the related settlements section of the Inheritance Tax Act 1984, s.62 which may attack the value of the other properties dealt with in the will under the related settlements section and these could be held to form part of the accumulative total of transfers inherited by the discretionary will trust.

One method dealing with this is to use a lifetime "pilot" trust with a small initial capital to which funds could be added by the will free from the "related settlements problem".

At termination of trust

3–18   Where property in the trust ceases to be relevant property, e.g. on distribution to a beneficiary, there is a charge to IHT. There is no charge if the property leaves the trust within three months of the start of the trust or the start of a 10-year exit charge. If this is before a 10-year anniversary, there is a proportionate charge. This is calculated on the basis of three-month periods, i.e. 10 years divided by 40.

It is likely that these sums can be minimised in practice. Thus, a mini discretionary trust set up under a will "to safeguard the interest of a

---

[7] "Discretionary trust and wills" in Taxation Magazine April 6, 1995 at p.13.

surviving spouse" may only last a brief period until matters crystallise, e.g. by a surviving spouse deciding that she has enough to live on and that the balance can be distributed.

CGT—discretionary trust

When trust commenced

It may be that the truster will be required to realise assets to fund the **3–19** trust and, in this event, he will be required to bear CGT as an individual. There may be some merit in carrying this out beforehand to utilise the higher personal CGT annual tax exemption. The annual exemption for the CGT annual exempt amount is £8,800 for the tax year 2006/07 for individuals, personal representatives of deceased persons and trustees of certain settlements for the disabled. The annual exempt amount for most other trustees is one half of the personal rate, i.e. £4,400. Please note that this amount may be proportionately reduced if the truster has set up other trusts.

The transfer of assets to trustees will constitute a disposal for CGT purposes even where no consideration is paid. Since the truster and the trustees are connected persons under TCGA 1992, s.286(3) the consideration is deemed the market value.[8]

While therefore disposal at a gain will trigger a CGT liability subject to possible hold over relief, any loss arising cannot (somewhat unsportingly) be set off, except against a gain arising on the subsequent disposal by the same truster to those trustees. It is only possible, and has been so since March 14, 1989, to make a hold over election in the case of a chargeable transfer, that is to say to a discretionary settlement within TCGA 1992, s.260 or a transfer of business or defined business interest assets under s.165 such as business property, unquoted shares or otherwise.

During the trust

During the trust, trustees are entitled to an annual exemption equal to **3–20** half the individual's exempt amount.[9]

This presently stands at £4,400[10]. Please note that this should be contrasted with executries where the executors are given the full exempt amount for the year of death and the two following tax years. The trustees' exemption is divided where the same truster has made more than "qualifying trust" since June 6, 1978, subject to a minimum of one tenth of the exempt amount, i.e. £420 for 2006/07. Capital gains tax is charged at the rate applicable to trusts ("RAT") of 40 per cent. The trustees will be entitled to taper relief.

Disposals by trustees are at the rate of 40 per cent, as is a transfer to a beneficiary; this is a deemed disposal also, although holdover relief will be available. Exemptions and reliefs are the same as for the liferent trusts but death and retirement relief for trustees may not apply.

---

[8] See also ss.17 and 18.
[9] Para.2 Sch.1 TCGA 1992.
[10] 2006/07.

Trustees pay CGT when they sell trust assets or pass them to beneficiaries. The rate is at 40 per cent of the net gain. The usual reliefs such as taper apply. The exemption for 2006/07 is £4,400.

At termination of trust

3–21 Trustees pay CGT when they sell trust assets or pass them to beneficiaries. However, hold over relief may be available when the assets are passed to beneficiaries.

Income tax–discretionary trust

When trust commenced

3–22 There are no special considerations when the trust is set up.

During trust

3–23 When the trust is set up it is necessary for the trustees or their agents to intimate this to HMRC by means of form 41G.

Trustees of a discretionary trust complete a trust tax return each year and pay tax on the trust income at the following flat rates:

Type of income	Trust income up to £1,000	Over £1,000
Dividends and distributions	10%	32.5%
Savings income, e.g. bank interest	20%	40%
Rent and trading income	22%	40%

In some circumstances the trustees may have to pay extra when they pay income to the beneficiaries.

Tax on the beneficiaries

3–24 All discretionary trust income paid to beneficiaries is treated as if tax **has already been paid at 40 per cent**. For example, and assuming that the first under £1,000 has already been used up, if the beneficiary is paid £600 out of trust income the beneficiary's total income (before tax) from the trust is considered to be £1,000, with £400 (40 per cent) having already been paid in tax. As a result, a beneficiary who is a non-taxpayer, a 10 per cent or a 22 per cent taxpayer may be able to reclaim all or some of the tax back.

A higher rate tax payer cannot reclaim, but has nothing to pay. They simply enter the income and 40 per cent tax already paid (the "tax credit") on their tax return.

Extra trust tax based on payments to beneficiaries

3–25 When paying income to beneficiaries, the trustees must make certain that they have paid enough tax to cover the 40 per cent being declared (or in some cases reclaimed in part or full) by the beneficiary.

Keeping track via the "tax pool"

To ensure that they have paid enough, the trustees must maintain a **3–26** record of payments called the "tax pool".

Broadly speaking this is the tax which the **trustees have paid at the special trust rates, but excluding the non-refundable 10 per cent on dividends and under deduction of any 40 per cent tax credits on payments to beneficiaries.**

If the amount in the tax pool does not cover the beneficiary's 40 per cent "tax credit" in a given year, the trust must pay extra tax to make up the difference. The effect is that the trust pays tax at 40 per cent on all income it pays to the beneficiaries. It may be that, over and above the first £1,000 of trust income, if the trustees wish to pay the beneficiaries out the sum of a further £2,000 there is a tax credit of, at the rate applicable to trusts, 40 per cent of £400. The beneficiary is regarded as receiving £2,000 from which £800 has been deducted. The balance on the pool is £900 which covers the tax credit and reduces the pool to £100. The trustees do not have to pay any more tax that year. If the pool did not have sufficient credit or the pool was empty, the trustees would be required to pay.

Thus extra tax is not always payable when dividend income is paid out since unused amounts in the tax pool can be carried over from year to year.

The rate is 40 per cent apart from the 10 per cent tax credit on non-recoverable dividend income, which has to suffer tax at 25 per cent, i.e. an additional 15 per cent. If these are paid to a beneficiary, they suffer tax at 34 per cent gross.

Example

Trustees of a discretionary trust receive a net dividend of £1,800 (over and above other trust income of £1,000). Tax of 10 per cent amounting to £200 has already been deducted from the gross dividend of £2,000. This is irrecoverable.

The trustees will have to pay tax at 32.5 per cent on the gross dividend, i.e. £650, less the 10 per cent already paid (£200) = £450.

Danger Warning!!!

Only this figure of £450 goes into the tax pool. The tax credit does not qualify for inclusion.

If the trustees wish to make a distribution

If the trustees distribute the net sum, i.e. £2,000 less the 32.5 per cent **3–27** (£1,350) it will have to be grossed up at 40 per cent

$$\frac{100}{(100 - 40)} \times £1,350 = £2,250$$

The trustees will have to account to the HMRC for tax at 40 per cent on £2,250 = £900. They have already accounted for £200 tax credit and the balance of the 32.5 per cent, namely £450, totalling £650. They

discover, somewhat to their horror, that the tax pool is empty! They will
have to pay an additional amount of tax of £250 (£900 minus £650).

The trustees use a R185 (Trust Income) form to advise the beneficiaries of their income.

Depending on his circumstances, the beneficiary may have to pay
more tax or may receive a refund.

The effect of receiving dividend income for a basic or higher rate
taxpayer will be that he will be worse off than if he had received the
dividend direct. A non-taxpayer will be the same.

By well thought investment, it may be possible to structure the
position to mitigate the effects of income tax. Thus, e.g. investment
could be made in zero type investments if income was not required.
Alternatively, the balance of trust investment could be skewed towards
investments which bear tax at the rate of 20 per cent.

However

However, the trustees in the above example, who are now in blind
panic because they do not have enough to pay the extra tax, decide that
they do not wish to have to pay any more tax than they need. They look
for ways in which to avoid this and still pay out as much as possible.
They recap and realise that the net income is £1,800, i.e. £2,000 minus
the tax credit of £200. This sum, namely the £1,800, should suffer tax at
40 per cent leaving 60 per cent available to pay out namely £1,080. It is
interesting (and also quite depressing!) to note that that of the £2,000,
tax has now been suffered of £920, which equates to 46 per cent!

At termination of trust

3–28   There are no special features regarding income tax at the termination
of the trust

ACCUMULATION AND DISCRETIONARY TRUSTS[11]

3–29   There are special tax rates that apply to the income of trusts which can
accumulate income or pay it out at discretion, as set out in the Taxes Act
1988, s.686. On April 6, 2004 the rate applicable to trusts, which applies
to trust income apart from dividend type income, went up from 34 per
cent to 40 per cent. The dividend trust rate, which applies to dividend
type income, went up from 25 per cent to 32.5 per cent.

The new rate of 40 per cent also applies to the capital gains of
accumulation and discretionary trusts and interest in possession trusts
from April 6, 2004.

A trust which makes discretionary income payments to beneficiaries
should take the increased rates into account when making net payments
to beneficiaries after April 5, 2004. Trustees' tax at the end of the year
will be higher and consequently there will be less net income available to
pay to beneficiaries.

---

[11] There is a very helpful article on this in *Taxation Magazine* July 1, 2004 reprinted from
Tax Bulletin.

The new rate applicable to trusts also means that discretionary income payments to beneficiaries should carry a tax credit at the rate of 40 per cent instead of 34 per cent after April 5, 2004, even if the income out of which the payment is made was taxed only at 34 per cent or 25 per cent in the hands of the trustee. This tax credit has to be covered by the amount in the trustees' tax pool. If there is a shortfall, the trustees have to pay additional tax.

When trustees make discretionary income payments to beneficiaries they have to ensure that they have paid enough tax to cover the tax credit at the rate applicable to trusts. Trustees therefore need to keep a record of tax payments known as the tax pool.

The tax pool consists of tax paid by the trustees on income they have received, and tax deducted at source, e.g. by banks or building societies on interest. It does not include non-payable tax credits, such as the tax credit on dividends.

ACCUMULATION AND MAINTENANCE TRUSTS

As stated, these are not really a specific category from discretionary **3–30** trusts but are popular because they provide, as set out in IHTA 1984, s.71, certain clear advantages over discretionary trusts. Unfortunately, at time of writing it appears that the benefits will accrue only if the date when the trust funds are to be paid over to the beneficiary is not later than age 18. To a certain extent, this undermines the benefits of the accumulation and maintenance provisions, which were meant to allow testators/trusters to defer benefit to children or grandchildren until they were of an age to deal responsibly with their gift or inheritance. It allowed a window to testators/trusters to defer payment without the relative harshness of the discretionary trust regime. The favoured age in Scotland was 25. Issue would become entitled to the revenue of the trust at the age of 21 and at age 25 the capital.

Now we are faced with three regimes:

1. Existing regimes.
2. Where the beneficiary is 18.
3. Where the beneficiary is 25.

Definition

Accumulation and maintenance trusts are defined in IHTA 1984, s.71. **3–31** Three conditions must be satisfied:

> **71.**—(1) Subject to subsection (2) below, this section applies to settled property if—
>
> **(a) one or more persons (in this section referred to as beneficiaries) will, on or before attaining a specified age not exceeding twenty-five, become beneficially entitled to it or to an interest in possession in it, and**
>
> **(b) no interest in possession subsists in it and the income from it is to be accumulated so far as not applied for the maintenance, education or benefit of a beneficiary.**

(1A) This section does not apply to settled property at any particular time on or after 22nd March 2006 unless this section—

(a) applied to the settled property immediately before 22nd March 2006, and
(b) has applied to the settled property at all subsequent times up to the particular time.

(1B) This section does not apply to settled property at any particular time on or after 22nd March 2006 if, at that time, section 71A below applies to the settled property.

(2) This section does not apply to settled property unless either—

(a) **not more than twenty-five years have elapsed since the commencement of the settlement or, if it was later, since the time (or latest time) when the conditions stated in paragraphs (a) and (b) of subsections (1A) to (1) above became satisfied with respect to the property, or**
(b) **all the persons who are or have been beneficiaries are or were either—**

  (i) **grandchildren of a common grandparent, or**
  (ii) **children, widows or widowers or surviving civil partners of such grandchildren who were themselves beneficiaries but died before the time when, had they survived, they would have become entitled as mentioned in subsection (1)(a) above.**

(3) Subject to subsections (4) and (5) below, there shall be a charge to tax under this section—

(a) where settled property ceases to be property to which this section applies, and
(b) in a case in which paragraph (a) above does not apply, where the trustees make a disposition as a result of which the value of settled property to which this section applies is less than it would be but for the disposition.

(4) Tax shall not be charged under this section—

(a) on a beneficiary's becoming beneficially entitled to, or to an interest in possession in, settled property on or before attaining the specified age, or
(b) on the death of a beneficiary before attaining the specified age.

(5) Subsections (3) to (8) and (10) of section 70 above shall apply for the purposes of this section as they apply for the purposes of that section (with the substitution of a reference to subsection (3)(b) above for the reference in section 70(4) to section 70(2)(b)).

(6) Where the conditions stated in paragraphs (a) and (b) of subsection (1) above were satisfied on 15th April 1976 with respect

to property comprised in a settlement which commenced before that day, subsection (2)(a) above shall have effect with the substitution of a reference to that day for the reference to the commencement of the settlement, and the condition stated in subsection (2)(b) above shall be treated as satisfied if—

(a) it is satisfied in respect of the period beginning with 15th April 1976, or
(b) it is satisfied in respect of the period beginning with 1st April 1977 and either there was no beneficiary living on 15th April 1976 or the beneficiaries on 1st April 1977 included a living beneficiary, or
(c) there is no power under the terms of the settlement whereby it could have become satisfied in respect of the period beginning with 1st April 1977, and the trusts of the settlement have not been varied at any time after 15th April 1976.

(7) In subsection (1) above "persons" includes unborn persons; but the conditions stated in that subsection shall be treated as not satisfied unless there is or has been a living beneficiary.

(8) For the purposes of this section a person's children shall be taken to include his illegitimate children, his adopted children and his stepchildren.

The qualifying conditions thus are:

(a) One or more persons (the beneficiaries) will, on or before attaining a specified age not exceeding 25, become beneficially entitled to an interest in possession in it;
(b) no interest in possession subsists in it and the income from it must be accumulated so far as not applied for the maintenance, education or benefit of a beneficiary; and
(c) not more than 25 years have elapsed since the commencement of the trust or, if it was later, since the time (or latest time) when the conditions stated in paragraphs (a) above became satisfied with respect to the property; or
(d) all the persons who are or have been beneficiaries are or were either:

    (i) grandchildren of a common grandparent; or
    (ii) children, widows or widowers of such grandchildren who were themselves beneficiaries but died before the time when had they themselves survived, they would have become entitled as mentioned in (a) above.[12]

The accumulation and maintenance trust as chameleon

It is interesting to note that accumulation and maintenance trusts may **3–32** start out their "life" as discretionary trusts; it may become a liferent trust during the age of a beneficiary or beneficiaries from age 21 to 25; finally

---

[12] This is sometimes known as the "the common grandparent test".

it may become a "bare trust" when a beneficiary becomes 25; it may then, if the power exists, go back to a liferent trust. Of course, all these trusts may be occurring with different beneficiary or beneficiaries in the one accumulation and maintenance trust!

Uses

3–33   They were utilised in providing for trust income to be used for maintenance, education or benefit for under age beneficiaries. Generally, they were used for beneficiaries under 25, usually by will, where the funds were likely to be substantial. They would normally be used in place of the usual clause for "providing for beneficiaries not of full capacity" although this may also be included in the will. It cannot be stated often enough that it was a type of discretionary trust without some of the punitive tax aspect. It should be considered where the bequest to the children is potentially of the order of £300,000 or more.

It may also be possible to benefit children in different proportions and a class of children as yet unborn.

In addition, an *inter vivos* transfer into an accumulation and maintenance trust was a PET.

IHT—accumulation and maintenance trust

When trust commenced

3–34   When a truster *inter vivos* places funds in an accumulation and maintenance settlement this was regarded as PET for IHT purposes under IHTA 1984, s.3A. This became chargeable if the truster died within seven years. If the accumulation and maintenance trust is set up by discretionary trustees, it will incur an exit charge. If commenced by will, there will be IHT on death in the usual way. It was sometimes used by trusters where the trust fund contained family company shares where there was a wish to retain some measure of control.

During trust

3–35   There was no 10-year charge.[13] Payments to a beneficiary or beneficiaries during the accumulation and maintenance trust did not give rise to an IHT charge.

At termination of trust

3–36   If all the conditions were satisfied, there was no IHT payable on the beneficiary becoming entitled or on the death of the beneficiary attaining the specified age.

It is possible to continue the trust as a *liferent* trust after the expiry of the accumulation and maintenance trust age limit(s) when there would be no IHT (or CGT) charge on "disposal" on conversion to the liferent. Provided the accumulation and maintenance trust beneficiary received the trust capital (and accumulated interest) at the specified age, the IHT

---

[13] IHTA 1984, s.58.

regime would not apply, and there would be no exit charge payable on the trust capital.

It was possible for the trustees to allocate unequal shares amongst beneficiary or beneficiaries. It should be borne in mind that, if a partial termination of interest in possession occurs, a charge under IHTA 1984, s.52(1) may occur if a beneficiary fails to survive for seven years.

There is no exit charge on the death of a beneficiary or beneficiaries before attaining the age specified.

If the conditions are not satisfied, an IHT charge is imposed. The charge is fixed based on the amount of the reduction in the value of assets in the accumulation and maintenance trust. In terms of IHTA 1984, s.70, the charge is one quarter of a percent for each of the first complete consecutive quarters in the "relevant period". One fifth for each of the next 40 quarters, 15 per cent for each of the next 40 quarters, 10 per cent each of the next 40 quarters and 5 per cent for each of the next 40 quarters. The maximum (30 per cent) is reached when 50 years have elapsed. If the trustees make a disposition a change arises, calculated on the foregoing basis.

This summarised the old regime.

Under the present regime, namely after March 22, 2006, the privileges only apply if the beneficiary receives the trust funds on or before age 18 years.

It seems likely that testators and truster alike will wish to continue to defer payment until age 25 **notwithstanding the loss of accumulation and maintenance trust advantages**. In this event the trust will become, in effect, a discretionary trust. There are transitional provisions regarding accumulation and maintenance trusts from the age of 18 until 25 which have previously been referred to. It is likely that the accumulation and maintenance trust regime will be replaced by the bereaved minor's trust. This only applies to trusts by parents, not grandparents.

CGT—accumulation and maintenance trust

When trust commenced

There may be a CGT charge on realising assets to place in the trust or **3–37** transferring them into the trust. However, there is no holdover relief under the Taxation of Chargeable Gains Act 1992 ("TCGA"), s.260 as there may be for transfers into a discretionary trust. There may be a possibility of election for "business assets" for holdover under TCGA 1992, s.165.

Under the post March 22, 2006 regime, as the trust may now become a discretionary trust, holdover relief will be available as for discretionary trusts.

During and at termination of a trust

Whilst accumulation and maintenance settlements enjoyed privileged **3–38** treatment as far as IHT is concerned, there is and was no special treatment in respect of CGT. The trustees will be liable to CGT at 40 per cent on disposals during the trust. When a beneficiary acquires capital, the trustees will be deemed to dispose of assets at market value and reacquire them. This is an advantage over discretionary trusts where CGT may need to be paid by the trustees on sale, transfer or disposal.

Holdover relief is available for business assets on creation or when assets leave the trust, and payment by instalments may also be possible (TCGA 1992, s.165). If a beneficiary is not already entitled to an interest in possession, holdover relief may be available for all assets (TCGA 1992, s.260(2)(d)).

Income tax—accumulation and maintenance trust

3–39 Until the beneficiary attains (usually in Scotland) the age of 21 the trustees will be liable for tax at the rate applicable to trusts under the Income and Corporation Taxes Act 1988, s.686 ("ICTA"). If the income is applied for the maintenance, education or benefit of the beneficiary, the beneficiary receives a credit for the tax paid by the trustees, and may be able to recover some of the tax paid. When he attains 21, he acquires a liferent (an interest in possession), and the trustees will be liable only for basic rate tax.

If the income or capital can be applied for the benefit of the "infant" unmarried child of the truster, it will be deemed to be the income of the truster (ICTA 1988, s.660B). These provisions do not apply to trusters who are grandparents, or whose children are over 18. This provision that a parent who sets up an accumulation and maintenance settlement for his children will not be taxed on the trust income, which they might otherwise be under ICTA 1988, Pt 15, c.147A was of considerable benefit but is likely not to be available.

LIFERENT TRUST

Uses

3–40 In the texts and in statute these are often referred to as "trusts with an interest in possession". It is important to differentiate between setting up a liferent trust and giving a right of enjoyment. The use of the wording such as "leave a liferent of my house at . . ." may not be sufficient. Regard should be had to the differences. The most common in Scotland is where the estate is left to a spouse in liferent and to the children in fee. Its advantage was that under the old "estate duty" (death duty) regime the liferented estate only suffered estate duty on the first death, usually the husband's. When the widow died the liferented fund went to the children who were usually the fiars.

The introduction of capital transfer tax, the forerunner of inheritance tax, removed the benefit by, in effect, equating liferent with beneficial ownership. IHT would be payable on the liferented fund which was aggregated with deceased's estate for IHT purposes. From being an advantage most practitioners regarded them as a fiscal disaster.

After almost dying out, however, they appear to be making a comeback, being used very commonly in second marriages, where the testator or donor will attempt to safeguard the inheritance of the children of the first marriage, while still providing for his second wife. A liferent trust can also be utilised for an adult child who suffers some kind of disability, although the preference now would be for a discretionary trust. Usually this will also give trustees power to advance capital to beneficiaries when the trustees consider it suitable. Another use is for retired employees, often in domestic service, to be given a liferent of a house, and on their death the fee will pass to the former employer's family. As the employee may be a person of low capital, the IHT implications of aggregation will often be minimal. There are situations where a liferent is extremely appropriate, particularly where second marriages are involved, and both spouses to the second marriage have children of their own by their first marriages.

A testator might well wish to provide for their surviving second spouse, but may well wish to ensure that the capital ultimately passes to their own children.

Other instances where a liferent trust is appropriate might be where a testator is adamant that the capital is to pass to his or her children, and they fear that in the event of their death, their surviving spouse might re-marry. A rich widow/widower could, for some, be an attractive prospect and unless the estate is protected by a liferent, the new spouse could put pressure on the newly remarried widow/widower to make available cash even on a short-term basis in order to assist business or maintain certain lifestyle. It would be difficult for the recently re-married spouse to refuse such a request. The recent changes, relative to equating the rules with those as for discretionary trusts in the Finance Act 2006 may make these less attractive.

IHT–liferent trust

When trust commences—Pre March 22, 2006

There are no clear IHT advantages where the first to die of a married **3–41** couple leaves their estate in liferent for the surviving spouse. Assuming the spouse is UK domiciled,[14] on the death of the survivor the value of the liferent trust is added to the estate of the survivor and IHT is payable on the combined total with only one NRB exemption available. The tax is payable from the liferent trust, and from the estate of the second spouse to die in the proportions which the two estates bear to each other. It is important to remember and to stress to clients that the NRB is not personal to the individual, and the only way in which a surviving spouse can ensure that the NRB is available for their personal estate, and not shared with the liferent trust, is for the survivor to make a lifetime transfer from their estate, which being a lifetime transfer will either become exempt if there is no gift with reservation, and the seven-year period elapses, or if it becomes a failed PET, it will fall within, and could utilise the NRB, as it pre-dates the transfer on death.

As regards existing liferent trusts which run on until the interest in the trust property at March 22, comes to an end, it is provided that if someone, the fiar, takes absolute ownership this will be a transfer by the person with the interest in the property—either a transfer on death or a PET if they are still alive—and will still receive the same IHT treatment as now.

If, however, the interest, i.e. the liferent, comes to an end so that the property remains on trust, this will be treated as the creation of a new

---

[14] If not the exemption is limited to £55,000.

trust. If this new trust comes to an end during the lifetime of the person entitled to it, this will be a transfer creating "relevant property" and will be immediately chargeable. New trusts for chargeable properties are of course excluded from this. If the interest comes to an end on death, it will form part of the person's IHT estate as at present. Any new liferent trust arising when a liferent trust created before March 22, 2006 comes to an end and before April 6, 2008, whether on death or otherwise, is to be treated as a liferent trust which was existing on March 22, 2006.

Danger Warning!!!

The old rules are likely only to apply to trusts made prior to March 22, 2006. Any new trust assets or indeed any transfer of assets into an existing trust are likely to fall within the new regime. In addition, when the liferent comes to an end before April 6, 2008 and is replaced by a new liferent within the same trust, the old rules also continue to apply to that new liferent.

There are four distinct possibilities where liferents prior to March 22, 2006 come to an end as follows:

1. The liferent ends on the death of the beneficiary before April 6, 2008.
   The trust fund is included in the beneficiary's estate for IHT purposes. Any new liferent coming into existence is also subject to the old rules.
2. The liferent ends during the beneficiary's lifetime but before April 6, 2008.
   Generally this will constitute a PET if the trust fund passes completely; any new liferent coming into existence will be subject to the old regime.
3. The liferent ends on the death of the beneficiary on or after April 6, 2008.
   The trust fund is included in the beneficiary's estate for inheritance tax purposes.
   Generally this will constitute a PET if the trust fund passes absolutely. Any new liferent coming into existence will be subject to the old regime.
4. Liferent ends during the beneficiary's lifetime on or after April 6, 2008. This will only be a PET if the trust funds pass without restriction. If they remain in a trust or remain in a trust there is a chargeable lifetime transfer and any new liferent coming into existence is subject to the new rules.

Post March 22, 2006

3–42   It seems that, as from 2008, these liferent trusts will suffer the exit charge and the 10 year "hit" presently at a maximum of 6 per cent. In addition, it seems that *inter vivos* trusts will also suffer the 20 per cent on the value above the NRB IHT lifetime charge on being set up. In addition, it may be that the surviving spouse exemption will not be available after March 23, 2006 to provisions in wills where a liferent is left to a surviving spouse with a power to advance capital.[15] In a helpful article "Will trust be lost?" in *Taxation* magazine Chris Whitehouse and Emma Chamberlain emphasise a real problem whereby in addition to the loss of surviving spouse exemption as before mentioned, the "practice of combining a nil-rate band trust with a 'liferent' trust of residue for the surviving spouse will result in tax charges on the nil-rate band trust being calculated by reference to the value of the residuary estate".[16] The learned authors underlie the potentially disastrous provisions:

> "Many existing family wills have been drafted to give the surviving spouse a life interest in residue, often with flexible overriding powers of appointment. There are a number of reasons why this is a relatively standard procedure, notably when the testator has been married more than once and has children from earlier marriages. All such wills have been drafted on the basis that the spouse exemption will be available on the testator's death. However, as a result of the Budget proposals currently in Finance (No 2) Bill 2006, it appears that such a trust will not satisfy the requirements for an immediate post-death interest (IPDI) and so spouse relief will not be available in the event of the testator dying without having altered his will."

While the initial worry has been, to some extent, alleviated in the Act, it nevertheless remains a real possibility that where the liferent trust provision contains a provision to advance capital, this will be sufficient to take the trust out of the surviving spouse exemption regime.

Under IHTA 1984, s.49, property, subject to a liferent trust is dealt with and treated as owned for IHT purposes. A new s.49, i.e. s.49A restricts the operation of the section to a tightly delineated class of trusts, which arise after March 22, 2006, to those qualifying for an immediate post-death interest ("IPDI"), a disabled person's interest and a transitional serial interest.

Immediate post-death interest

The concept of an immediate post-death interest is introduced in **3–43** order to satisfy the requirements for an interest to be treated as an IPDI. The interest **must arise as a result of a will or intestacy** and immediately on the death of the truster or testator. The termination of an IPDI in favour of a trust for a "bereaved minor" or a transitional serial interest will be a PET by the person whose interest ends. An IPDI in favour of a spouse is to be ignored when changing the trusts created in the death of the same testator.

A transitional serial interest occurs where a person is beneficially entitled to a liferent in trust property and the rules for this are as follows:

---

[15] Chris Whitehouse, "Will trust be lost?", Taxation, June 8, 2006, Vol.157 No.4061.
[16] Finance (No.2) Bill 2006.

The trust commenced before March 22, 2006 and immediately before March 22, 2006 the property then comprised in the will was property in which the liferentor was beneficially entitled to in the liferent; that interest came to an end at a time on or after March 22, 2006 but before April 6, 2008, at which point the liferentor became beneficially entitled to the trust.

Example

In his will, James Garfield bequeaths the residue of his estate in liferent to his wife, Mrs Jean Arthur or Garfield and to his children in fee. The will provides for the usual power on the trustees to advance capital to the widow.

On the death of Mr Garfield, it might be assumed that this would create an IPDI and the spouse exemption would be available in the normal way subject to the usual qualifications regarding domicile.

It could be argued that power to advance capital would nullify the effect of this **since it could bring to an end the liferent in whole or in part**.

Instead of this, Mr Garfield decides in his will to set up a NRB mini discretionary trust and leave his wife a liferent of the residue.

Prior to March 22, 2006, the effect was that under s.80 the trust was not treated as arising until the termination of the liferent. Thus, it could be argued that the two trusts were not related within IHTA, s.62

Section 62 provides:

> **62.**—(1) For the purposes of this Chapter two settlements are related if and only if—
>
> (a) the settlor is the same in each case, and
> (b) they commenced on the same day,
> but subject to subsection (2) below.
>
> (2) Two settlements are not related for the purposes of this Chapter if all the property comprised in one or both of them was immediately after the settlement commenced held for charitable purposes only without limit of time (defined by a date or otherwise).

However, it may be that the effect of the recent legislation could be that when the liferent in favour of the spouse arises after March 22, 2006 these two trusts will be created on the same day and will therefore be related settlements within IHT 1984, s.62. The effect of this could be potentially disastrous in that the values of both trusts will require to be taken into account for IHT purposes and in fixing the rate!

During trust

3–44   Until March 22, 2006, the incidence of IHT during the administration was uncommon. It might occur if the capital is paid out during a renunciation but, if correctly drafted, IHT should not be a problem during the administration of a liferent trust.

It should be that if there are no capital payouts or advances then there should be no IHT problems.

If, of course, the liferent trust does not fall within the strict guidelines as before mentioned, then it will in fact be treated as a discretionary trust and the appropriate regime will apply.

At termination of trust

IHT occurs on the death of the testator setting up the trust if it is **3–45** made by will. If it is made *inter vivos* then it was regarded as a PET. However, under Budget 2006 speech proposals it would appear that 10 year charges and on the death of the Liferentor or Liferentrix of the trust there will also be the possibility of a charge to IHT. If the trust is set up *mortis causa* in favour of a spouse, the surviving spouse exemption will apply at one of these stages. Under present rules, the termination of the liferent by the trustees is not regarded as a gift by the individual benefiting from the liferent.

Capital gains tax—liferent trust

When trust commenced

If set up *inter vivos* there may be CGT payable by the truster on **3–46** investments sold or transferred into the trust. The usual reliefs, such as hold over, taper, indexation and retirement, may apply.

As regards trusts which do not qualify as IPDIs there is the possibility of hold over relief under TCGA 1992, s.260(2)(a).

During trust

Disposals during the trust will attract CGT in the usual way and are **3–47** taxed at 40 per cent. During the administration, there is an annual exemption of half the lifetime rate (presently £4,400 for 2006/2007), always assuming that only one trust has been set up.

At termination of trust

On the death of the liferentor, no chargeable gain or loss will accrue. **3–48** There is assumed to be a disposal and reacquisition by the trustees at date of death of the liferentor.

Income tax—liferent trust

Whilst the Finance Act 2006 made drastic changes to the IHT **3–49** treatment of discretionary trusts and liferent trusts, some of which have had the effect of equating the two for IHT purposes, nevertheless, income tax was not altered!

The trustees are liable to pay tax in the usual way. They were not liable if the income went direct to the beneficiary. Trustees suffered tax at basic rate (20 per cent), Schedule F dividend rate (10 per cent) or lower rate (22 per cent). However, the new provisions suggest that the treatment of non-qualifying trusts will be similar to discretionary trusts.

Expenses

The beneficiary is entitled to a credit for the amount of tax paid by the **3–50** trustees in respect of that income. If expenses have been deducted, the credit will not be for the full amount of the tax paid by the trustees. If the beneficiary is entitled to a refund of income tax, the trustees' should have power to charge the expenses to capital as otherwise the beneficiary will not be able to obtain a complete refund; this could be important in the case of chargeable beneficiaries or beneficiaries who pay little or no tax.

Social security and other benefits from public funds

3–51   Obviously, these and other benefits have to be taken into account in determining which form of trust. Some benefits are not means tested (e.g. NIRP, DLA) but others are (e.g. income support, local authority housing benefit, and local authority help with residential or nursing home care fees). Clearly, the liferent trust may not be appropriate for a beneficiary who is receiving means tested benefits.

TRUSTS FOR DISABLED PERSONS

3–52   There are certain benefits from the point of view of IHT and CGT for "Disabled Trusts". Because of the incidence of benefits from public funds, these are rarely used but they may be of use where the beneficiary is not in receipt from public funds or where the same is not "means tested". However, it should be noted that practically the same effect can often be obtained by skilful drafting of a discretionary trust deed where the beneficiary's right to assistance from public funds may be safeguarded.

It would appear that this type of trust will still enjoy some protection and will be excluded from the more stringent provisions of the new regime. Indeed, trusts for disabled beneficiaries are now to be the only trusts, which do not now trigger an IHT charge on a lifetime gift. However, the definition of "a disabled person" within this regime is so strict that many vulnerable individuals do not qualify.

Inheritance Tax Act 1984 provides: Trusts for disabled persons

89.—(1) This section applies to settled property transferred into settlement after 9th March 1981 and held on trusts—

(a) under which, during the life of a disabled person, no interest in possession in the settled property subsists, and
(b) which secure that not less than half of the settled property which is applied during his life is applied for his benefit.

(2) For the purposes of this Act the person mentioned in subsection (1) above shall be treated as beneficially entitled to an interest in possession in the settled property.

(3) The trusts on which settled property is held shall not be treated as falling outside subsection (1) above by reason only of the powers conferred on the trustees by section 32 of the Trustee Act 1925 or section 33 of the Trustee Act (Northern Ireland) 1958 (powers of advancement).

(4) The reference in subsection (1) above to a disabled person is, in relation to any settled property, a reference to a person who, when the property was transferred into settlement, was—

(a) incapable, by reason of mental disorder within the meaning of the Mental Health Act 1983, of administering his property or managing his affairs, or

(b) in receipt of an attendance allowance under section 64 of the Social Security Contributions and Benefits Act 1992 or section 64 of the Social Security Contributions and Benefits (Northern Ireland) Act 1992, or

(c) in receipt of a disability living allowance under section 71 of the Social Security Contributions and Benefits Act 1992 by virtue of entitlement to the care component at the highest or middle rate.

(5) The reference in subsection (1) above to a disabled person includes, in relation to any settled property, a reference to a person who, when the property was transferred into settlement—

(a) would have been in receipt of attendance allowance under section 64 of either of the Acts mentioned in subsection (4)(b) above had provision made by regulations under section 67(1) or (2) of that Act (non-satisfaction of conditions for attendance allowance where person is undergoing treatment for renal failure in a hospital or is provided with certain accommodation) been ignored, or

(b) would have been in receipt of disability living allowance by virtue of entitlement to the care component at the highest or middle rate had provision made by regulations under section 72(8) of either of the Acts mentioned in subsection (4)(c) above (no payment of disability living allowance for persons for whom certain accommodation is provided) been ignored.

(6) The reference in subsection (1) above to a disabled person also includes, in relation to any settled property, a reference to a person who satisfies the Commissioners for Her Majesty's Revenue and Customs—

(a) that he would, when the property was transferred into settlement, have been in receipt of attendance allowance under section 64 of either of the Acts mentioned in subsection (4)(b) above—

    (i) had he met the conditions as to residence under section 64(1) of that Act, and

    (ii) had provision made by regulations under section 67(1) or (2) of that Act been ignored, or

(b) that he would, when the property was transferred into settlement, have been in receipt of a disability living allowance by virtue of entitlement to the care component at the highest or middle rate—

    (i) had he met the prescribed conditions as to residence under section 71(6) of either of the Acts mentioned in subsection (4)(c) above, and

(ii) had provision made by regulations under section 72(8) of that Act been ignored.

One potential disadvantage of a disabled person's trust is that although assets in an interest in possession trust will automatically receive an uplift for capital gains tax purposes on the death of the income beneficiary, with a disabled person's trust, because the Principal Beneficiary would only have a "deemed" interest in possession for inheritance tax purposes, the uplift is not given.

Inheritance tax—trust for the disabled

3–53   A transfer into a disabled person's trust is a PET for IHT purposes.

However, the *incapax* is treated as equivalent to a liferentor for IHT purposes.

Usually the trust is discretionary in form, although the disabled person could be named as a "principal beneficiary", and the income may be held on discretionary trusts throughout the principal beneficiary's lifetime so it should not jeopardise his or her entitlement to state benefits. At least half of the capital, which is paid out during the principal beneficiary's life, must be paid to him or her or for his or her benefit. This does not mean that half of the capital **has** to be paid out—only that if there is a distribution of capital the Principal Beneficiary must receive at least half of it.

Although the trust is discretionary in form, the principal beneficiary would be treated as liferentor for inheritance tax purposes. In other words, the principal beneficiary would be the revenue beneficiary, even though there was power to accumulate income. This means the trust will not be subject to the penal inheritance tax charges which usually apply to discretionary trusts. Therefore there would be no charge on setting up the trust, and no 10 year or exit charges.

When trust commenced; During trust; At termination of trust

3–54   Section 89(1) IHTA applies to property transferred after March 9, 1981 and held in trust:

(a) under which, during the life of a disabled person, no interest in possession in the settled property subsists, and
(b) which secure that not less than half of the settled property which is applied during his life is applied for his benefit.

Section 89(4) defines a disabled person as a person who, when the property was transferred into settlement was:

(a) incapable, by reason of mental disorder within the meaning of the Mental Health Act 1983, of administering his property or managing his affairs, or
(b) in receipt of an attendance allowance under section 64 of the Social Security Contributions and Benefits Act 1992 or section 64 of the Social Security Contributions and Benefits (Northern Ireland) Act 1992, or

    (c) in receipt of a disability living allowance under section 71 of the Social Security Contributions and Benefits Act 1992 by virtue of entitlement to the care component at the highest or middle rate.

Under s.89(3) a trust is still within the section even though the trustees have the power to advance. The disabled person is treated as beneficially entitled to an interest in possession of the settled property.

The practical effect of these provisions is to treat these trusts as if the disabled person had a liferent of the trust property, even though they are really discretionary trusts.

Capital gains tax—trust for the disabled

Disabled persons' trusts can also obtain capital gains tax advantages **3–55** under the Taxation of Chargeable Gains Act 1992, Sch.1 para.1 ("TCGA 1992, Sch.1 para.1") namely, a full annual exemption compared to half the annual exemption usually applicable to trusts. However, the conditions required to meet this are not entirely compatible with IHTA 1984, s.89.

The annual exemption for many trusts is usually one-half of the personal exemption. However, a disabled person's trust is entitled to exemption amounting to the full personal entitlement, i.e. £8,800.

The rules for this are somewhat restrictive. The disabled beneficiary must be incapable of administering his property by reason of mental incapacity or be physically disabled. This latter qualification is linked to receipt of certain benefits from public funds. In addition, the trust must provide that not less than one-half of the property applied is for the benefit of the *incapax* and for no other person.

As if this was not restrictive enough the other problem is that the trust can lose the benefit of the relief if the *incapax* loses their disability or ceases to qualify.

When trust commenced; During trust; At termination of trust

    Schedule 1(1) to the TCGA 1992 provides that;   **3–56**

    1.—(1) For any year of assessment during the whole or part of which settled property is held on trusts which secure that, during the lifetime of a mentally disabled person or a person in receipt of attendance allowance or of a disability living allowance by virtue of entitlement to the care component at the highest or middle rate—

    (a) not less than half of the property which is applied is applied for the benefit of that person, and

    (b) that person is entitled to not less than half of the income arising from the property, or no such income may be applied for the benefit of any other person.

The IHT and CGT provisions appear to conflict.

However, these provisions should be carefully considered when advising elderly clients as trusts of which they are beneficiaries may qualify (they may be in receipt of an attendance allowance).

Full exemption as for an individual for CGT purposes is available under TCGA 1992, Sch.1 para.1, but the conditions are very restricted, so much so that it could be argued that they completely undermine setting up such a trust in the first place, unless reducing the truster's CGT exemption is the main purpose.

One of the main problems is that at least 50 per cent of the trust income must be advanced to the disabled beneficiary each year. This might undermine the benefit of any benefits from public funds.

Income tax—trust for the disabled

3–57   As for liferent trusts.

CHARITABLE TRUSTS

3–58   These enjoy exemption from IHT, CGT and income tax.

OFFSHORE TRUSTS

3–59   The advantages of these for UK residents have largely been diminished by recent legislation.

CGT—offshore trusts

3–60   No chargeable gain accrues on the disposal of interest in settled property where both trustees and beneficiaries are further of UK. The main advantages of these are foreign domiciled persons who plan to come to live in the UK. They may be able to use these as a "tax shelter". Conversely, a UK resident emigrating may be able to use the IHT exemption for gilt-edged stock.

Income tax

3–61   Trustees resident abroad are not liable for income tax on income arising abroad; they will be liable for income tax on income arising in the UK.

BARE TRUSTS

3–62   These occur when a beneficiary has a vested right to capital but has not received it, e.g. on the death of a liferentor some time will elapse before the fee is conveyed to him and the trustees are still holding it for him, or where executors are holding a legacy or an "ascertained" share of residue for a beneficiary. Trusts for administration are a form of bare trust.

As regards IHT, CGT, and income tax, the income and capital of the trust are treated as if they were the beneficiary's.

PILOT TRUSTS

3–63   These are not a specific category. They are generally used to format or set up the mechanism or trust deed which will be later utilised to transfer funds into where, e.g. a testator wishes to set up more than one trust in his will, and it is thought that this may fall foul of the related settlements rule.[17]

Inheritance Tax Act 1984 provides:

62.—(1) For the purposes of this Chapter two settlements are related if and only if—

(a) the settlor is the same in each case, and
(b) they commenced on the same day,

but subject to subsection (2) below.

(2) Two settlements are not related for the purposes of this Chapter if all the property comprised in one or both of them was immediately after the settlement commenced held for charitable purposes only without limit of time (defined by a date or otherwise).

Instead the testator merely leaves the legacy to be paid into the previously created pilot trust. As the trust is not actually set up on the same day as his, e.g. accumulation and settlement trust (also to be set up under his will), the consequences of related settlements rule are avoided.

Trusts for a Bereaved Minor

It looks as if under current proposals the status and exemptions which **3–64** were previously effeiring to accumulation and maintenance trusts will be changed to the more restricted class of trusts known as "a trust for a bereaved minor". The assets of this trust will be exempt from inheritance tax and no charges will apply if the beneficiary dies or assets are transferred from the trust.

This will be an exemption from the proposed new 'mainstream' rules. To qualify as a trust for a bereaved minor the following requirements are necessary:

1. The beneficiary of the trust must be under 18 years of age.
2. At least one of his parents is dead.
3. The trust requires to be set up under intestacy or the criminal injuries compensation scheme or the will of a deceased parent. It is this last one with which we will be principally concerned in this text.
4. The beneficiary must become absolutely and fully entitled to the assets at the age of 18. Reference has already been made to transitional arrangements for accumulation and maintenance trusts but for the pure trust for a bereaved minor it is necessary that he is entitled to benefit from the assets at this age.

This will be a somewhat disappointment to many testators who will consider that the age is far too young for children to have assets. It is not so much the fact that they, themselves, may not be mature enough. It is that they may be subject to pressure from other parties!

---

[17] IHTA 1984, s.62.

Until the beneficiary reaches 18 the trust fund may only be applied for the benefit of the beneficiary.

The trust income may be either applied for the benefit of the minor given directly to them or accumulated. As stated there will be a partial exemption up until the age of 25. What is likely to happen is that the trust assets will become relevant property when the beneficiary reaches the age of 18. There will be no inheritance tax charge then but there will be an exit charge at the age of 25.

A Word about Stamp Duty

3–65   Arguably the oldest form of taxation in Scotland, stamp duty goes back to 1694. The format did not materially change until it did so radically with the introduction in 2003 of what is virtually a new tax, Stamp Duty Land Tax ("SDLT"). This is leviable on transfers of heritable property in Scotland. The legislation repealed stamp duty on all other property excluding stocks and shares. Special rules apply to marketable security transactions.

Thus, if heritable property is conveyed to trustees SDLT at rates of up to 4 per cent may be chargeable depending on whether the property is in a disadvantage area, for business use or otherwise. It may well be the case that the truster, on starting the trust, will give shares or heritable property; in this case no stamp duty or SDLT will apply. If shares are transferred the transfer will be certified under Category L of the schedule to Stamp Duty (Exempt Instruments) Regulations 1987[18] and avoid the fixed duty of £5. In the case of heritable property the trustees themselves certify the deed as exempt.[19] Form SDLT 60 is used for this purpose.

Joint Property

3–66   This single topic causes many more problems than it should. It occurs in, and has separate rules for, both heritable and moveable property.[20]

Heritable

3–67   Often the main focus of difficulty relates to the family house; this may be:

>   1. In the sole name of one of the spouses. Here it will be necessary to execute a disposition conveying it into joint names (no survivorship) as for 2.
>   2. In the joint names of both spouses (no survivorship).

Joint name, joint names and the survivor

3–68   Reference is made to Chapter 23 of *Conveyancing* (1993) by Professors Gretton and Reid on destinations, and which specifically deals with special destinations.

---

[18] SI 1987/516.

[19] FA 2003, Sch.3, para.1.

[20] This topic is covered from a different perspective under the section regarding deeds of variation.

There have of course been further developments in the law of destinations and these are dealt with by the same authors in Reid/ Gretton *Conveyancing 2005*.[21]

It relates to a matter which has been covered elsewhere in this text. It is extremely common in the west of Scotland and elsewhere for survivorship destinations to be included in the titles for heritable properties particularly where these are owned by husband and wife or son and daughter or elsewhere. Clearly, this is a matter which has caused a certain amount of trouble over the years as evidenced by the various cases. These cases have stemmed mainly from the disposition by an inexperienced practitioner of a one-half *pro indiviso* share where the original title is affected by a survivorship destination.

If there is a survivorship destination then this may affect parties' ability to deal directly with their own one-half share since this will be affected by the survivorship.

It is possible for survivorship destination to be evacuated or cancelled by *mortis causa* deed.

It is also competent for the survivorship destination to be evacuated by deed of variation and the style of this is included together with a style of conveyance to the discretionary trust and the sale by the discretionary trustees of the one-half share to the surviving spouse. In addition, there is also a form of standard security which may be of assistance also.

The authors point out the problems of incorporating destinations in deeds with particular reference to wills. Their remarks may well apply to trust deeds as well. They cite the example of where the destination is in favour of "A" whom failing to "B". They cite the common law presumption that if the subject of the legacy is moveable or partly heritable and partly moveable, the testator is presumed to have intended conditional substitution, that is to say A would take in preference to B. However, if the subject of the legacy is exclusively heritable the testator is presumed to have intended a substitution.

There have, of course, been further developments in the law relating to destinations in particular as contained in the Family Law (Scotland) Act 2006.[22]

In joint names and the survivor[23] to the joint account—which, certainly, in the West of Scotland—is likely to be the preferred method of joint holding (despite strictures to the contrary). For a legacy of the half share of the house to be effective it is really necessary to revoke/ evacuate any destination so that each spouse has a *pro indiviso* (half) share. This may mean that a fresh disposition by both parties is necessary. Alternatively, a separate deed or minute in the following form can be executed and recorded or registered. If it is registered the title number must be quoted. If recorded it must contain a conveying description.

Style

WE, **THOMAS PURSE** and **MRS CHRISTINE PATRICIA HANDBAG** or **3–69 PURSE**, Spouses, both residing together at Forty six Millionaires Avenue, Milngavie G62 1XX, heritable proprietors of ALL and WHOLE that plot or

---

[21] (2006), p.72 (update series).

[22] These and other aspects are also dealt with by Professors Gretton and Reid *Conveyancing 2005"* (2006), p.72 ff.

[23] This is similar to the English "joint tenancy".

area of ground in the Burgh of Milngavie and County of Dumbarton containing Nine hundred and eighty five square yards or thereby Imperial Measure marked "Plot No. 1" on the plan annexed and subscribed as relative to and described in the first place in the Feu Contract between Colonel Archibald Vivian Campbell Douglas of Mains on the one part with consents therein mentioned and The Gerry Building Company Limited on the other part dated First and recorded in the Division of the General Register of Sasines applicable to the County of Dumbarton on Fifteenth both days of January in the year Nineteen hundred and forty three; WHEREAS we are infeft in the said subjects by virtue of Disposition by me, the said Thomas Purse in our favour dated twenty eighth June and recorded in the said Division of the General Register of Sasines on the twenty fifth day of August in the year Nineteen hundred and thirty nine and WHEREAS the said last mentioned Disposition contains a survivorship destination in favour of the survivor of us AND CONSIDERING that we, the said Thomas Purse and the said Mrs Christine Patricia Handbag or Purse HEREBY AGREE and CONFIRM that the said survivorship destination should be evacuated THEREFORE WE HEREBY EVACUATE the aforementioned destination to the effect that the subjects hereinbefore described will be held by us to the extent of a one-half share by me, the said Thomas Purse (husband) and the remaining one-half share by me, the said Mrs Christine Patricia Handbag or Purse (wife) and WE HEREBY AGREE and DECLARE that either of us shall be entitled to dispone and convey our respective one-half share in the subjects by way of inter vivos or mortis causa Deed; and We hereby certify that this deed falls within Category L in the Stamp Duty (Exempt Deeds) Regulations 1987; and we consent to registration hereof for preservation; IN WITNESS WHEREOF

Both the disposition and the minute attract registration/recording dues of £22.

However, sometimes there is a power reserved to the grantor to revoke/evacuate. Here, it is possible for the party granting the deed containing the destination to unilaterally revoke the destination.

It might be appropriate when preparing a deed in joint names and the survivor for a power to be reserved to revoke for either or one party as appropriate. Instructions should be taken before this is done.

After the destination is cancelled it can be included as a separate bequest.

The half *pro indiviso* share can then be left directly to children or issue.

> I direct my executors to make over such interest in the subjects known as Twelve [...] Irvine as I may own at the time of my death, free of all expenses of transfer, heritable debts and securities and other capital burdens affecting my interest in the said subjects to my children namely, my son the said [...] my daughter, the said Mrs [...] or [...] and my son, [...] residing at Number [...] Ontario, Canada DECLARING THAT in the event of any of my said children failing to survive me their share in the said subjects shall pass hereunder to their respective surviving spouses.

Incapax spouse

3–70   The operation of the survivorship destination can cause difficulty where one of the spouses becomes incapax and perhaps is unable to live at home. If the spouse who resides in the house dies then, unless something is done, the incapax spouse will be entitled to the whole house by survivorship. This may cause difficulties. A costly guardianship or intervention order may be necessary and the deceased spouse has, of course, lost the right to leave "his" half share direct to his children.

It may be possible prior to his death to include a provision in his will to evacuate the destination as follows:

Legacy Evacuating Special Destination

I direct my Executors to make over to my son, the said James Aaron Burr, my **3–71** interest in the house known as Eighty Madison Avenue, Jordanhill, Glasgow, which house is held by myself and my wife, MRS ELLEN ADAMS or BURR, on a special destination contained in the Disposition by The City of Glasgow District Council with consent therein mentioned, in favour of myself and the said Mrs Ellen Adams or Burr and the survivor of us dated First and Seventh August and recorded in the Division of the Sasine Registers for the County' of the Barony and Regality of Glasgow on Twenty second July Nineteen hundred and seventy five and which destination I hereby evacuate.

As an alternative

Some thought might be given to bequeathing a liferent of the one half share to the surviving spouse, but it might be as well to consider either not giving the spouse a liferent or leaving him or her to negotiate with the children or issue or giving a liferent and also giving the trustees power to terminate the liferent in whole or in part.

> I direct my trustees to hold the one half share *pro indiviso* of the house owned by me at [. . .] in liferent for my wife, the said [. . .] Declaring that my trustees shall be entitled in their absolute discretion to terminate and revoke said liferent, upon giving written notice to my said wife, in which event the said half share shall be dealt with as hereinafter provided

Moveable

The position with heritable estate should be contrasted with deposits **3–72** in joint names. A receipt for money deposited in the bank may include names on it other than the owners. This is merely for administrative convenience and gives those named on it the right to uplift the money from the bank. However, this is not a document of title in the strict legal sense, in that it does not prove who actually owns the money. The person depositing the money in principle is the owner. If he were to put a destination on the receipt or the account it has no testamentary effect. The survivor can uplift the funds but must pay them to the depositor's executor as part of the estate.

As Professor McDonald points out in *Succession*,

> "there is a further problem with share certificates. In England a simple joint holding by 'A and B' implies a survivorship destination although none is expressed; in Scotland that is not so. However, the English rule applies apparently to shares held by Scots in English companies. The rule has been doubted and does not apply to government stock, which is deemed to be British rather than English".

Danger Warning!!!

Please take care not to include a survivorship clause to children or issue in the legacy.

Chapter Four

TRUST DRAFTING GENERALLY

"He mended his pen, however, marked half a dozen sheets of paper with an amply marginal fold, whipped down Dallas of St Martin's styles from a shelf, where that venerable work rousted with Stair's institutions, Dirleton's Doubts, Balfour's practiques, and a parcel of old account books—opened the volume at the article Contract of Marriage and prepared to make what he called a "sma-minute, to prevent parties frae resiling.""[1]

INTRODUCTION

If only it were as simple for us as this. Scott's superb character, the **4–01** eccentric notary, Mr MacWheeble, would perhaps be more than bemused at the array of tools available to the modern drafter. While present day drafters would not sustain themselves as with Scott's character on ample mouthfuls of porridge and whisky (unfortunately), it could be argued that the drafting process has not materially changed. Instead of Martin's styles and Dirleton's Doubts we have in-house styles, diploma styles and those on our computer software. Very few people are able from memory to draft out on the dictating machine or otherwise a trust deed to fit the given situation. Most people will start with a style or part of a style. Word processing software makes this simpler and, as we shall presently see, at the same time more complex.

Fast forwarding several hundred years to the 1950s and 1960s, a student entering the class of conveyancing at the University of Glasgow would acquire a helpful booklet entitled *Styles of Deeds and Practice Notes* 1954.[2] In the Preface the author/editor pays credit to the late Professor of Conveyancing for the use of his styles and indicates, with a certain amount of respectful diffidence, that he has included some Styles and Notes, which he has found useful. However, the author strictly enjoins the would-be drafter: "Forms should not be slavishly copied. In the case of statutory forms the requirements of the statute must be observed, but in general forms should be used as guides and adapted to suit the circumstances of each case". This probably encapsulates the most useful advice which can be given to a trust drafter, or indeed any other drafter.

Following on from such joys as procuratory of resignation, writs of Clare Constat and the like we find at art.50, a style of general trust

---

[1] Sir Walter Scott, *Waverley*.
[2] *Styles of Deeds and Practice Notes*, 1954 October 1, 1954. Robert Maclehose and Co Ltd, Glasgow.

disposition and settlement, at art.51, a checklist of discretionary powers, at arts 52 and 53 styles of clauses, and finally at art.54, a marriage contract.

These were the starting points for trust drafters. From then progression would take place to Green's *Encyclopaedia of Styles*. In those days training was by apprenticeship. Practical experience in the office was combined with attendance at classes.

Apprentices in law offices in Scotland, when making their first attempts at drafting, were entrusted with two "pearls" of wisdom. First, never witness a deed unless you are present at the signing and, secondly, always draft a deed with the idea at the back of your mind that it will be read over in court some day. The advice usually came with the joke, "I doubt if Lord President Blank has ever seen, much less had to draft a writ". While the maxim is appropriate to all writs, it should apply to drafting trust deeds with even greater relevance today. It may seem a high standard because only an infinitesimal fraction of writs will be the subject of litigation; nevertheless, it is the criterion at which to aim. If, instead of Judges of the Court of Session, there is substituted another solicitor appointed by a disappointed beneficiary, agent or counsel appointed by the solicitor's professional negligence insurer or counsel employed to give an opinion, the fraction increases exponentially. The purpose of this Chapter is to deal with the preliminary aspects of drafting but it is an appropriate point to underline the aspects of professional negligence as it applies to solicitors in general and to trust drafters in particular. The trust drafter cannot ignore this aspect.

Negligence

4–02 This section is not meant to be a sustained and comprehensive treatment of the law of professional negligence. For this, reference should be made to Professor Rennie's excellent book *Solicitor's Negligence* and/or to one of the many English law texts such as *Jackson and Powell on Professional Negligence*.

Before considering the aspect of professional negligence it is worthwhile having in mind a clear picture of what a professional is. Generally speaking, the professional is characterised by the nature of their work being highly specialised, mental rather than manual and requiring a considerable period of theoretical and practical training. In addition there is the moral aspect whereby practitioners or professionals are usually perceived to be committed to certain moral standards, which go beyond general levels. They also, generally speaking, belong to a society or a professional association, which seeks to regulate training and uphold the standards of the profession. Finally, they tend to be of a high status, social or otherwise and are vested in certain privileges, which are granted by Parliament. The legal profession in Scotland embodies all these four characteristics.

It is also perhaps worth stating, although not strictly relevant, that professionals by their very nature operate in situations where success cannot always be achieved; thus in litigation, it could be argued that one person is successful and the other is not. However, high degrees of skill may have been utilised by the agents or solicitors acting for both parties.

In matters of tight judgment on aspects of great complexity no human being can be right every time.

The basic problem for professional negligence, therefore, is to define what standards the law will require of a professional person in general and of a trust drafter in particular and which provides protection for the client, customer or consumer. Generally, professional persons who possess a certain minimum degree of competence should exercise reasonable care in the discharge of their profession. In the old English case of *Lanthier v Philpos*, in particular Lord Chief Justice Tindals remarks

"every person who enters into a learned profession undertakes to bring to the exercise of it a reasonable degree of care of skill. He does not undertake, if he is an attorney, that at all events you shall gain your case, nor does a surgeon undertake that he will perform a cure; nor does he undertake to use the highest possible degree of skill."

An extremely useful definition and one which is often referred to is by Lord President Clyde in *Hunter v Hanley*[3] at p.205

"to establish liability . . where deviation from normal practice, three facts require to be established. First of all it must be proved that there is a usual and normal practice; secondly, it must be proved that the defender has not adopted that practice; thirdly, it must be established that the course adopted is one which no professional man of ordinary skill would have taken if he had been acting with ordinary care. This is clearly a heavy onus on a pursuer to establish these three facts, and without all three his case will fail. If this is the test, then it matters nothing how far or how little he deviates from the ordinary practice. For the extent of deviation is not the test. The deviation must be of a kind which satisfies the third requirement . . ."

Thus, where there is a contract between the professional person and the client whereby services are provided in return for a fee, it is generally implied that the professional person will exercise a reasonable degree of skill and care. This is as opposed to the question of delict where the professional has owed yet breached duty of care to the claimant who has suffered damage or loss as a result.

It should be borne in mind of course that the test for the person to whom the professional (solicitor) owes a duty of care is fairly circumscribed.

Examples of failure could include, in the context of trust deeds, the failure to actually prepare a trust deed at all, the failure to follow the instructions given by the client, the failure to take reasonable steps to ascertain the wishes as regards the estate, to see that the deed is validly executed and that all time limits have been observed. It may well be that

---

[3] 1955 S.C. 200.

proper advice has not been given on life or pension policies, foreign law aspects or transactions relating to abroad.

However, the duty may not extend to other estates to which the testator may be entitled, or to tax savings schemes in respect of them. The damages, of course, will be mitigated or restricted by the usual rules for damages as to remoteness etc.

Certain factors can be identified in identifying an increase in claim "potentialability":

Culture of litigiousness

4–03   There can be no doubt that we live in a time when clients are more ready to question the judgments of professional persons. It is sometimes argued that this emanates from the USA. There is some merit in the argument that people should challenge and question advice rather than as perhaps in the past being more ready to accept advice from a professional. Paradoxically, the "difficult" client is the one to cherish as this is the one who may draw your attention inadvertently to a mistake you have made.

It is alleged that society has developed a culture of "blame and claim", although lawyers naturally resent this assertion and point to contrary evidence.[4]

Although this statement refers to personal injury claims the authors go on to state "for accidents involving physical injury, there can appear to be a knee-jerk reaction. The injured party often thinks about financial compensation before they have even had a chance to assess their physical injuries!" Unfortunately this type of ethos is spreading to other aspects of loss. Practitioners, their insurers and those now formerly dealing with complaints about solicitors regularly see this type of ethos developing in executry and trust practice.

Increased specialisation

4–04   In days gone by there was little if any specialisation. Solicitors routinely appeared in the courts in the morning and dealt with chamber practice in the afternoon. There may have been specialisation into court and chamber practice. Now there is a bewildering list of specialisations. Indeed the Law Society of Scotland operates a well-developed and mature accreditation scheme which was established in 1990. The exceptional quality and skill of accredited specialists under the scheme is recognised by practitioners throughout Scotland. Entry to the scheme is difficult and there are only about 400 accredited specialists out of over 10,000 solicitors in Scotland.

While solicitors will see accreditation as a way of developing their skills and career, the qualification assures clients that they are having access to specialist advice of a highest standard. This is particularly important in difficult cases.

The Law Society of Scotland accredits about 23 specialisms, including agricultural law, charity law, child law, commercial leasing, family law,

---

[4] Mark McLaughlin and David Coldrick, Blame and Claim?—Personal Injury and Disabled Trusts, Taxation Magazine, November 11, 2004 p.158.

insolvency law, incapacity & mental disability law, intellectual property law, liquor licensing law, medical negligence law, medical negligence (defender only) and trusts law.

The problem is that solicitors, for various reasons, continue to take on work for which they are not really qualified, lack the necessary experience or have no one in a firm (especially where it is a small or medium-sized one) to consult. They may wish to retain a client or it may be that a client who trusts them may not speak to any one else. Unless the solicitor is prepared to pass the work on to someone more qualified or to take detailed advice from a more experienced colleague or counsel, he runs the risk of making a costly and expensive mistake.

Competition for legal services

There is now much more competition for what was considered **4–05** traditionally legal work from outside the profession. The legal profession in Scotland has shown itself to be singularly skilful in losing vast areas and trenches of work to other professions or *quasi* professions. Accountancy, tax work and town and country planning law are just the tip of the iceberg. If you add to this financial planning, financial services, employment law, trust and executry work a more realistic picture can be seen.

The problem here is that, by losing this work, solicitors do not build up the expertise in that type of work, and when they take it on or are consulted, it is likely to be the difficult case!

Law Society of Scotland

It may seem to members that the Society is more concerned with **4–06** protecting the interests of the public than championing the interests of solicitors! The Society would probably accept this to a limited extent. This is likely to change drastically in the near future as the Society is to lose its "policing" power as complaints against practising lawyers face major changes as a result of the recently published Scottish Executive bill, Legal Profession and Legal Aid (Scotland) Bill, which is now nearing the end of stage one in the Scottish Parliament. Broadly, the Bill proposes a Scottish Legal Complaints Commission (SLCC) to handle service complaints against lawyers. According to the Society's website

> "This announcement followed the Society's decision to call for an independent body for service complaints in order to increase confidence in the system. That decision was reached despite the many improvements made to the Society's own complaints system since 2003. The Society's view is that many criticisms are based on perception rather than reality."

In a recent statement, Deputy Justice Minister Hugh Henry said the bill would provide "greater consumer choice, increase public confidence in the justice system" and that "consumers [clients!] are right to expect high standards of service, and the time is now right for this culture change in our society to be extended into Scotland's legal system."

This Commission is to deal with all complaints against practising lawyers. Any complaints which relate to professional misconduct, or a new category of unsatisfactory conduct, will still be referred to the

Society or Faculty of Advocates to investigate. The Society retains its power to prosecute before the Scottish Solicitors Discipline Tribunal. If the complaint concerns inadequate professional services, the Commission will decide that it is eligible, that is to say, not frivolous or vexatious, and not premature in that no attempt has been made to resolve it at source. The Commission may offer mediation but both sides have to accept.

Needless to say the Commission will have much stronger financial powers than the Society. In addition to ordering a refund of fees, or action at the practitioner's own expense to remedy matters, it is to have power to order compensation of up to the staggering amount of £20,000; it is unlikely that there will be a right of appeal from the Commission.

It is also to have a supervisory role over the professional bodies' handling of conduct complaints, with power to award up to £5,000 in compensation for loss, inconvenience or distress, plus costs, to a complainer if an investigation has been badly handled.

All solicitors will pay a flat rate annual levy, set by the Commission and collected by the Law Society, to fund its work. It does seem slightly bizarre that in addition a further levy will be made as a result of the number of complaints made. This could rise at an ever increasing rate with greater and greater numbers of complaints made, whether or not the complaint is upheld. Somewhat unsportingly, complainers will not be expected to pay even if their complaint turns out to be frivolous.

The Society is to have power to censure, fine up to £2,000 and award compensation up to £5,000 for unsatisfactory professional conduct, defined as conduct beyond inadequate professional services but falling short of professional misconduct. A right of appeal will be provided to the Discipline Tribunal.

While the public should be protected it does seem that there is an element of a "sledgehammer to crack a nut" about the whole thing given the small number of complaints as a proportion of the millions of pieces of work undertaken satisfactorily by solicitors every year.

The problem is that this may encourage dissatisfied clients to complain who have no business doing so. Every practitioner is familiar with the client who, after work has been carried out, says "I do not like your fee; I am reporting you to the Law Society".

Indemnity Policy aka the Master Policy For Professional Indemnity Insurance

4–07   Solicitors working in private practice have Professional Indemnity Insurance cover for claims against them. The Master Policy is the compulsory Professional Indemnity Insurance arrangement which covers all Scottish solicitors working in private practice. The Society arranges the Master Policy for Professional Indemnity Insurance. Claims are handled by the Master Policy insurers. The insurance provides cover of up to £1.5million for any one claim.

The problem is that this may encourage clients to make specious claims in the belief that there are deep pockets or that the solicitor himself may not be liable since it is not "him who is paying but the insurer"!

Effect of foreign attitude

Anecdotal evidence suggests that the influence of foreign practices **4–08** almost solely from North America initiating proceedings is contributing to an increasing number of claims in this country.

Duty of care: what is it?

What indeed?

The basic problem therefore for professional negligence is to define **4–09** what standards the law will require of a professional person and which provides protection for the consumer.

The problem of the duty of care has bedevilled courts not only in Scotland but elsewhere and a full discussion of the scope is outwith the scope of this text.

Some help may be found in the "Partnership Law" (report) [2003] A.W.L.C. 283 (November 15, 2003) of the Law Commission. Admittedly, this relates to partnerships but the fiduciary duty of care, which partners owe to each other, may be of assistance. The Commission identify a duty of good faith. Some institutional writers in Scotland suggest that the partner is expected to show in relation to the partnership "that diligence which he would show in his own affairs".[5] However, as the report goes on to say in *Ross Harper & Murphy v Banks*[6] Hamilton rejected this subjective standard. Instead, he maintained that there should be an objective standard of reasonable care and that standard should be qualified by reference to the way in which that particular partnership carried on its business. It is suggested also that there is no duty to devote full time and attention to a particular matter, however, there is a duty of skill and care as "such care and skill as can reasonably be expected of those with the general knowledge, skill and experience that the partners have or purport to have".

Financial services

The Financial Services Authority is the principal regulator for invest- **4–10** ment business in the UK. It came into operation on December 1, 2001; its powers are set out in the Financial Services and Markets Act 2000.

This provides that no individual or firm may carry on a regulated activity unless that individual/firm is authorised by the FSA. From December 1, 2001 to October 31, 2004 the FSA's regulatory regime was confined to the conduct of investment business. However, with effect from October 31, 2004, the FSA's regulatory regime is extended to incorporate mortgage business and with effect from January 14, 2005, the regime is extended to include general insurance business.

Solicitors may carry out certain regulated activities and be exempt from the requirement to be authorised by the FSA if they are licensed by the Law Society regime, known as the "Incidental Financial Business

---

[5] *Mair v Wood* 1948, S.C. 83, at 90, *Blackwood v Robertson*, 1984 S.L.T. (Sh Ct 68) and also Stairs *Institutions*, 1.16.7 and Erskine, *Institute* III.iii.21.
[6] 2000 S.L.T. 699.

(IFB) Regime". This allows solicitors to carry out certain activities which would otherwise require FSA authorisation. It is paramount that these activities are integral to other business, e.g. trust administration, and must not under any circumstances be advertised as "stand-alone" activities.

If the correct authorisation is not held solicitors are vulnerable to a claim. It is important to realise that a breach could occur very easily. For example, if the solicitor passes on a copy of the stockbroker's letter recommending the sale of certain shares to pay off the loan taken out to pay IHT and a trustee asks the solicitor what he thinks; if the solicitor were to voice an opinion he might well have contravened the terms of his firm's incidental business authorisation.

Third Parties

4–11   Until the decision in the case of *Holmes v Bank of Scotland*, it was probably the law that a disappointed beneficiary had no claim for negligence against the solicitors who had caused them to lose their inheritance. In this case, relatives sought damages from a bank, for losses caused by the bank's failure to have the will executed. Lord Kingarth held that the principle in *White v Jones*,[7] a leading English case, would be followed in Scotland and that an intended beneficiary would be allowed a remedy; that the duty alleged was a matter for evidence, and prima facie the loss which was reasonably foreseeable was the loss of the legacies to be provided. This case may open the floodgates by disappointed beneficiaries. It is clearly likely that this will extend to trust drafters.

Increase in standards/expectations

4–12   All of the foregoing, it is suggested, may give rise to an increase in the expectations of clients and this may have a "knock-on" effect on claims.

AVOIDING CLAIMS OF NEGLIGENCE

4–13   There is no special magic for avoiding claims. Generally speaking, these methods will fall into six tried and tested groupings as follows:

1. Taking full particulars.
2. A letter of engagement.
3. Observing and including realistic time scales.
4. Use of checklists and styles.
5. Keeping in regular contact with the client.
6. Reviewing the foregoing and files.

Full particulars

4–14   This, of course, includes a full client information sheet and obtaining documentary evidence of their identity. Think of the problems which could arise if you took instructions from an impostor.

---

[7] *White v Jones* [1995] 2 A.C. 207.

There is no substitute for taking full particulars at the outset of the instructions for the will or trust deed. Many clients' wishes are vague and amorphous. Beyond arranging their affairs, they have only a rough and unformed idea.

Some clients have a very clear idea as to what they want to achieve and look to you for the means to put this into practice. Some have ideas which their asset and prospects make impracticable to achieve. As previously indicated, trust drafting, in common with other forms of drafting, is a professional skill requiring a knowledge of various branches of the law and the ability to efficiently keep up to date; it also requires a degree of empathy and what are now called "good communication skills".

In addition, for reasons of a psychological nature which are well beyond the scope of this modest work, clients may not immediately tell you what they want; instead they will talk round this and you are expected to show your cleverness by guessing what it is they actually want or what they wish you to achieve.

In these circumstances, a checklist is usual and one is appended for wills and trusts produced for the students for wills.[8]

All too often obtaining instructions is rushed. There are often good reasons for this, e.g. obtaining information from trusters who have only a limited amount of time, but this type of excuse will not save liability. It is as well to be as prepared as possible looking out title deeds, copies of the wills and other papers as are available and studying these in advance. In trusts of any complexity, e.g. where it is likely IHT will apply or where there is heritable property or other difficulty, it would be as well to leave aside the best part of a morning or afternoon for this purpose. The notes should be extended as soon as possible then sent out at the same time as the letter of engagement or as soon as possible thereafter. It seems obvious that file entries should be made for telephone and face-to-face instructions and that these are regularly maintained.

Letter of engagement

The letter of engagement, a copy of which is shown at the Appendix[9] **4–15** should also be sent out. It is important that care should be given to this and that where, say, work is to be carried out by another professional, e.g. a chartered accountant in connection with tax, that this is expressly specified. If you are agreeable to accepting instructions by email you should specify that, e.g. your emails are only checked say twice a day. In these days, when there are considerable difficulties as regards financial services and otherwise, it would also be as well to spell out exactly what the firm's responsibility is under this heading. To some practitioners this is a tiresome piece of additional work. However, it can be such a useful tool, not only for safeguarding your position against a negligence claim but also in the matter of feeing. It is important to spell out exactly what you are to do but also what you are to be paid for; accordingly, if what

---

[8] APPENDIX A.1.
[9] APPENDIX A.2.

you are asked to do is over and above what you originally contracted for then you are entitled to be paid for this.

Timescales/diaries

4–16   By far the most effective tool in preventing claims is an efficient and regular diary service and bring/forward system. It does not really matter whether this is a hand-written diary or other commercial product or the most sophisticated online diary system, which the computer can produce, but it is essential that this is used. It is suggested that all the relevant critical dates are incorporated in the diary system such as the end of September; it may be important to have R185 (Trust Income) certificates in the hands of beneficiaries as they or their profession advisors may wish to have their tax returns submitted timeously to have them checked by HMRC.

If all of these three steps are carried out and the position and the diary checked and progressed then it is likely that 95 per cent of possible claims will be avoided. There are many diary systems on the market of an electronic nature; the one, which is sometimes found most useful, is "Time and Chaos". However, Microsoft Outlook is equally good and there are others on the market, which can be secured for a modest outlay.

Use of checklists and styles

4–17   This is dealt with in more detail elsewhere and in the appendix of checklists and styles. The list is by no means exhaustive. Others can be found in other publications such as "Ensuring Excellence". Styles of trust deeds are included in Ch.6 and in the Appendix. Testamentary trust deed styles are generally outwith the scope of this text but you should build up your own "bank" of styles from Barr, Elder, Kerrigan, Diploma notes course, CPD notes, etc. It may be permissible to "steal" styles from other practitioners. They may find it very flattering when they see something which they have drafted being used by another agent!

Keeping in contact with the client

4–18   After the initial consultation try to get something back to a client **within two weeks** at the most and thereafter keep in contact.

This may be the last thing you want to do but the opportunity should not be lost to keep in regular contact with truster or the testator. Do not let weeks go past without some form of communication. The opportunity to speak will often alert you by "reading between the lines" to something worrying a client and to give you early warning of a client's dissatisfaction. The Law Society may consider it professional negligence if you fail to follow up. You cannot send out the initial correspondence and draft and sit back. **Some clients think that after the initial consultation that it is their part of the procedure finished without signing of documents etc**.

Reviewing the foregoing and files

4–19   While your inclination may be to throw the files out the window, there is no substitute for reading the file and especially the notes of the original interviews and checking that all matters raised have been addressed. It might be worth taking a copy of this and keeping it beside the file as you read through it.

Please watch out particularly for deeds of variation and ensure you are clear who your client is. Clearly it is the beneficiary making the DEED OF VARIATION (not the executors); and therefore the costs incurred are not an expense of the estate. For the estate or legatees to pay the cost could constitute "consideration" preventing s.142 (or, for CGT, TCGA 1992, s.62) from applying. The cost of the variation should be clearly identified if rendering an executry fee.

Making Deeds User Friendly

The actual appearance of the deed can make a great deal of difference. 4–20 Now even more than ever there is an emphasis on making deeds easily comprehensible and, to use the much abused modern cliché, "user friendly". This trend is to be encouraged as much as possible but at the same time, we must be vigilant not to sacrifice effectiveness at the false altar of simplification.

A typical trust disposition and settlement of bygone days is shown at Appendix I. This bears similarities to that found in the University Styles. These, or variations thereof, were commonly used by legal practitioners from the start of the last century until several decades after the Second World War. This was known as a direct form of will. It conveys the deceased's estate to trustees and enjoins them to carry out certain purposes. It has many advantages principally of adaptability and flexibility. However, it has been largely replaced by the indirect form of will, which appoints executors and lists the purposes. This usually comes with marginal headings, which can be helpful particularly to the lay client. To drafters above a certain age this new format, taught at all major Scottish Diploma Courses, lacks the flexibility of the earlier trust disposition and settlement. The new format of will seems to straightjacket testamentary provisions particularly where a will trust is envisaged.

Plain English

The other emphasis is on so-called plain English and clarity of 4–21 expression. For a generation who, according to one source, has stated that Scottish schoolchildren are linguistically incapable of understanding Scott or Dickens this presents something of a challenge. We have all gritted our teeth when we hear or read the quite bizarre use or misuse of the words "got", "done" and "that". We have heaved a sigh of sadness when we hear or read Scottish terms spelled with an English (or even American) spelling by such an august body as our own beloved Scottish Parliament.

We have all experienced the frustration of computer "spellcheckers" which compound the foregoing. However much we look back with fondness to older days it is clear that plain English is here to stay.

Plain English in drafting

There is a burgeoning movement in the UK for the use of "plain" 4–22 English. This was and is spearheaded by the "Plain English Campaign" (*www.plainenglishcampaign.com*). They define "plain English" **as lan-**

guage which the reader can "understand and act upon from a single reading". Their guides should be prescribed reading for all drafters.

In drafting we should aim to produce writs which the lay reader can read and understand after a single reading. This is a difficult ideal to achieve. However, it should be the objective for which to aim in all cases.

The actual appearance of the deed can also make a difference to comprehension. Traditionally **BLOCK CAPITALS** were used for the first mention of the name and designation of parties; other sections such as words of disposition, e.g. **DISPONE**, were also shown in blocks as were important expressions, e.g. "the sum of **TWENTY THOUSAND POUNDS (£20,000) STERLING**". With modern word processing equipment and software it is the work of a nanosecond to use **bold**; this also can be a useful aid to comprehension particularly for the lay reader. The Plain English Campaign website has references to resources for using plain English in legal matters. The article on using plain English in legal drafting refers to problems stemming from "legalese" such as:

1. long sentences;
2. often trying to cover several points;
3. verbiage (unnecessary padding-out of sentences);
4. too many double negatives and over-formality.

"Legalese" came from laws being originally written in a language other than English, such as Latin or French. Many of the common terms is still being used, e.g. *per stirpes*. Moreover, drafters were paid by the word, not by the hour; precedents were seen as "tried and tested" and drafters are and were reluctant to use original language because if something had worked in the past, why change it?

The need for legalese has now largely disappeared. Many old Latin terms have equivalent English terms (although we may not yet use them!). Although clients may think to the contrary, we do not always charge by the word. Modern styles are available for perusal in books or on the internet. On the other hand, modern computer word-processing facilities have enabled us to store large amounts of text which can be reproduced or copied into a document in an instant and make documents longer and more complex than is necessary.

Many of the problems can be avoided by the following:

Use shorter sentences

4–23   Traditionally, solicitors in Scotland and elsewhere drafted deeds as one long sentence. Although stylistically correct it was difficult to comprehend, particularly when written in longhand continuously over the whole page with only the occasional *Primo* or *Secundo* to break it up. This may have been for a valid reason, perhaps to save paper which was expensive or to avoid fraudulent insertions. Sentences are easier to understand. Breaking up a clause into shorter sentences can make the meaning clearer.

Use indentation

4–24   Acts of Parliament routinely use indentation to make the appearance of the text user friendly by splitting up text into smaller pieces.

Indentation makes it easier for the eyes to skip from one part of a document to another. As mentioned, former styles of deeds had continuous, often handwritten, text across the page which was difficult for the practitioner to follow and practically impossible for the lay reader to follow.

Courts have been known to take account of indentation to ascertain meaning.[10]

A good example of the older style is given in the Appendix—the old fashioned trust disposition and settlement.

Singular and plural

The singular includes the plural. Usually a phrase such as "the trustee **4–25** or trustees" can be replaced, safely, by "the trustee". Where there is doubt, a short "interpretation" section can be inserted. A simple clause in the deed spelling out the law would prevent such mistakes.

Avoid outdated expressions

Here are some examples: **4–26**

1. accretion	add to
2. as the case may be	[omit]
3. notwithstanding that	even though, whether or not
4. moneys	money
5. the trustees shall have the power to/the right to	the trustees may
6. it is hereby stipulated that	[omit]

Sir Ernest Gowers' excellent book, (although written for civil servants) *"The Complete Plain Words"* refers to certain words and phrases to be used with care, such as replacing "According to our records" with "Our records show". The book also contains a table showing simplifications of compound prepositions, such as:

- as a consequence of (because of)
- by means of (by, with, using)
- by virtue of (by, under).

The plain English Campaign continues this. In one of their guides they give hundreds of alternative words, e.g:

Acquiesce	agree
Adjacent	next to
Accede to	allow, agree to

However, some practitioners will consider this "dumbing down".

Above all, use article headings

This is probably the greatest aid to comprehension for both lay and **4–27** professional readers alike. Clause headings are now commonplace to aid the reader of a document and help to fulfil the criteria of making it

---

[10] But see the English case, *Macarthur v Greycoat Estates Mayfair*, 67 TC 598 (at 613).

comprehensible at one reading. They can quickly identify the relevant part of a deed. If Microsoft Word or a similar product is used there may be a "document map" facility which makes location of the section much quicker. Sometimes a clause may be inserted in the deed to the effect that clause headings are for ease of reference only and are not to affect the construction of the deed. This should be superfluous because, in a well-drafted deed, there should be no clash between the clause headings and the actual clauses themselves. At most, the clause heading is an aid to the construction of the clause. An example of a heading might be "Trust purposes". It is a matter of preference whether these are in the body of the deed or in the left margin. Word processing software makes this much easier to achieve.

Aims of Clients

4–28 Of paramount importance are our clients' objectives in drawing up a trust. The objective is certainly not to confuse them with long-winded and difficult to understand deeds but rather to help them put their assets in trust for a specific purpose. Deeds of trust should reflect that purpose and should, if at all possible, be in language which they can understand.

As with most things, a compromise must be reached; between dumbing down and losing drafting effectiveness on the one hand and going back to stone age drafting but preserving effectiveness on the other.

We must bear in mind that clients pay lawyers to draft effective trust and other deeds and where there these are complicated to be able to explain them clearly to the lay client.

It is important for us to focus on drafting what the client wants to achieve instead of trying to fit his requirements into one of our styles. For example it may be that a person of very modest means wishes a very simple will trust for liferent to his (second) wife with fee to his issue.

Generally speaking the truster will be concerned with providing for a beneficiary but retaining some measure of control. As Bill Pagan states in his excellent paper[11] "keeping control" is a natural wish, and control is often retained far too long. For some estate owners, it is no easier to give up control than it is for the proverbial Aberdonian to write a cheque. A shorthand, but dangerous, comfort to give to a reluctant donor is that putting the estate into trust and selecting the trustees carefully allows control to be retained.

Selection of Trustees

4–29 Careful selection of trustees is vital. Traditionally, trusters and testators have liked to have "professional" trustees such as solicitors, stockbrokers and factors. This was something which was of help to both the professional and the testator. The testator had the comfort of knowing

---

[11] "The Role of Trusts in Estate Planning" extracted in *Trusts & Estates*, December /January1998.

that he had secured the care and assistance which a trusted professional would give. In addition, if the professional was a co-trustee, a professional could usually be relied on to do what he was instructed. On the other hand the professional saw it as a way of keeping the testator's business particularly in the event that it was a testamentary trust.

From the point of view of the professional this matter should now be reconsidered. New legislation is likely to place additional duties on "professional" trustees. In a recent case the Inland Revenue (as it then was) successfully pursued a professional trustee, a solicitor, for outstanding IHT instalments where the beneficiary who had received the instalment option property had become insolvent.

However, the main reason why professionals should consider this carefully is related to the higher standards of care which are required from the professional trustee. It is likely that even higher standards will be required if the English model of the Trustees Act comes into force in Scotland. In particular, careful thought should be given to avoiding having partners as trustees without considering fully the possible exposure to the firm.

Before we consider particular styles of clauses, there are some particular points to consider. These relate to restrictions on drafting powers.

RESTRICTIONS

Vesting in beneficiaries[12]

A beneficiary who has vested is entitled to payment provided the trustees **4–30** retain sufficient funds to make payment to any beneficiaries who have not yet vested or are not yet payable.

Anomalies arise where vesting and right to payment occur on different dates or events and the solution is to ensure as far as possible that vesting and the right to payment arise at the same time.

When the trust asset or assets vest in whole or in part the beneficiary has rights to those assets. The significance of the date of vesting is that from that date onwards the **asset is the property of the beneficiary; prior to that date the beneficiary only has the possibility of acquiring the property**.

Vesting, of course, is not dependent on possession. Once vested the beneficiary has the power of disposal over the asset.

Certain conditions may have to occur before vesting occurs, as follows *videlicet*:

Suspensive conditions—These suspend vesting until a previously ordained uncertain event occurs, e.g. conditional on beneficiary attaining a certain age or it may be conditional on survivorship; vesting may only occur at the time or occasion when it is ascertained who are the survivors; destination-over vesting occurs at the time fixed for payment.

---

[12] Candlish Henderson on Vesting.

Resolutive conditions—They will allow immediate vesting but render it liable to withdrawal in the event of the condition occurring. This is known as vesting subject to **defeasance**:

(1) to A in liferent and to A's issue in fee, whom failing to B in fee. B therefore takes a vested right in the fee subject to defeasance if A has issue.

The question is whether the fiar was known and existing at the time of truster's death, if so then the fee vests in the fiar *mortis causa*. There are several variations of this.

- to A in liferent and to A's issue in fee whom failing to B in fee provided B attains the age of 18 years.

B takes a vested right in fee, not on the testator's death but when B attains the age of 18 years, subject to defeasance if A has issue.

- to A in liferent and to A's issue in fee, whom failing to B in liferent and B's issue in fee, whom failing to C in fee.

C takes a vested right in the fee at the testator's death subject to defeasance if either A or B has issue.

- to A in fee with subsequent direction to trustees to hold for A in liferent and A's issue in fee.

A takes a vested right in fee, subject to defeasance if A has issue.

- to A in liferent and B in fee, whom failing to B's issue.

B takes a vested right in fee, subject to defeasance if B predeceases A and leaves issue. The fiars, depending on the facts, will be B's executors or B's issue. It cannot be stated forcibly enough that this matter must be addressed at the drafting stage. Make sure payment goes to the right party!

Anti-avoidance legislation

4–31   ICTA 1988, ss.660–694 contains income tax anti-avoidance provisions for trusters. If these provisions are breached, the trust income is treated as being the truster's income for income tax purposes.

Clearly, most of these provisions do not apply in testamentary trusts because the truster is dead. Similarly, the restrictions on spouses apply during the marriage only and do not apply to former spouses, widows and widowers. The NRB discretionary trusts in wills take advantage of this rule.

Trust funds for truster's children (ICTA 1988, ss.663–670).

4–32   If the trust income is paid to the truster's children while they are aged under 18 and unmarried, the income is treated as being the truster's income for income tax, subject to a *de minimis* limit of £100 per child (s.663(4)). There is no objection to the income being accumulated, but it will be taxed at the higher discretionary trust rate.

The definition of truster in s.670 is wide enough to cover "shadow" trusters who provide funds indirectly. There is a risk of accidental breach of these provisions by a parent joining in an arrangement and so becoming a truster without his knowing it, such as in a deed of variation whereby a parent passes part of his entitlement under the will to his children who are aged under 18. Or it might occur where the parent disclaims or renounces his entitlement if the will has destination-over to his children on renunciation.

Revocable settlements and retained interests. (ICTA 1988, ss.671–682).

The abuses attacked by these sections are the receipt of trust income **4–33** or capital or other benefit by the truster or his/her spouse.

Sections 673 and 674 deal with receipt of income and contain exceptions for income received after the death, bankruptcy, etc. of a beneficiary. There is a potential trap under these sections if the truster or spouse is allowed in the trust deed to receive payment for services rendered to the trust or for management of the trust's business. **All benefit must be excluded**.

Danger Warning!!!

The receipt of trust income could also indicate that there has been a GIFT WITH RESERVATION for IHT with adverse consequences on the truster's death.
Section 674A attacks temporary settlements of capital.

Sections 677 and 678 attack capital sums (and loans) received by the truster or spouse funded from trust income. Temporary borrowing by the trustees from the truster or spouse (e.g. to finance the taking up of a rights issue) is just as bad from an HMRC point of view.

Trust deeds therefore almost invariably disallow any payment of the trust's capital and income to the truster and his/her spouse, loans to them from the trust and receipt by them of any benefit from the trust.

A truster has a radical or reversionary interest in a trust estate on failure of the trust purposes under common law. If the truster does not divest himself absolutely of his reversionary right, failure of the trust purposes can lead to a resulting trust for the truster with the consequences under s.683 already noted. Many trust deeds have ultimate destinations to charities to prevent reversion to the truster on failure.

Also forbidden are the receipt by the truster or spouse of trust property or income or benefit from them (under some exceptions) and it is provided that on a breach the trust's capital gains will be assessed on the truster without the benefit of the trust's annual capital gains tax exemption.

Bequests for short periods (ICTA 1988, ss.660–662)

A transfer of income is ineffective for tax purposes if the arrangement **4–34** does not exceed three years. Charitable covenants are therefore granted for four years or more. A truster usually intends the arrangements in the trust to be permanent and the deed therefore incorporates a declaration that the trust is "irrevocable" to avoid any problems under these sections.

Perpetuities

4–35   Scottish trusts are generally more flexible than their Southern counterparts. In England and Wales there is a prohibition against perpetuities. This is not the case with Scotland, e.g. public trusts such as charitable trusts, which can go on forever.

Under this head comes the prohibition on entails whereby heritable property passed from one generation to another with liferents. These were abolished at the beginning of the last century.

Illegal purposes

4–36   At first sight this might be a strange restriction. However, we are thinking of something other than a trust to promote drug usage in Milngavie. There may be questions of public policy, e.g. McCaig's Follies.

Accumulations

4–37   It is important to bear in mind restrictions on **accumulation periods**. These are of particular importance in discretionary trusts and accumulation and maintenance trusts, which may be *inter vivos* trusts or testamentary trusts. The conditions for accumulation and maintenance trusts under IHTA 1984, s.71 require the accumulation of income not applied for the maintenance, education or benefit of the beneficiaries. The periods of phases for which income may be accumulated are specified in the Trusts (Scotland) Act 1961, s.5 as amended by the Law Reform Miscellaneous Provisions) (Scotland) Act 1966, s.6 and are:

1. the life of the grantor;
2. 21 years from the death of the grantor;
3. the minority of person(s) alive at the grantor's death;
4. the minority of person(s) entitled to the income at full age;
5. 21 years from the date of the settlement;
6. the minority of person(s) alive at the settlement date.

The life of the grantor

4–38   It goes without stating that the period of the life of the grantor clearly does not apply to wills since these only become effective on the death of the testator. This period is of limited use for *inter vivos* trusts because the grantor may die soon after the date of the trust deed.

4–39 21 years from the death of the grantor

The minority of person(s) alive at the grantor's death

4–40   These two phases are applicable to testamentary settlements because they begin with the date of death of the testator.

The minority of person(s) entitled to the income at full age

4–41   This is the one to use in *inter vivos* trusts but only if the young person is entitled to receive the income from the age of 21 years. The persons need not be alive at the date of the deed or the grantor's death if there is an intervening interest such as a liferent. This period is extremely useful for a "class" gift to beneficiaries who may be born **after the trust comes into operation**, but there must be at least one person in minority at the commencement or an intervening interest such as a liferent. Otherwise the fixed period of 21 years from the death of the grantor will apply because the accumulation would otherwise exceed the periods permitted[13] under s.5.

This period may also be used in wills.

21 years from the date of the settlement 4–42

The minority of person(s) alive at the grantor's death

These two phases are applicable to testamentary settlements because 4–43 they begin with the date of death of the testator.

It should be noted that:

In this context minority means the period from birth to the age of 21 years.

Only one period may be chosen. Section 5 prohibits accumulation of income for longer periods

If accumulation starts during the grantor's life under an *inter vivos* trust, the presumption is that the **period of his life will apply** and that accumulation after his death will be prohibited unless another period has been clearly selected.[14]

The restriction appears to apply to directions to accumulate and powers to accumulate, but there seems to be no objection to the creation of a reserve fund of income for future expenditure after the 21 years or respective minorities **because the prohibition is against increasing the fund by adding income to capital**.[15]

If, for any reason:

(1) the accumulation of income becomes unlawful, and
(2) the trust deed does not allocate the income,

it will regress to the truster as a resultant trust from his reversionary right with the consequence that the trust income will be treated as his under ICTA 1988, s.673.

As if that was not bad enough the regression will probably also be a gift with reservation under IHTA 1984, s.65. However, this can usually be overcome in the trust deed by allocating the income illegally accumulated to the beneficiaries prospectively entitled to the capital and by appointing any reversionary right to charities.

To summarise, the appropriate periods for *inter vivos* trusts are:

- Number 5 above (21 years from the settlement). This will allow accumulation to the age of 25 **if all the beneficiaries are alive and aged over 4 years at the date of the settlement**. However,

---

[13] *Carey's Trustees v Rose*, 1957 S.C. 252.
[14] *McIver's Trustees v Lord Advocate*, 1973 S.C. 189.
[15] *Stair Memorial Encyclopaedia*, Vol.24 para.47 on Trusts etc.

the period will end if a destination-over to issue comes into operation as a result of the death of a beneficiary. In that event the issue will have to receive the income from the end of the 21 years.

- Number 6 above allows accumulation to the age of 21 years, but all the beneficiaries must be alive at the date of the deed.
- Number 4 above may be used if all the beneficiaries are not alive, but they must be entitled to the income from 21 years. This length of time may be employed in accumulation and maintenance trusts by a grandparent for grandchildren when further grandchildren may be born.
- Number 2 above (21 years from date of death) corresponds with number 5 for *inter vivos* trusts and has the same potential problem.
- Number 3 above corresponds with number 6 and requires all the beneficiaries to be alive at the testator's death. There will be no more children if the bequest is to the testator's children or to those of a beneficiary who has predeceased. This period will therefore be the normal choice.
- Number 4 above may be useful if there is a liferent and will allow accumulation during the minority of fiars born after the testator's death but they must receive the income from 21 years.

It is absolutely paramount that the drafter makes a clear selection of the period in the deed or will to avoid the above presumptions coming into force.[16]

Note on liferents

4–44   If the person who is in minority at the date of creation of the trust and survives to reach majority then the capital must be paid over. However, if a beneficiary does not reach majority (age 18), then the liferent can continue for the next beneficiary and so on.

It should also be noted that liferents are only available for actual living persons at the time of creation of the trust. It is, of course, possible and competent to provide for a liferent for children as yet unborn in a will. The saving for live persons is extended to persons *in utero* but here the liferent can only subsist for the period to age 18.

The Auctor Principle

4–45   Bill Pagan identifies this in his paper as a trap for trustees who are members of the family or involved in the same activity as the trust. He cites the example of farming. The Auctor Principle is extremely relevant to trust drafting and basically provides that trustees should not benefit from any transaction with the trust or in any other way from a decision or action of the trust. Even where the trust has not suffered any loss in

---

[16] For additional reading, see Wilson & Duncan *Trusts, Trustees & Executors* (2nd edn), Ch.9 on Accumulation of income.

strict legal terms the trustee should reimburse the trust and perhaps these requirements are not often mentioned to trustees. Most styles will provide a suitable clause (as does the one in the latter part of the notes). However, this should not be regarded as full proof and it should be mentioned to the trustee and of course the truster. Although in the Article Bill Pagan refers to agricultural matters it is relevant in many cases such as a family business or where shares are held in a private company where one of the trustees is a director or person who contracts with the company.

Reference can be made to the case of *Sarris v Clark*, 1995 S.L.T. 44, in which a farmer entered into partnership with his wife and granted a lease to the partnership. It was decided some time later that the farms should be sold and negotiated with the widow who was the tenant and one of the executors. The challenge by her stepchildren on the grounds of the auctor principle failed in this particular case but it underlines the difficulties involved.

A more recent restriction on drafting is the pre-owned assets tax.

THE PRE-OWNED ASSETS TAX

In a text such as this it is only possible to provide a brief outline of what **4–46** is one of the most complex pieces of tax legislation produced in recent years, if not ever. It does impact on trust drafting. In fact the third limb of the tax relating to intangibles or incorporeal moveables only occurs in trusts and in particular types of trusts. It is vital with these trusts to ensure that all is done to avoid the tax or to minimise its operation.

The pre-owned assets tax ("POAT") is an income tax charge, which is to operate alongside the IHT gift with reservation of benefit rules. Its *raison d'être* is to deter "contrived and artificial" IHT saving strategies. It is only possible to give here a brief summary of what is an extremely complex tax, which may impact quite disastrously on trust arrangements. The drafter should have a clear grasp of this tax and how it may affect, generally speaking, an *inter vivos* trust.

POAT is a freestanding charge to income tax; it is not under any existing schedule and operates from 2005 to 2006 onwards. It is a "stand-alone" charge. The charge is to be the equivalent under the Income Tax (Trading and Other Income) Act 2005 and came into operation in place for 2005/2006 of a Sch.D Case VI charge and that Sch.D Case VI losses can be set off against the chargeable amount. There is a *de minimis* restriction of £5,000 *per annum.*

The tax was first announced in the December 2003 pre-budget report and found legislative form in s.84 and Sch.15 of the Finance Act 2004.

The tax applies where a former owner of land (and buildings) or corporeal moveables,[17] disposed of after March 17, 1986, benefits in certain prescribed ways from the said land or corporeal moveable disposed of, or is a beneficiary of a "interested trust" created after the date. It might be observed that there would be a limited number and type of corporeal moveables which generate an annual value of over

---

[17] The legislation refers to the English expression "chattels".

£5,000 *per annum!* Although it was targeted at abuses of the gift with
reservation ("GWR") rules, the POAT rules have a potentially much
wider ambit and are not restricted to gifts. Neither are all the statutory
exemptions to the GWR rules found in the POAT rules.

There are three distinct POAT charges in relation to land, corporeal
moveables and intangible property. Intangible property which roughly
equates to incorporeal moveables, is any property **other than** corporeal
moveables and interests in land.

A former owner can be liable to POAT in relation to these assets in
the following circumstances:

- Where he occupies land **which either he used to own**[18] or **which
  was purchased using the proceeds of sale of land**[19] which he
  used to own or which was acquired using consideration provided by him (Finance Act ("FA") 2004, Sch.15, para.3).
- Where he is in possession of or has the use of a corporeal
  moveable **which either he used to own or which was purchased
  using the proceeds of sale of a corporeal moveable** item which
  he used to own or which was acquired using consideration
  provided by him.
- **Where intangible property is comprised in a settlement in
  which he has an interest as defined by ICTA 1988, s.660A (FA
  2004, Sch.15, para.8).**

In relation to land and corporeal moveables **but not to intangibles** a
former owner will escape a POAT charge if the land or corporeal
moveable was disposed of or if the consideration was provided by way of
an *excluded transaction* (FA 2004, Sch.15, para.6).

The legislation has also a number of exemptions, two of which are
where the property potentially subject to the charge is otherwise
contained within the former owner's estate, or where that property is
already property subject to a reservation for IHT purposes.

**Where the charge applies the former owner is charged to income tax
on an amount calculated by reference to an assumed market rental of
any interest in land or an assumed rate of interest in relation to the
value of any corporeal moveables or intangible property.**

The legislation also has rules, para.21, which enables the former owner
to avoid the tax by electing for the land, corporeal moveable or
intangible property to be treated as property to be subject to a
reservation for IHT purposes.

The most striking aspect of POAT is its "retrospective" effect.
Individuals who have adopted IHT planning in the past which was then
outside the gift with reservation rules will in many circumstances find
themselves now facing a charge.

The other striking aspect of the POAT legislation is its width. It is as if
the charge was to be made as wide as possible and then the exemptions
and exclusions were listed.

It is with the third of these categories, namely intangible property,
with which we are concerned under the context of trust drafting since it

---

[18] The disposal element.
[19] The contribution element.

relates to trusts specifically. The first heading, land, and the second, corporeal moveables, may, if they form part of trust estate, come into the context of trust drafting; however, it is the third which exclusively relates to trust drafting.

POAT in relation to intangible property

Intangible property, as mentioned before, is any property other than **4-47** corporeal moveables or interests in land. Accordingly it includes cash, shares, life policies, insurance bonds or anything else which does not fall within the previous definition; the charge arises under the Finance Act 2004, Sch.15, para.8 where the individual has settled any property at any time after March 17, 1986 which is now intangible and the individual has an interest in the income from that property in terms of the settlement and in relation to which he is the truster.[20]

The definition of a settlement comes from the ICTA 1988, s.660A.[21] A taxpayer is deemed to have an interest in settled property "if that property or any derived property is or will or may become payable to or applicable for the benefit of the settlor or his spouse in any circumstances whatsoever".

The income must arise under the terms of the settlement in such a way that *it is treated as income of the truster.*

Please watch out for badly drafted trust deeds where, because all beneficiaries or potential beneficiaries have died out, the trust assets may revert back to the grantor.

The scope of the rules is extremely wide; thus, where an individual has intangible property by way of a liferent trust or discretionary trust, of which he is a potential beneficiary, any income of the trust would be assessed on him under the ICTA 1988, s.660A. However, in the first of these cases the property would be treated as part of his estate for IHT purposes and in both as property subject to a reservation for GWR purposes. In that event a POAT exemption could apply.

The trusts which are therefore likely to be caught in relation to intangibles are those which have been outside the GWR rules but caught by s.660A and the type of trust which will be most commonly falling within this category will be those in which the truster retains a reversionary interest.

Many clients may have invested in packaged trust arrangements usually involving bonds or life policies. "Flexible trusts", "discounted gift" and "gift and loan" schemes are popular examples. The position of these types is far from clear. While HMRC have given certain informal assurances it, nevertheless, seems clear that they will look at these closely to see if there is any possible POAT exposure.[22]

Excluded transactions

There are basically five circumstances which constitute excluded **4-48** transactions in more detail, as follows:

---

[20] The English expression "settlor" is used in the legislation.
[21] Taxes Act 1988.
[22] A useful article on this is by John Woolley: "Loans and Gifts" *Taxation Magazine*, November 25, 2004.

- sale for a full consideration; there must be no element of gift;
- outright transfers to spouses or former[23] spouses;
- settlements for spouses or former spouses;
- gifts of cash more than seven years ago; and
- where certain GWR exemptions apply, e.g. where the disposition falls within the IHTA 1984 as a distribution for family maintenance or an outright gift to an individual that is a transfer of value which is wholly exempt such as by annual exemptions or an outright gift which is wholly exempt by virtue of the small gifts.

Exemptions from a POAT charge

4–49   There are two sets of circumstances where an exemption to the POAT charge will apply where it would otherwise be chargeable; first, if it is included in the chargeable person's estate for IHT purposes or secondly if it is property subject to a reservation for GWR purposes. These exemptions apply to all three categories.

Property forming part of the chargeable person's estate for IHT purposes

4–50   These will be the types of cases where the taxpayer gives something away and later comes to own it "back again"!

The IHT legislation defines a person's estate as "the aggregate of all the property to which he is beneficially entitled" and further provides "that the estate of a person immediately before his death does not include excluded property".

Example One

In 1998 Mr Talisman transferred £200,000 to a liferent trust in which he was the liferentor. Shortly after that the trustees invested the funds in shares.

As Mr Talisman is both the truster and the liferentor of the settlement TA1988, s.660A is in point. Because the settlement holds intangible property there is a potential for a POAT charge in these circumstances. However because the **relevant property** is the intangible property in which the truster now has an interest and Mr Talisman had an interest in that property, there will be a POAT exemption.

It does not actually matter whether the property is subject to an IHT relief, e.g. business property relief, it will nevertheless form part of an individual's estate for the purposes of IHT.

Another aspect of this occurs where the replacement or derivative property is included in an individual's estate. Where the property which is now included in an individual's estate is not the **relevant property**, but other property which derives its value from the **relevant property**, the extent of the exemption can be limited depending upon the value of that other property as compared to the **relevant property**. It is difficult to give a definitive list of situations where this might occur because of the wide definition of replacement or derivative property.

---

[23] As regards former spouses this will only be where it has been by order of the court.

Example Two

Mr Antiquary transferred shares into a discretionary trust for his adult children in 2000. Under the terms of the trust the shares are to revert to Mr Antiquary in 2020.

He thus has a reversionary interest in the trust which owns intangible property and it will therefore be caught by the POAT rules in relation to intangibles.

The **relevant property** in these circumstances is the intangible settled property, i.e. the shares, and these are not included in Mr Antiquary's estate. However, the reversionary interest which derives its value from these shares is.

It should be noted that where replacement or derivative property is included in a person's estate the POAT exemption may be limited.

If that part of the value of the replacement or derivative property is not substantially less than the value of the **relevant property** the POAT exemption will apply in full.

Conversely, if it is substantially less than the value of the **relevant property** there will be no absolute POAT exemption. Instead, it is likely that the amount of the POAT charge, i.e. the appropriate rental value in the case of land, the appropriate amount in the case of corporeal moveable and the chargeable amount in the case of intangibles will be reduced by "such proportion as is reasonable to take account of the inclusion of the property in his estate" FA 2004, Sch.15, para.11(2). It is hoped that the HMRC will be able to publish guidelines in this given the possible fall in market values or reductions in value caused by damage.

Where a taxpayer's estate includes **relevant property** or replacement or derivative property then if any transaction by virtue of which the chargeable person's estate came to include the **relevant property** or by virtue of which the value of the replacement property came to be revived from **relevant property** when associate operation then that liability is an excluded liability.

There is other property which would have been the property subject to a reservation. POAT will not be due in those circumstances where the statutory exemption provides relief from an IHT charge. In these circumstances there will be no POAT charge also.

Post death variations[24]

A disposition made by an individual in relation to an interest in estate is to be disregarded for the purposes of the POAT rules if it is not treated as a transfer of land by the individual for the purposes of IHT. The most common instance of this is with a deed of variation which may be made within two years of the date of death. **4–51**

Example

Mr Robroy inherits a house on the death of his father. Within two years of his father's death he executes a deed of variation relative to his father's estate providing for the property to devolve jointly to his two

---

[24] . . . . More detailed reference will be made to deeds of variation in Ch.9.

adult children. Notwithstanding the variation it is Mr Robroy rather than the children who take up the occupation of the property.

Mr Robroy's disposition of the property falls within IHTA 1984, s.142(1) and is therefore to be disregarded for POAT purposes. No POAT charge therefore arises in relation to Mr Robroy's continuing occupation of the property.

Calculating the charge

4–52   **As regards the charge in relation to intangibles** this is slightly simpler than the calculation for the other two categories and is represented by

N-T

Where N is the amount of interest payable at the prescribed rate and T is the amount of tax which the taxpayer has otherwise to pay in respect of that interest.

The *de minimis* exemption. Where, in relation to an individual for a particular year, the total aggregate amount potentially subject to income tax under the POAT rules in relation to land, corporeal moveables and intangibles does not exceed £5,000, that individual is not subject to a POAT charge under FA 2004, Sch.15, para.13. The *de minimis* level is roughly equivalent to £100,000 of capital value taking the official interest rate of 5 per cent as a guide. If, however, it comes to £5,001 or more it is subject to tax on the entire amount.

It is vital to identify those cases where arrangements might be struck at.

Any schemes, e.g. home loan schemes, which have been entered into with a view to allowing the taxpayer to reside in the property and gift it away, thus saving IHT, should be examined very carefully. It is an "odds on" bet that it will come within the wide ambit of POAT.

Because many individuals will find themselves caught by the POAT rules in relation to transactions undertaken as long ago as March 18, 1986, the legislation contains **limited transitional provisions** enabling individuals to elect out of a POAT charge. Unfortunately, in doing this the individual has to choose to be subject to the GWR rules.

The election has to be made in respect of the first year of assessment in which a POAT charges and it must be made before January 31, in the following year of assessment unless a reasonable excuse can be shown.

The form is to be in the prescribed manner and a form is being prepared for this purpose by the HMRC.

The effect of the election for POAT purposes will operate so that in making the election the taxpayer elects that POAT charge shall not apply to him for the initial and any subsequent years of assessment. However, so long as the individual continues to occupy the land or possess or use the corporeal moveable, a chargeable portion is treated as property subject to the reservation.

When drafting *inter vivos* trusts it is important to make sure there is no possibility of a reversion to the truster, or of a truster receiving benefit inadvertently, perhaps by including a charitable trust as a back up.

FLEXIBILITY

4–53 Trust drafters must have flexibility at the forefront of their minds. To a certain extent this may involve crystal ball gazing but the changing pace of modern life and in particular the necessity for provision of investment decision making must be borne in mind. The trust drafter must write in as much flexibility as possible. Modern trusts need to be flexible to cope with change and a faster change of rate of fiscal and social changes and still be tax efficient. As always, we must guard against the "tax tail" wagging the dog.

Danger Warning!!!

Under the Civil Partnership Act 2004, s.131, where a person dies survived by a civil partner, unless he is also survived by issue, the civil partner has right to one half of the moveable net estate belonging to the deceased at time of death. If issue is involved the civil partner has a right to a third. This attempts to equate matters with *jus relictae*. **This means issue, however remote; every will executed after the commencement of the section in which provision is made in favour of the civil partner of the testator and which does not contain a declaration to the effect that the provision so made is in full and final satisfaction of the right to any share in the testator's estate to which the civil partner is entitled in effect, unless the disposition contained an express provision to the contrary, is read as if it contained such a declaration.**

SPOUSES, CIVIL PARTNERS, COHABITANTS AND OTHERS?

A matter to be borne in mind when considering will trusts is the impact **4–54** of the Family Law (Scotland) Act 2006, s.3. This is relevant to the rights of a co-habitant who is defined in s.25 of the Act as a man or woman who are (or were) living in a relationship as if they were husband and wife or two persons of the same sex who are (or were) living together as if they were civil partners. In determining this, the court has to have regard to the length of the period during which they had been living together, the nature of their relationship during that period and the nature and extent of any financial arrangements subsisting. Under s.29 the surviving co-habitant may apply to the Sheriff Court for provision on intestacy. The deceased must have been domiciled in Scotland before he or she died and must have been co-habiting with the survivor immediately before death. If parties have split up the former co-habitant does not appear to have any rights under s.29. The expression used is "immediately" and this might give some grounds for ambiguity. In his text, *Family Law Reform*, Professor Joe Thomson indicates that there may be a question of the deceased having been in hospital or a nursing home for several months before he died.

The court could make an order for:

- payment of a capital sum out of the deceased's net intestate estate.
- heritable or moveable property to be transferred.

The date on which it is to be paid, whether by instalments or otherwise, is also within the jurisdiction of the court, but it should be noted that the application must be made within six months beginning with the day in which the deceased died.

It should be noted that if the deceased died with a surviving spouse or civil partner then the claim of the applicant only comes into effect after these rights have been satisfied. The co-habitant's right is taken before the question of legitim is considered.

This introduces a matter whereby the certainty is introduced to the estate and parties would be well advised not to make any disposal prior to six months after the date of death.

Under s.131 of the Civil Partnership Act 2004, it is provided that:

> **131.**—(1) Where a person dies survived by a civil partner then, unless the circumstance is as mentioned in subsection (2), the civil partner has right to half of the moveable net estate belonging to the deceased at the time of death.
>
> (2) That circumstance is that the person is also survived by issue, in which case the civil partner has right to a third of that moveable net estate and those issue have right to another third of it.
>
> (3) In this section—
> "issue" means issue however remote, and
> "net estate" has the meaning given by section 36(1) (interpretation) of the Succession (Scotland) Act 1964 (c. 41).
>
> (4) Every testamentary disposition executed after the commencement of this section by which provision is made in favour of the civil partner of the testator and which does not contain a declaration to the effect that the provision so made is in full and final satisfaction of the right to any share in the testator's estate to which the civil partner is entitled by virtue of subsection (1) or (2), has effect (unless the disposition contains an express provision to the contrary) as if it contained such a declaration.
>
> (5) In section 36(1) of the Succession (Scotland) Act 1964 (c. 41), in the definition of "legal rights", for "and legitim" substitute "legitim and rights under section 131 of the Civil Partnership Act 2004".

This means that issue, however remote, and every will executed after the commencement of the section in which provision is made in favour of the civil partner of the testator, and which **does not contain an express declaration to the effect that the provision so made is in full and final satisfaction of the right to any share in the testator's estate to which the civil partner is entitled in effect** and unless the disposition contained an express provision to the contrary, it will be read as if it contained such a declaration.

Chapter Five

CONDITIONS AND POWERS OF TRUSTEES

"Despite the extent of the growth of the trust in the modern world, the law relating to the power or duties of trustees has not kept pace with their evolving social and economic role. . ."[1]

INTRODUCTION

It may be trite to state but, apart from (first) successful application to the **5–01** court to vary the terms of the trust under the Trusts (Scotland) Act 1921 and (secondly) the fact that certain powers may be inferred, the powers of trustees can only come from the trust deed or from statutory or common law rules. Indeed the statutory powers are only to be included if these are not at variance with the purposes of the trust. A distinction may need to be drawn between powers and duties but for the purposes of this chapter these will be "lumped" together.

It may be possible to divide these powers into two: first, general or administrative powers, e.g. power to purchase heritable property, which may relate to all or most trust deeds, and, secondly, those which relate to a particular trust, e.g. power to purchase a motor car for a carer of an *incapax*.

This chapter will attempt to address these types of powers with particular reference to the first of these. The next chapter will attempt to incorporate the second of these groups under the different types of trusts.

One of the perennial problems facing the drafter of trust deeds relates to the question of powers.

On the one hand, a large number of powers are now contained in statute such as the Trusts (Scotland) Act 1921, the Trusts (Scotland) Act 1961, the Trustee Investments Act 1961, all as amended, and the Charities and Trustee Investments (Scotland) Act 2005. In England the Trustee Act 2000 has given further detail and further powers which many practitioners south of the border find helpful. However, there are no immediate plans for similar legislation in this country at the time of writing. These will be referred to later. Powers exist in the new Charities and Trustees Investment (Scotland) Act 2005,[2] which was passed on June 9, 2005 but these do not go as far as those of the English Act. It is considered by many that the present structure of trust law and practice in

---

[1] Hudson, *Second Reading Committee Reports*, July 11, 2000, Mr Lock.
[2] The provisions of the Trusts (Scotland) Act 1921 are shown at page 87 with the new powers incorporated.

Scotland is insufficient and inadequate to deal with the speed and administration necessary. In particular, it is considered that the powers of investment and the levels of expertise necessary for some trusts cannot now be dealt with unless some greater measure of delegation can be given.

On the other hand trustees, particularly lay trustees, like to have a note of the powers *in gremio* the trust deed; that is to say they like to be able to refer to one deed and see all the powers they have. While this may be a chimera in many cases, they still prefer it.

This generally means repeating *ad longum* many of the powers which are enshrined in statute anyway. It is also necessary for the statutory provisions to be amplified and/or expanded and this can be carried out by conventional provision.

If a trust deed is silent on the matter of powers of investment then, generally speaking, the statutory provisions will apply. Most trust deeds will give the trustees wide powers of investment; a typical trust deed will give them, e.g. power to invest as if they were *absolute beneficial owners*. On the face of it, this is potentially very wide. However, it may be that the court would construe such a power very strictly.

The provision of the "shotgun" approach to drafting powers is often to be welcomed although the drafter knows that many of the powers which he has included in a draft will be superfluous. This is the dilemma facing the drafter. On the one hand he does not wish to make his deed like a larger version of *War and Peace*. On the other hand he must include all those powers which he considers the truster may need. Generally speaking he will, and should, try to err on the side of length. Indeed, with a view to avoiding claims, it is recommended that these be as comprehensive as possible.

Recent events have introduced, and to a certain extent restored, the suggestion that these powers should be included in a schedule.

In England and Wales it is possible for the trustees' powers merely to be incorporated by reference to the Society of Trust and Exemptory Practitioners ("the STEP provisions") but there does not appear to be any plans afoot for this at present north of the border, and the position with English law is so different in many aspects that this is of limited use. It is recommended that each firm should produce its own "house style". It may be worth having this printed, or rendered into a semi-permanent form. The possibility of having it registered in the Books of Council of Session and thereafter refer to it *in gremio* the deed may be considered. A copy can be given to the client for perusal prior to a meeting. At the first meeting this can be referred to. A possible style of this is shown later and statutory provisions have been included. Many banks now offer trustees' services and they will have a style of printed powers.

What happens if the particular statutory provision changes? If the document has this enshrined, then the power may still be available to the trustees perhaps with some additional benefit conferred by statute or otherwise. These powers should only be regarded as the starting point.

Particular care should be paid to individual trust provisions and for individual trustees and these are shown in more detail in succeeding chapters where particular trust deeds for particular situations and particular individuals are concerned. It may be helpful to take the statutory powers as a starting point.

The statutory powers are summarised here for reference. These can be regarded as "the default powers", that is to say, if the deed or statute is silent these powers may be implied.

Prior to the passing of the Trusts (Scotland) Act 1921, the common law would allow the trustees to invest consolidated stock or heritable securities.

<h2 style="text-align:center">TRUSTS (SCOTLAND) ACT 1921[3]</h2>

The investment powers of the 1921 Act are set out here with the **5–02** amendments made by the subsequent Trustee Investments Act 1961 and the Trusts (Scotland) Act 1961 as well as the recent changes made by the Charities and Trustee Investments (Scotland) Act 2005.[4]

Trusts (Scotland) Act 1921

5–03

General powers of trustees

    4.—(1) In all trusts the trustees shall have power to do the following acts, where such acts are not at variance with the terms or purposes of the trust, and such acts when done shall be as effectual as if such powers had been contained in the trust deed, viz.:—

(a) To sell the trust estate or any part thereof, heritable as well as moveable.

(b) *[Repealed by the Abolition of Feudal Tenure etc. (Scotland) Act 2000, (asp5), Sch.13(1), para.1 (effective November 28, 2004)]*.

(c) To grant leases of any duration (including mineral leases) of the heritable estate or any part thereof and to remove tenants.

(d) To borrow money on the security of the trust estate or any part thereof, heritable as well as moveable.

(e) To excamb any part of the trust estate which is heritable.

(ea) **To make any kind of investment of the trust estate (including an investment in heritable property).**

(eb) **To acquire heritable property for any other reason.**

(f) To appoint factors and law agents and to pay them suitable remuneration.

(g) To discharge trustees who have resigned and the representatives of trustees who have died.

(h) To uplift, discharge, or assign debts due to the trust estate.

(i) To compromise or to submit and refer all claims connected with the trust estate.

(j) To refrain from doing diligence for the recovery of any debt due to the truster which the trustees may reasonably deem irrecoverable.

(k) To grant all deeds necessary for carrying into effect the powers vested in the trustees.

---

[3] As amended by subsequent legislation.

[4] Recent changes made by the Charities and Trustee Investments (Scotland) Act 2005 (effective January 1, 2006) are highlighted in bold in the text.

(l) To pay debts due by the truster or by the trust estate without requiring the creditors to constitute such debts where the trustees are satisfied that the debts are proper debts of the trust.

(m) To make abatement or reduction, either temporary or permanent, of the rent, lordship, royalty, or other consideration stipulated in any lease of land, houses, tenements, minerals, metals, or other subjects, and to accept renunciations of leases of any such subjects.

(n) To apply the whole or any part of trust funds which the trustees are empowered or directed by the trust deed to invest in the purchase of heritable property in the payment or redemption of any debt or burden affecting heritable property which may be destined to the same series of heirs and subject to the same conditions as are by the trust deed made applicable to heritable property directed to be purchased.

(o) to concur, in respect of any securities of a company (being securities comprised in the trust estate), in any scheme or arrangement—

  (i) for the reconstruction of the company.
  (ii) for the sale of all or any part of the property and undertaking of the company to another company.
  (iii) for the acquisition of the securities of the company, or of control thereof, by another company,
  (iv) for the amalgamation of the company with another company, or
  (v) for the release, modification, or variation of any rights, privileges or liabilities attached to the securities or any of them,

in like manner as if the trustees were entitled to such securities beneficially; to accept any securities of any denomination or description of the reconstructed or purchasing or new company in lieu of, or in exchange for, all or any of the first mentioned securities; and to retain any securities so accepted as aforesaid for any Period for which the trustees could have properly retained the original securities;

(p) to exercise, to such extent as the trustees think fit, any conditional or preferential right to subscribe for any securities in a company (being a right offered to them in respect of any holding in the company), to apply capital money of the trust estate in payment of the consideration, and to retain any such securities for which they have subscribed for any period for which they have power to retain the holding in respect of which the right to subscribe for the securities was offered (but subject to any conditions subject to which they have that power); to renounce, to such extent as they think fit, any such right; or to assign, to such extent as they think fit and for the best consideration that can reasonably be obtained, the benefit of such right or the title thereto to any person, including any beneficiary under the trust.

(1A) The power to act under subsection (1)(ea) or (eb) above is subject to any restriction or exclusion imposed by or under any enactment.

(1B) The power to act under subsection (1)(ea) or (eb) above is not conferred on any trustees who are—

(a) the trustees of a pension scheme,
(b) the trustees of an authorised unit trust, or
(c) trustees under any other trust who are entitled by or under any other enactment to make investments of the trust estate.

(1C) No term relating to the powers of a trustee contained in a trust deed executed before 3rd August 1961 is to be treated as restricting or excluding the power to act under subsection (1)(ea) above.

(1D) No term restricting the powers of investment of a trustee to those conferred by the Trustee Investments Act 1961 (c.62) contained in a trust deed executed on or after 3rd August 1961 is to be treated as restricting or excluding the power to act under subsection (1)(ea) above.

(1E) The reference in subsection (1D) above to a trustee does not include a reference to a trustee under a trust constituted by a private or local Act of Parliament or a private Act of the Scottish Parliament; and "trust deed" shall be construed accordingly.

(1F) In this section—

"authorised unit trust" means a unit trust scheme in the case of which an order under section 243 of the Financial Services and Markets Act 2000 (c.8) is in force,

"enactment" has the same meaning as in the Scotland Act 1998 (c.46),

"pension scheme" means an occupational pension scheme (within the meaning of the Pension Schemes Act 1993 (c.48)) established under a trust and subject to the law of Scotland.

(2) This section shall apply to acts done before as well as after the passing of this Act, but shall not apply so as to affect any question relating to an act enumerated in head (a), (b), (c), (d), or (e) of this section which may, at the passing of this Act, be the subject of a depending action.

Exercise of power of investment: duties of trustee

4A.—(1) Before exercising the power of investment under section 4(1)(ea) of this Act, a trustee shall have regard to—

(a) the suitability to the trust of the proposed investment, and
(b) the need for diversification of investments of the trust, in so far as is appropriate to the circumstances of the trust.

(2) Before exercising that power of investment, a trustee shall (except where subsection (4) applies) obtain and consider proper advice about the way in which the power should be exercised.

(3) When reviewing the investments of the trust, a trustee shall (except where subsection (4) applies) obtain and consider proper advice about whether the investments should be varied.

(4) If a trustee reasonably concludes that in all the circumstances it is unnecessary or inappropriate to obtain such advice, the trustee need not obtain it.

(5) In this section, "proper advice" means the advice of a person who is reasonably believed by the trustee to be qualified by the person's ability and practical experience of financial and other matters relating to the proposed investment.

Exercise of power of investment: power to appoint nominees

4B.—**(1)** The trustees of a trust may, for the purpose of exercising the power of investment under section 4(1)(ea) of this Act—

(a) appoint a person to act as their nominee in relation to such of the trust estate, heritable as well as moveable, as they may determine, and

(b) take such steps as are necessary to secure the transfer of title to that property to their nominee.

(2) A person may not be appointed as a nominee unless the trustees reasonably believe—

(a) that the appointment is appropriate in the circumstances of the trust, and

(b) that the proposed nominee has the skills, knowledge and expertise that it is reasonable to expect of a person acting as a nominee.

(3) The power to appoint a nominee is subject to any restriction or exclusion imposed by or under—

(a) the trust deed, or

(b) any enactment (within the meaning of the Scotland Act 1998 (c.46)).

(4) An appointment as a nominee shall—

(a) be made in writing,

(b) be subject to the trustees' retaining power to—

   (i) direct the nominee, and

   (ii) revoke the nominee's appointment, and

   (c) subject to subsection (4), otherwise be on such terms as to suitable remuneration and other matters as the trustees may determine.

(5) The trustees may not appoint a nominee on any of the following terms unless it is reasonably necessary for them to do so—

(a) a term permitting the nominee to appoint a substitute,

(b) a term restricting the liability of the nominee, or of any substitute, to the trustees or to any beneficiary,

(c) a term permitting the nominee, or any substitute, to act in circumstances capable of giving rise to a conflict of interest.

(6) While a nominee continues to act for the trust, the trustees shall–

(a) **keep under review the arrangements under which the nominee acts and how those arrangements are being put into effect,**

(b) **if circumstances make it appropriate to do so, consider whether there is a need to exercise their power—**

   (i) **to direct the nominee, or**

   (ii) **to revoke the nominee's appointment, and**

(c) **exercise either or both of those powers if they consider that there is a need to do so.**

Declaration of power to delegate investment management functions

4C.—(1) It is declared that the trustees of a trust have and have always had the power, subject to any restriction or exclusion imposed by or under the trust deed or any enactment, to authorise an agent to exercise any of their investment management functions at the agent's discretion or in such other manner as the trustees may direct.

(2) In this section—

"enactment" has the same meaning as in the Scotland Act 1998 (c.46), and

"investment management functions" means functions relating to the management of investments of the trust estate, heritable as well as moveable.

At a glance it may be considered that these powers as constituted in the original 1921 Act were reasonably comprehensive. However, although they were "ground breaking" for the time, they are now very much out of date. (Unfortunately this is still the case even after the changes following on from the 2005 Act.) The next statute did not help much.

Trusts (Scotland) Act 1961

About 40 years later the next act was passed. This is only of passing **5–04** interest to drafters dealing as it does with powers of the court to vary trust purposes, validity of transactions by trustees and accumulations. The next Act was somewhat more innovative.

Trustee Investments Act 1961

The 1921 Act authorised only a limited range of investments, nearly all **5–05** of which have a fixed rate of interest and were repayable at par such as Bank of England fixed interest stocks and heritable securities. In periods of inflation, this proved to be unduly restrictive and the powers of investment were extended by the Trustee Investments Act 1961 which authorised trustees, on certain conditions, to acquire and hold a much more extensive and indeed risky range of investments. The Schedule is divided into three parts. The significant change is effected by Part III (Wider-Range Investments) which includes certain shares and debentures of UK incorporated companies.

The Trustee Investments Act 1961 was an attempt to provide a comprehensive framework for investment of trust funds where the deed was silent. It attempted to give trustees more scope for better returns on investments without exposing the trust funds to imprudent risk. Although it now seems a bit dated, it is difficult to underestimate the effect of this legislation. It is hard to believe that earlier last century the most risky investment allowed at common law was consolidated stock. The 1921 Act allowed fixed interest investments but in an age of inflation this was considered unduly restrictive. The Trustee Investments Act 1961 tried to strike the balance for capital appreciation (for the fiars) and income (for the liferentor) and authorised trustees under certain conditions to invest as set out in the first Schedule. The powers are divided into three parts.

Broadly speaking under its terms the trust funds were to be divided into two equal parts, namely, the Narrow Range, as specified in Part I and Part II of Sch.1 of the Act, and Wider Range, as specified in Part III. Narrow Range investments are also divided into those not requiring advice and those requiring advice. Wider Range investments, however, *always* require advice. Narrow Range investments not requiring advice are basically bank deposits and National Savings Certificates. Narrow Range Investments requiring advice are mainly fixed interest securities. Wider Range investments are UK company securities, unit trusts and Building Society shares.

The Trustee Investments (Division of Trust Fund) Order 1996[5] increased the proportion of wider range investments from a ratio of one: one to a narrower range of three: one.

There is also "Special Range" property. These may consist of the testator's non-qualifying investments which the trust deed authorises the trustees to retain. This includes Wider Range but not Narrow Range, it is not divided and forms a separate part of the fund. The most common would be heritable property. If the testator's house was held in the fund it would constitute Special Range property. Special Range property requires advice. If Special Range property is disposed of the funds must be divided equally between the Narrow and Wider Ranges.

In terms of the Trustee Investments (Division of Trust Fund) Order 1996, which came into force on May 11, 1996, any division of trust funds made after that date shall be in proportion three parts in the Wider Range to one part in the Narrow Range.

Part IV imposes restrictions on the investments which can be held. Additions may be made to the Parts by Order in Council.

Advice when required is to be taken from someone authorised in terms of the Financial Services Act. The trustees must decide how frequently to obtain advice and review their investments and keep a full record.

Section 15 of the Act safeguarded the saving powers of the court by providing that:

> "The enlargement of the investment powers of trustees by this Act shall not lessen any power of a court to confer wider powers of

investment on trustees, or affect the extent to which any such power is to be exercised."

No property was to be transferred from one part of a fund unless either the transfer is authorised or required by the following provisions of this Act, or a compensating transfer was made at the same time.

It is competent for the truster to provide for investments which are more restricted than those authorised by the Act but these must be specified in the Deed. Thus, the truster might provide that no investments be made in any company which had anything to do with the production and/or sale of alcohol.

Although also considered groundbreaking when passed, it is now considered that the requirements of the Trustee Investments Act 1961 are too restrictive and aimed at protecting the capital of the trust fund without much risk. Usually this will mean that the return on the fund will be low if there is little risk and this may not be in the interests of the beneficiaries.

It is much more preferable when drafting the trust to ensure that the truster gives the trustees the widest possible powers of investment to allow more flexibility to react to prevailing events and circumstances and maximise the return to the trust. For the purpose of the draft deed, we often see the power given to the trustees to be that of investing "as if the beneficial owners thereof".

In applications to the *nobile officium*, the court at one time would not extend the trustees' powers of investment beyond what was authorised by the trust deed and what was authorised by the Trustee Investments Act but this seems to be no longer the law.

As Alan W Eccles in his outstanding article *"Investing in the Future"*[6] wrote:

> "Whilst the 1961 Act relaxed the restrictions on trustees, it created a significant administrative burden on trustees, was itself restrictive and was overtaken by modern drafting. Therefore, the 1961 Act provided default rules which were, it is submitted, unsatisfactory for practical realities and practical requirements. The experience of the 1961 Act was such that it quickly became a target for reform and modernisation. This culminated in the Law Commission and Scottish Law Commission s Joint Report on Trustees Powers and Duties (No 260 and No 172)."

Sections 92 to 95 of the Charities and Trustee Investment (Scotland) Act 2005 provide an extension to the investment powers of trustees (of all trusts, whether charities or not). The Trusts (Scotland) Act 1921 is amended by adding a provision (s.92(2)) allowing a trustee to make any kind of investment of the trust estate (including an investment in heritable property). The effect is that trustees will generally have the same powers of investment as if they were the beneficial owners of the trust estate. Subsection (2) also provides a new wide power for trustees

---

[6] S.L.T. 2006, Vol.5, pp.23–27.

to acquire heritable property for any other reason. These wider powers are subject to any restriction or exclusion imposed by other deeds.

The 2005 Act also introduces new rules for the administration and decision making processes of trusts in relation to investment. However, the innovative investment opportunities for trustees are counter balanced with the need to obtain proper advice and the general underlying duties of care of trustees.

There are slight problems in the Act. As Eccles points out, "Trustees and advisers therefore must ensure that the apparent extension of investment powers in fact applies to the trust deed in question."

Looking at matters overall he poses the question: "Will the 2005 Act change practice in respect of the constitution and administration of trusts?" He suggests the answer:

> "It is unlikely that the constitution and administration of modern trusts will be greatly affected by the extension and clarification of trustees powers and duties. It may operate as a useful reminder to trustees and advisers to review portfolios, clearly communicate and consider decisions that are being made. Nevertheless, rather than provide a set of provisions that proactively develop the law, the 2005 Act's intentions appear to be more modest: to ensure that the default law of trusts keeps apace with contemporary investment practice and provides parity to less modern trust deeds while ensuring trustees are aware of their overarching duties to consider the trust fund's performance. The Scottish Law Commission is currently undertaking a comprehensive review with the aim of providing a more appropriate, responsive and coherent default law of trusts. The overhaul of the 1921 Act and a coherent updating is required, especially as the law of trusts operates in a more complex investment climate and has a greater exposure to corporate and commercial transactions."

THE TRUSTEE ACT 2000

5–06 The Trustee Act 2000, which, unfortunately, applies only to England and Wales, specifically to trusts which are governed by English Law, off and onshore, came into effect in England and Wales on February 1, 2001. It is worth looking at because it may be a precursor to what might occur in Scotland. The Act, which is an impressive piece of drafting in itself, attempts to provide a comprehensive framework for trustee's powers and duties. It has conferred powers on trustees and also imposed obligations and placed restrictions upon them to safeguard the beneficiaries.

The main new duties and obligations imposed by the Act are such duties as the statutory duty of care (s.1), the duty to consider the standard investment criteria (s.4), the duty to review the activities of agents, custodians and nominees (s.22), and the duty to obtain "proper advice" (s.5). There are restrictions on the terms of appointment of agents, custodians and nominees (ss.14 and 20), and in relation to the delegation of "asset management functions" (s.15).

Section 15 deals with the delegation of asset management functions. Subsection 5 defines asset management functions as functions relating to the investment of assets subject to the trust, the acquisition of property which is to be subject to the trust and managing property which is subject to the trust and disposing of, or creating and disposing of an interest in, such property.

Where trustees seek to delegate their asset management functions, they may not do so without complying with the requirements of this section, namely:

(a) an agreement made or evidenced in writing;
(b) a written "policy statement" setting out how the functions should be exercised; and
(c) a term in the agreement whereby the trustees secures conformity with the policy statement.

Danger Warning!!!
The duties in relation to delegation of asset management functions may not be excluded or restricted by any provision in the trust deed.

It is unfortunate that the practice of the two countries is dissimilar since this may affect the competitive edge of Scotland to attract private trusts. As Eccles puts it:

"**The pre 1 January 2006 position is an example of unnecessary divergence between the jurisdictions which can lead to confusion in practice. Furthermore, levelling the investment playing field between Scottish and English trusts is a sensible and overdue development.**"

POLICY STATEMENT

The trustees are bound by s.4(3) of the Act (like the Trustee Investments **5–07** Act 1961, s.6(1)) to have regard to the standard investment criteria of (i) the suitability of the investments and (ii) the need for diversification as appropriate to the trust. Where the asset management functions are delegated by the trustees to an asset manager, the asset manager is similarly bound by the standard investment criteria. The policy statement should contain the criteria for such suitability and diversification, to draw the trustees' attention to these matters.

A style of policy statement is contained in the Autumn 2001 edition of the *STEP Journal* at p.16 (by Owen Clutton, senior member of the technical committee of STEP). The "precedent" or style was written for *Tolley's Administration of Trusts* and will therefore be widely followed by practitioners.

The matters in the Policy Statement would include:

- Aim of the investment portfolio in the context of the trust's overall objectives, e.g. beneficiaries' needs, role of portfolio in relation to other assets in the trust.
- Summary of the trust's investment clause.
- Restrictions: as to markets in which transactions are to be effected; as to investments that may not be disposed of unless

expressly directed or authorised; on the amount or proportion of the funds under management which may be invested in any particular investment or category of investment, e.g. not more than 10 per cent in a single line of stock.
- Minimum yield requirement.
- Objective in terms of return on capital.
- Level of acceptable risk.
- Spread of investments/degree of diversification required.
- Whether there is a "total return" objective.
- Timescale and base currency in which performance to be assessed.
- Initial asset allocation, benchmark(s), frequency of review, use of collective investments.
- Anticipated additions or withdrawals of capital.
- Timing and extent of likely realisations.
- Requirement as to marketability of portfolio/part and any restrictions as to investments which may be difficult to realise.
- Tax considerations having an impact on investment decisions, e.g. as to *situs* of investments, e.g. whether any jurisdictions are "off limits"; as to gains, e.g. constraints on timing and frequency of realisations; as to impact on trustees'/beneficiaries'/ trusters' income and capital taxes position generally.
- Ethical investment considerations.
- Degree of freedom to exercise voting rights.
- Whether transactions may be entered into under which the trustees could incur obligations.

The policy statement may encompasse a wider range of matters than the agreements currently used by asset managers in Scotland.

The policy statement is prepared by or on behalf of the trustees and managers. It is in addition to a written agreement with the asset manager regulating their relationship with the trustees.

The trustees are themselves responsible for ensuring that the asset managers, who may be stockbrokers or other financial advisors, comply with the policy statement. This means that the trustee cannot simply depend on the asset managers to comply with the policy statement but must themselves ensure compliance. The written agreement entered into with the asset manager must reflect the policy statement and any changes to the policy statement should be intimated to the asset managers immediately.

Drafters may wish to familiarise themselves with policy statements as they are likely to have to draft or revise these in the near future.

The Scottish Law Commission produced a Report on Trustees' Powers and Duties in 1999 and has identified trusts as an area for medium-term consideration. The Sixth Programme of Law Reform (laid before the Scottish Parliament in March 2000):

"2.31 The powers and duties of trustees need to be reviewed. In the Report on Trustees' Powers and Duties the Commission, together with the Law Commission, made recommendations regarding powers of investment and the power to buy land. The core recommendation was to repeal the Trustee Investments Act 1961 and give trustees powers of investment as if they were absolute owners of the trust funds. Sections 29, 30 and 33 of the Trusts (Scotland) Act 1921 should be reviewed if this recommendation is implemented. Other topics that should be considered include the holding of investments in nominee accounts, the delegation of administrative functions, and the charging of remuneration by professional trustees in the absence of a charging clause. It is apparent that the list of powers in section 4 of the 1921 Act should be overhauled and restated in more general terms"

In Scotland there is no requirement for a policy statement. However, the Act provides that the appointment of nominees be made in writing. The trustees are required to obtain advice from a person who they reasonably believe to be a person qualified by that person's ability and experience. For reasons which are not entirely clear, as lawyers say, there is no duty on the trustees to obtain advice where the trustees consider that it is unnecessary or inappropriate to do so.

GENERAL POWERS

As can be seen there is a considerable amount of help from statute for **5–08** trustees' powers and conditions. However, it is suggested that these be used as "back up" and the bulk of the general conditions (by which is meant those conditions which will be required for all trusts) should be enshrined in a schedule which can be incorporated in the individual deed leaving the drafter free to concentrate on the specific provisions which he requires.

The following is a suggested style which drafters may wish to adapt and to retain in a semi-permanent form to annex to deeds of trust whether by will, deed of trust or deed of variation. It is appreciated that it is extensive and clients may initially baulk at a document which may extend to five or six pages and 80 per cent of which is unlikely to apply to them. These reservations may evaporate after it is explained to them that it may be simpler and cheaper to have the whole schedule, on the off chance, that their trustees may need one or more of the more unusual conditions. The drafter is also protecting himself against a claim at a future time arising from an omission.

SCHEDULE OF CONDITIONS

SCHEDULE of POWERS referred to in the foregoing Deed of Trust by JASON BOURNE

5–09

Definitions	In this Schedule: "Trustees" means the trustees acting under the Deed of Trust/Will. "Trust estate" means the property, heritable and moveable, administered at any time under the Trust Fund. "Income" and "Capital" refer to the income and capital respectively of the trust estate or any part thereof.

	Words indicating the plural include the singular, and vice versa. Words indicating the masculine may include the feminine. Marginal headings do not from part of the Schedule.
Conditions	The trust estate will be administered according to the following conditions:
Quorum of trustees	(A) A majority of the trustees under the Deed of Trust who may from time to time be in Great Britain shall be a *quorum*, and if at any time there shall be only one in Great Britain such one alone shall be a quorum, the power of any of the trustees to act being suspended during his absence from Great Britain.
Vesting of interests and advances	No beneficiary shall take a vested interest in any part of the trust estate until the due date for payment thereof, except that all advances made by the Trustees in terms of powers conferred on them by the Trust Deed shall vest in the recipient at the date of the advance.
Indemnity to trustees	The Trustees shall not be liable for loss or depreciation of investments retained or made by them, nor for omissions, nor for neglect in management, nor for insolvency of debtors, nor for the acts, omissions, neglect or default of each other or of any bankers, solicitor, factor or other agent employed by them.
Discharge	(B) Where a payment is made to a charity, unincorporated body or similar organisation the receipt of the treasurer or other appropriate official shall be sufficient discharge and my Trustees make payment of any sum to any charitable body which may have changed its name, been wrongly designed or amalgamated with any other body to that body, as my Trustees may in their sole discretion decide.
Powers	(C) In the administration of the trust estate or any part thereof my Trustees shall, in addition to the powers and discretions hereinafter expressly conferred upon them, and in addition to the powers, privileges and immunities conferred upon gratuitous executors in Scotland by statute or at common law, have the fullest powers of and in regard to investment, realisation, administration, management and division of the trust estate or any part thereof as if they were the beneficial owners thereof; and shall have power to do everything they may consider necessary or expedient for the administration of the trust as well as anything which is incidental or conducive to the exercise of their functions and, in particular, but without prejudice to the foregoing generality my Trustees shall have the following powers, which powers may be exercised by the Trustees at their absolute discretion and from time to time as necessary:
Sale of trust estate	(1) To retain, sell, purchase, lease or hire the trust estate or any part thereof in such manner and on such terms and conditions as the Trustees think proper including holding trust estate jointly with any other person.

Purchase of trust estate by trustees	(2) My Trustees may purchase any part of the trust estate or any part thereof as long as the purchaser is not the sole Trustees.
Retention of estate	(3) To retain any property comprised in the trust estate for such time as the Trustees think proper.
Investment	(4) To lend or invest the whole or any part of the trust estate, in any manner as if they were beneficially entitled thereto, in the purchase or on the security of heritable or real property, whether situated in Great Britain or elsewhere, corporeal moveables, stocks, shares (including partly paid shares), deposits, securities (including securities payable to bearer), unsecured loans, units of unit trusts, investments in property or other bonds and other assets of whatever description, whether producing income or not, whether or not falling within the class of investments authorised for trust funds or not, whether or not payable to bearer, and generally in investments or securities of any company, undertaking or body incorporated or carrying on business in any part of the world, and to sell, vary, exchange and transfer any such investments or securities.
Lend estate	To lend or allow to be used the whole or any part of the Trust estate at such rate of interest or rent as they may consider appropriate, or free of interest or rent, or by any person who is for the time being entitled to payment of a share of the income of the trust estate or to whom or for whose benefit the income may be paid or applied in the exercise of a discretion then available to the Trustees
Borrowing	(5) To borrow on the security of the trust estate or any part thereof on such terms and conditions as the Trustees may think proper.
Policies of assurance	(6) To effect or acquire policies of assurance, whether whole life, endowment, term, accident, contingency or otherwise, on the life or lives of any person; to pay the premiums thereon out of income or capital or partly from one and partly from the other; to cash bonuses on such policies; to convert such policies into fully paid policies for the same or reduced amounts or into any other from of assurance; to exercise any option available under such policies; to increase or decrease the amount of the annual premiums; to alter the period during which such premiums are payable; to surrender such policies and to do any such things notwithstanding that the sums assured may thereby be reduced; and to insure any property on whatever terms they think fit including on a first loss basis.
Borrow or lend	(7) To borrow or lend with or without security; to grant or continue with any guarantee or indemnity for the benefit of any beneficiary actual or prospective and to grant standard securities or other forms of charge against the trust estate or any part of it.

Nominees	(8) To allow the trust estate or any part thereof to be registered in the names of or held or the documents of title to be held by any person, firm, company or corporation or other body as a nominee of the trustees, whether in paper, electronic or other from, any part of the trust estate and to pay reasonable fees to such nominee or person.
Management of heritable property	(9) To administer and manage any heritable or real property forming part of the trust estate; to repair, maintain, renew and improve the same and to erect additional buildings and structures; to grant, vary and terminate leases and rights of tenancy or occupancy; to plant, thin and cut down timber; to work or let minerals; all as the Trustees may think proper and as if they were absolute owners of the trust estate
Companies	(10) To exercise in relation to any company or corporation in which shares or securities are held by the Trustees all powers competent to them, including power to promote or concur in any reconstruction or amalgamation, with power to any of their number to continue or to be appointed as a director or officer of any such company or corporation and to retain personally any remuneration paid to him in respect of that office.
Proxies	(11) To grant proxies in favour of any of their number or any other person to attend, act and vote for the Trustees at meetings of any company, corporation, trust or undertaking or in any bankruptcy or winding-up proceedings in which the executors may be interested or at any class meeting of shareholders, stockholders or debenture holders of any such company, corporation, trust or undertaking or of creditors in any such company, corporation, trust or undertaking.
Compromise of claims	(12) To compromise or settle by arbitration or by the advice of counsel or in the discretion of the Trustees all disputed claims by or against the trust estate.
Apportionment between capital and income	(13) To decide what money represents capital and what represents income and the proportion in which expenses are to be charged against capital and income respectively, notwithstanding any rule of law or practice to the contrary, and all similar questions which may arise in relation to the trust estate.
Loans to beneficiaries	(14) To make personal loans with or without interest and with or without security to any beneficiary actual or prospective of the trust estate, provided the Trustees are at least two in number
Accommodation for beneficiaries	(15) To acquire for the occupation of any beneficiary in the trust estate any dwelling-house which the Trustees may consider suitable and to improve, decorate, reconstruct or add to it in such manner as the Trustees may consider necessary or desirable.

Appropriation of investments	(16) To set apart and appropriate specific investments or property of the trust estate of any description to represent the whole or part of the particular share of any beneficiary or any share to which such beneficiary shall be entitled, prospectively or otherwise, and that at such valuations as the Trustees shall determine, so that the particular share shall have the whole benefit and the whole risk of the appropriate investments or property. A Minute signed by the Trustees, though not probative, shall be sufficient evidence of such appropriation
Satisfaction of bequests in cash or in kind	(17) To settle any share of a beneficiary in the trust estate either in cash or by conveyance or transfer of any part or parts of the trust estate, or partly in one way and partly in the other, all as the Trustees may decide and the valuation at which parts of the trust estate are so conveyed or transferred shall be determined conclusively by the Trustees, to any beneficiary or to the legal guardian of said beneficiary with power to require said beneficiary or any such guardian to accept such asset or assets at such value or estimate of value as the trustees in their uncontrolled discretion shall consider fair and, subject to any of the foregoing provisions to set apart and appropriate specific investments or assets to represent the whole or any part or parts of the share or shares , prospective or otherwise, of any beneficiary under this deed at such valuation as the trustees may in their absolute discretion, so that thereafter the particular share or shares shall have the full benefit and the whole risk of the appropriated investments or assets.
Delegation	(18) To appoint an investment adviser and revocably to delegate any power or powers, including discretion, of making, managing, realising or otherwise dealing with any investment or deposit comprised in the trust estate to such advisor or to any person or persons upon such terms as to remuneration or otherwise as the Trustees may think fit and no trustee shall be responsible for the default of any such agent if the trustee in question employed him in good faith
Resignation of Trustees	(19) To resign office as long as he is not the sole Trustees.
Appointment of agents	(20) To appoint one or more of their own number or, in the case of **any corporate trustee**, one or more of its directors, secretary or other officer or shareholders, or any firm or company or similar of which he, she or they may be a member, partner, shareholder or employee or consultant, to act whether as solicitors, stockbrokers, accountants or factors or any of these or in any other professional capacity to the trustees, in carrying out the purposes of this Will and to allow them their usual charges and professional remuneration, but always excluding from such appointment the grantor or any spouse hereof; under declaration that neither the grantor, no any spouse thereof should in any way receive benefit under this power.

Payment of expenses	(21) To reimburse any of the Trustees out of the trust estate for all expenses reasonably incurred by them in the administration of the trust estate.
General	(22) To do everything the Trustees may consider necessary or expedient for the administration of the trust estate.
Accept additional assets	(23) To accept as an addition to the Trust estate any other property as may be made over to them.
Business	(24) To continue, to carry on or to commence any business, whether alone or in conjunction or in partnership with any other persons, or through any companies, for such period as the Trustees may think proper; to appoint or employ any Trustee and/or any other person in any capacity in relation to such business and to pay to them suitable remuneration for services, including pension provisions for any employees or their dependants; and to delegate or entrust to any persons the control and management of such business to such extent as the Trustees may think fit; and (a) the Trustees may employ for the purposes of such business such part of the income or capital as they think proper; (b) the Trustees may enter into any agreement or partnership or other conditions; (c) the Trustees shall exercise only such control or supervision of said business as they shall think fit; (d) the Trustees shall be entitled to be relieved from the trust estate from all personal responsibility for any loss arising from such business operations, and (e) any Trustee appointed or employed in any such business shall be entitled to retain personally any remuneration for his services.
Promotion of companies	(25) To promote or concur in the flotation and reconstruction or amalgamation of any company with limited liability including, but without prejudice to that generality, any company framed to take over any business, company or concern carried on by the executors or in which they may be interested, and to subscribe for and hold the debentures, stocks, shares or other scrip or obligations of such new company or to accept the debentures, stocks, shares or other scrip or obligations of such reconstructed or amalgamated company in view of or in substitution for the debentures, stocks and shares or other scrip or obligations held by the Trustees executors prior to such reconstruction or amalgamation, and to contribute to the expenses of such flotation, reconstruction or amalgamation.
Participation in discretion	(26) To participate in the exercise of any discretion granted to the Trustees notwithstanding that a trustee is or may be a, or the sole, beneficiary in whose favour the discretion is then exercised provided that there is at least one trustee not so favoured.

Conflict of interest	(27) To enter into any transaction or do any act otherwise authorised by law or by this deed notwithstanding that any trustee is or might be acting as *auctor in rem suam* or with a conflict of interest between such trustee and himself as an individual or as trustee of any other trust or any partnership of which a trustee is a partner or any company of which a trustee is a shareholder or director or in relation to any combination of these capacities provided that the trustee or trustees with whom there is or may be such conflict are not the sole trustee or trustees.
Non-resident Trustees	(28) To appoint any one or more trustees resident out of Great Britain and themselves to resign office.
Administration abroad	(29) To carry on the administration of the trust hereby created in some place out of Great Britain.
Change of proper law	(30) To change the proper law of this trust by deed or deeds and therein to make such consequential variations or additions to this trust as the Trustees may consider expedient but no such deed shall be valid if or to the extent that it would result in any of the provisions hereof or of any appointment hereunder not being enforceable or exercisable or being revoked or revocable.
Renunciation of powers	(31) To renounce for themselves and their successors in office the power to exercise any of the foregoing powers in this purpose as if the same were vested in them beneficially and not as trustees; Declaring that none of the powers contained in this Purpose shall be exercised so as to benefit me or during my lifetime any spouse of mine in any way whatsoever.
Irrevocability	(32) I declare that this trust is irrevocable by me.
Scots law	(33) This trust shall be governed by and construed according to the law of Scotland:
	Place. . . . . Date. . . . . This is the Schedule of Powers referred to in the foregoing deed of trust/will by me,. . . . . Signed. . . . .

There follows a brief commentary on these powers. For those who prefer a non-tabular type of format there is shown the powers as in narrative form with headings in the body of the text. This is mainly a matter of personal preference.

The commentary is shown below in lower case text.

SCHEDULE OF CONDITIONS WITH COMMENTARY

SCHEDULE of POWERS referred to in the foregoing Deed of Trust by JASON BOURNE

Definitions

In this Schedule:

5–10

"Trustees" means the trustees acting under the Deed of Trust/Will.

"Trust estate" means the property, heritable and moveable, administered at any time under the Trust Fund.

"Income" and "Capital" refer to the income and capital respectively of the trust estate or any part thereof.

Words indicating the plural include the singular, and vice versa.

Words indicating the masculine may include the feminine.

Marginal headings do not from part of the Schedule.

It is useful to have a definitions section at the outset; it may be appropriate to have other definitions. Thus if it was wished to use the schedule as an attachment to a simple will the definition of the term trustees could include executors; the trust deed could include a will.

Conditions

5–11   The trust estate will be administered according to the following conditions:

Quorum of trustees

5–12   A majority of the trustees under the Trust Deed who may from time to time be in Great Britain shall be a *quorum*, and if at any time there shall be only one in Great Britain such one alone shall be a quorum, subject as aftermentioned, the power of any of the trustees to act being suspended during his absence from Great Britain.

This is standard. It does not preclude appointment of trustees of foreign-based trustees in the event of the trust being "exported". It may be important to arrange matters so that the wife and "outside trustee" can outvote the children. It may be appropriate to give one trustee (but not a spouse in a mini-discretionary trust) an overriding power or a power of veto. It is important to actually run the trust. It is not enough to have minutes of meetings. It must be possible to demonstrate that trust meetings have taken place. It is considered that the HMRC will use this as a means of challenging that a trust has actually taken place!

It is useful to have this to demonstrate to the beneficiaries that the trust is an entity from their own property, e.g. surviving spouses sometimes find it difficult to understand why in a mini-discretionary trust dividends should not be mandated directly to them!

Vesting of interests and advances

5–13   No beneficiary shall take a vested interest in any part of the trust estate until the due date for payment thereof, except that all advances made by the Trustees in terms of powers conferred on them by the Trust Deed shall vest in the recipient at the date of the advance.

This may seem obvious but it is as well to have it spelled out.

Indemnity to Trustees

5–14   The Trustees shall not be liable for loss or depreciation of investments retained or made by them, nor for omissions, nor for neglect in management, nor for insolvency of debtors, nor for the acts, omissions, neglect or default of each other or of any bankers, solicitor, factor or other agent employed by them.

This type of clause endeavours to protect trustees in what is after all basically a gratuitous office. It is likely that statute will in the future place greater duties on trustees which this type of clause will not cover. Scottish Law Commission published their first paper Breach of Trust *(number 123) which deals with breach of trust, standard of care and relief from liability by way of immunity clauses. As stated by Dr David Nichols in a recent article in the Scottish Law Commissions'* Trust Law Review *"Trust Deeds often contain a clause which purports to grant the trustees immunity from specific breaches of trust, such as neglect of management. Under the present law such clauses are effective in protecting trustees, lay and professional, unless they have been grossly negligent or fraudulent. The Commission suggested changes to the legal effectiveness of this immunity and other clauses which restrict liability and propose the professional trustees should not be able to rely on immunity or other clauses to avoid liability for their own negligence let alone for gross negligence or fraud. Dr Nichols differentiated between the position of lay trustees and suggested that the present laws should remain intact. The Commission also considered whether trustees should be able to protect themselves against liability for their own negligence by obtaining indemnity insurance at the trust's expense.*

Discharge

Where a payment is made to a charity, unincorporated body or similar **5–15** organisation the receipt of the treasurer or other appropriate official shall be sufficient discharge and my Trustees make payment of any sum to any charitable body which may have changed its name, been wrongly designed or amalgamated with any other body to that body, as my Trustees may in their sole discretion decide.

In days when charities are constantly changing their names this type of clause is absolutely vital. If used in the past it would probably have avoided about 90 per cent of disputed cases (and hundreds of thousands of pounds not being used for charitable purposes) of charities being wrongly or inaccurately designed.

Powers

In the administration of the trust estate or any part thereof my **5–16** Trustees shall, in addition to the powers and discretions hereinafter expressly conferred upon them, and in addition to the powers, privileges and immunities conferred upon gratuitous trustees and executors in Scotland by statute or at common law, have the fullest powers of and in regard to investment, realisation, administration, management and division of the trust estate or any part thereof as if they were the beneficial owners thereof; and shall have power to do everything they may consider necessary or expedient for the administration of the trust as well as anything which is incidental or conducive to the exercise of their functions and, in particular, but without prejudice to the foregoing generality my Trustees shall have the following powers, which powers may be exercised by the Trustees at their absolute discretion and from time to time as necessary.

It could be argued that this clause is all which is required. However, because it will certainly be construed contra preferentem it is necessary to insert ad longun the remaining clauses.

Sale of trust estate

5–17   To retain, sell, purchase, lease or hire the trust estate or any part thereof in such manner and on such terms and conditions as the Trustees think proper including holding trust estate jointly with any other person.

Part of this is included by statute but part not; it is as well to have it include so that trustees can see it in the deed.

Purchase of trust estate by trustees

5–18   My Trustees may purchase any part of the trust estate or any part thereof as long as the purchaser is not the sole Trustee.

Unless this clause is included the trustees may not purchase any trust property. This could prove embarrassing if a purchase by a close relative is later challenged.

Retention of estate

5–19   To retain any property comprised in the trust estate for such time as the Trustees think proper.

Sometimes a truster will transfer an investment which could not be justified under normal rules because it is, e.g. so speculative, into the trust fund. It could be shares in a company in which he was employed at some time. This clause protects the trustees.

Investment

5–20   To lend or invest the whole or any part of the trust estate, in any manner as if they were beneficially entitled thereto, in the purchase or on the security of heritable or real property, whether situated in Great Britain or elsewhere, corporeal moveables, stocks, shares (including partly paid shares), deposits, securities (including securities payable to bearer), unsecured loans, units of unit trusts, investments in property or other bonds and other assets of whatever description, whether producing income or not, whether or not falling within the class of investments authorised for trust funds or not, whether or not payable to bearer, and generally in investments or securities of any company, undertaking or body incorporated or carrying on business in any part of the world, and to sell, vary, exchange and transfer any such investments or securities.

This and the two following clauses are along with clause(s) 5–25 an attempt to make the powers as wide as possible. It is clear that this whole field will undergo vast changes as the variety of change and speed of decision making accelerate further. Gone are the days when the trustees would meet once a year to approve the trust investments for the succeeding year! The importance of powers to lend are relevant for the situation described elsewhere the one half share of the matrimonial home is sold to the surviving spouse (or partner) but the price is not paid. Instead the trustees accept a standard security or other document by the spouse/ purchaser/borrower. It could also be necessary where the trustees wish to lend as opposed to giving money to a young beneficiary to enable them to purchase an heritable property.

Lend estate

5–21   To lend or allow to be used the whole or any part of the Trust estate at such rate of interest or rent as they may consider appropriate, or free of interest or rent, or by any person who is for the time being entitled to

payment of a share of the income of the trust estate or to whom or for whose benefit the income may be paid or applied in the exercise of a discretion then available to the Trustees.
As above.

Borrow or lend

To borrow or lend with or without security; to grant or continue with **5–22** any guarantee or indemnity for the benefit of any beneficiary actual or prospective and to grant standard securities or other forms of charge against the trust estate or any part of it.
As above.

Nominees

To allow the trust estate or any part thereof to be registered in the **5–23** names of or held or the documents of title to be held by any person, firm, company or corporation or other body as a nominee of the trustees, whether in paper, electronic or other from, any part of the trust estate and to pay reasonable fees to such nominee or person.
It is questionable if this clause is necessary now given that it is now enshrined in the 2005 Act as the opinion of the Scottish Executive, in their infinite wisdom, that it was always competent!

Borrowing

To borrow on the security of the trust estate or any part thereof on **5–24** such terms and conditions as the Trustees may think proper.
This could have been included in one of the general clauses above but is listed separately as a clause to which the special attention of the truster should be drawn; it is always assumed that this will relate to heritable property. It is difficult to foresee the need for this power in a deed. However, it could be necessary over the moveable estate to obtain an overdraft to tale up or pay a "call" on a shareholding of the trust.

Policies of assurance

To effect or acquire policies of assurance, whether whole life, endow- **5–25** ment, term, accident, contingency or otherwise, on the life or lives of any person; to pay the premiums thereon out of income or capital or partly from one and partly from the other; to cash bonuses on such policies; to convert such policies into fully paid policies for the same or reduced amounts or into any other from of assurance; to exercise any option available under such policies; to increase or decrease the amount of the annual premiums; to alter the period during which such premiums are payable; to surrender such policies and to do any such things notwithstanding that the sums assured may thereby be reduced; and to insure any property on whatever terms they think fit including on a first loss basis.
As above for 5–20.

Management of heritable property

To administer and manage any heritable or real property forming part **5–26** of the trust estate; to repair, maintain, renew and improve the same and to erect additional buildings and structures; to grant, vary and terminate leases and rights of tenancy or occupancy; to plant, thin and cut down timber; to work or let minerals; all as the Trustees may think proper and as if they were absolute owners of the trust estate.

This is the type of clause which on balance it might be thought could be excluded as being appropriate to a larger heritable estate. However it is probably worth including it. If there is a large heritable estate much wider powers and more detailed powers are likely to be needed.

Companies

5–27   To exercise in relation to any company or corporation in which shares or securities are held by the Trustees all powers competent to them, including power to promote or concur in any reconstruction or amalgamation, with power to any of their number to continue or to be appointed as a director or officer of any such company or corporation and to retain personally any remuneration paid to him in respect of that office.

This and the following are extremely likely to be needed where there is a private company or family run business and there is no qualified adult to become involved in running the company. It would be unfair for a trustee to give up so much time without remuneration. It can have somewhat unusual results; in one instance a former partner of the writer became the chairman of a multi-national quoted company!

Proxies

5–28   To grant proxies in favour of any of their number or any other person to attend, act and vote for the Trustees at meetings of any company, corporation, trust or undertaking or in any bankruptcy or winding-up proceedings in which the executors may be interested or at any class meeting of shareholders, stockholders or debenture holders of any such company, corporation, trust or undertaking or of creditors in any such company, corporation, trust or undertaking.

As before; sometimes private companies will not allow beneficiaries or trustees to become registered stock or shareholders. This clause could be extremely important if the only method of challenge of the management of the company is at the Annual General Meeting.

Compromise of claims

5–29   To compromise or settle by arbitration or by the advice of counsel or in the discretion of the Trustees all disputed claims by or against the trust estate.

This clause could be excluded and is included merely for historical reasons and because it is the kind of clause which lay trustees like to see in a deed.

Apportionment between capital and income

5–30   To decide what money represents capital and what represents income and the proportion in which expenses are to be charged against capital and income respectively, notwithstanding any rule of law or practice to the contrary, in addition, all similar questions which may arise in relation to the trust estate.

If any one clause is to be inserted it is this one! Many trustees ignore apportionments but strictly speaking they do so at their peril!

Loans to beneficiaries

To make personal loans with or without interest and with or without **5–31** security to any beneficiary of the trust estate, provided the Trustees are at least two in number.

This is already included but it is included to underline the importance of the possible loan to the surviving spouse/partner in a mini-discretionary trust.

Accommodation for beneficiaries

To acquire for the occupation of any beneficiary in the trust estate any **5–32** dwelling-house which the Trustees may consider suitable and to improve, decorate, reconstruct or add to it in such manner as the Trustees may consider necessary or desirable.

This is the type of clause which used to be thought more specialised but is now standard. It would cover, e.g. complicated alterations for a handicapped or elderly person to a house.

Appropriation of investments

To set apart and appropriate specific investments or property of the **5–33** trust estate of any description to represent the whole or part of the particular share of any beneficiary or any share to which such beneficiary shall be entitled, prospectively or otherwise, and that at such valuations as the Trustees shall determine, so that the particular share shall have the whole benefit and the whole risk of the appropriate investments or property. A Minute signed by the Trustees, though not probative, shall be sufficient evidence of such appropriation.

These are of limited use; it might be helpful for the trustees from an accountancy point of view to identify a fund for a particular beneficiary but not to have it vested in the beneficiary who may be incapax and might stand to lose some benefit from public funds.

Satisfaction of bequests in cash or in kind

To settle any share of a beneficiary in the trust estate either in cash or **5–34** by conveyance or transfer of any part or parts of the trust estate, or partly in one way and partly in the other, all as the Trustees may decide and the valuation at which parts of the trust estate are so conveyed or transferred shall be determined conclusively by the Trustees, to any beneficiary or to the legal guardian of said beneficiary with power to require said beneficiary or any such guardian to accept such asset or assets at such value or estimate of value as the trustees in their uncontrolled discretion shall consider fair and, subject to any of the foregoing provisions, to set apart and appropriate specific investments or assets to represent the whole or any part or parts of the share or shares, prospective or otherwise, of any beneficiary under this deed at such valuation as the trustees may in their absolute discretion, so that thereafter the particular share or shares shall have the full benefit and the whole risk of the appropriated investments or assets.

This is extremely useful in that it may save brokerage realisation costs. It will not necessarily save CGT on trustees as this may count as a disposal. It may save brokerage or conveyancing/estate agency charges.

Delegation

5–35　　To appoint an investment adviser and revocably to delegate any power or powers, including discretion, of making, managing, realising or otherwise dealing with any investment or deposit comprised in the trust estate to such advisor or to any person or persons upon such terms as to remuneration or otherwise as the Trustees may think fit and no trustee shall be responsible for the default of any such agent if the trustee in question employed him in good faith.

In the past, i.e. pre-2005 Act, it was questionable just how effective this clause would be. However, with the passing of the 2005 Act and the specific power being given it seems likely that this will be the way forward. It might be worth considering extending this power.

Resignation of trustee

5–36　　To resign office as long as he is not the sole trustee.

This is included under statute. It seems reasonable, given the cost of applying to the court etc., to have a new trustee appointed, that a sole trustee should assume at least one trustee before he resigns. This is a matter, which should be raised with a prospective trustee before he takes up office. At the risk of repetition, trustees should always be asked to accept in writing the office of trustee after having matters explained to them.

Appointment of agents

5–37　　To appoint one or more of their own number or, in the case of any corporate trustee, one or more of its directors, secretary or other officer or shareholders, or any firm or company or similar of which he, she or they may be a member, partner, shareholder or employee or consultant, to act whether as solicitors, stockbrokers, accountants or factors or any of these or in any other professional capacity to the trustees, in carrying out the purposes of this trust and to allow them their usual charges and professional remuneration, but always excluding from such appointment the grantor or any spouse hereof; under declaration that neither the grantor, nor any spouse thereof should in any way receive benefit under this power.

This might be regarded as the second most important clause in the schedule! Obviously, it extends to professional partners of the trustees.

One aspect of the principal of "auctor rem suam" is that trustees are forbidden from receiving remuneration. The trust deed is and the office of trust deed is a gratuitous one. Accordingly, unless the trust deed specifically provides or authorises this or all the beneficiaries agree then no remuneration is possible.

It is vitally important therefore that the deed contains a "charging clause" authorising the trustees to appoint one or more of their number to carry out trust business at usual professional rates. The principal example of this would be where a legally qualified trustee might be appointed solicitor to the trust and to do all the legal and administrative work.

Payment of expenses

To reimburse any of the trustees out of the trust estate for all expenses **5–38** reasonably incurred by them in the administration of the trust estate.

This comes under the heading of something, which trustees like to see.

General

To do everything the trustees may consider necessary or expedient for **5–39** the administration of the trust estate.

This is a backstop all-inclusive power in case previous powers miss something out. As before, it would be construed strictly. It is very important.

Accept additional assets

To accept as an addition to the trust estate any other property as may **5–40** be made over to them.

It seems that this is hardly necessary. The original deed provides for £20 so that it is obvious that something extra is going to come into the trust. Presumably, additions will have their own taxation agenda.

Business

To continue, to carry on or to commence any business, whether alone **5–41** or in conjunction or in partnership with any other persons, or through any companies, for such period as the trustees may think proper; to appoint or employ any trustee and/or any other person in any capacity in relation to such business and to pay to them suitable remuneration for services, including pension provisions for any employees or their dependants; and to delegate or entrust to any persons the control and management of such business to such extent as the trustees may think fit; and

- the trustees may employ for the purposes of such business such part of the income or capital as they think proper;
- the trustees may enter into any agreement or partnership or other conditions;
- the trustees shall exercise only such control or supervision of said business as they shall think fit;
- the trustees shall be entitled to be relieved from the trust estate from all personal responsibility for any loss arising from such business operations; and
- any trustee appointed or employed in any such business shall be entitled to retain personally any remuneration for his services.

The necessity for this clause is more common than might, at first sight, be thought.

Promotion of companies

To promote or concur in the flotation and reconstruction or amal- **5–42** gamation of any company with limited liability including, but without prejudice to that generality, any company framed to take over any business, company or concern carried on by the executors or in which they may be interested, and to subscribe for and hold the debentures, stocks, shares or other scrip or obligations of such new company or to accept the debentures, stocks, shares or other scrip or obligations of such reconstructed or amalgamated company in view of or in substitution for the debentures, stocks and shares or other scrip or obligations held by the trustees' executors prior to such reconstruction or amalgamation, and to contribute to the expenses of such flotation, reconstruction or amalgamation.

It might be thought that this is a very specialised provision. However, it is worth considering for trusts, particularly charitable trusts where the trustees may wish the vehicle of a company for retaining control of a charitable donation. Readers will be aware of the somewhat cavalier attitude of the recipients of some charitable gifts in replying to requests regarding the outcome of, say, donations made for medical requests. In some instances, it may be discovered that the person or researcher or medical specialist who spearheaded the drive for funds has actually left the hospital or research facility.

Participation in discretion

5–43   To participate in the exercise of any discretion granted to the trustees notwithstanding that a trustee is or may be a, or the sole, beneficiary in whose favour the discretion is then exercised provided that there is at least one trustee not so favoured.

Unless this is included it will be questionable as whether a trustee, e.g. a spouse, can benefit under a discretionary power.

Conflict of interest

5–44   To enter into any transaction or do any act otherwise authorised by law or by this deed notwithstanding that any trustee is or might be acting as *auctor in rem suam* or with a conflict of interest between such trustee and himself as an individual or as trustee of any other trust or any partnership of which a trustee is a partner or any company of which a trustee is a shareholder or director or in relation to any combination of these capacities provided that the trustee or trustees with whom there is or may be such conflict are not the sole trustee or trustees.

At common law trustees are forbidden by reason of their fiduciary position from obtaining any personal benefit from the trust estate or from allowing a conflict to arise between their own personal interests. It is necessary therefore to permit this in terms of the trust deed.

As Doctor David Nichols stated in a recent article in the Scottish Law Commissions' Trust Law Review*:*

> *"any profit derived from the trust estate, even inadvertent profit or profit gained from dealings with the trust estate in good faith and at general commercial rates must be accounted for and paid back into the trust fund".*

The paper enquires whether the current rules are too strict.

Non-resident trustees

5–45   To appoint any one or more trustees resident out of Great Britain and themselves to resign office.

This could be important if it was decided to "export" the trust offshore and the law of the new home of the trustees required trustees to be nationals.

Administration

To carry on the administration of the trust hereby created in some **5–46** place out of Great Britain.
This is linked in with para.5–45 above.

Change of proper law

To change the proper law of this trust by deed or deeds and therein to **5–47** make such consequential variations or additions to this trust as the trustees may consider expedient but no such deed shall be valid if or to the extent that it would result in any of the provisions hereof or of any appointment hereunder not being enforceable or exercisable or being revoked or revocable;
As above.

Renunciation of powers

To renounce for themselves and their successors in office the power to **5–48** exercise any of the foregoing powers in this purpose as if the same were vested in them beneficially and not as trustees; declaring that none of the powers contained in this purpose shall be exercised so as to benefit me or during my lifetime any spouse of mine in any way whatsoever.
This could be an extremely useful power to have. It is likely that the change in the law of tax relating to trusts could penalise a trust with a particular power, e.g. power to accumulate. If the trustees were able to renounce this power it could be of great advantage.

Irrevocability

I declare that this trust is irrevocable by me. **5–49**

Scots law

This trust shall be governed by and construed according to the law of **5–50** Scotland.

This is a typical list of powers and will mirror the kinds which drafters have in their trust deeds. It can be used for trusts or in wills or in *inter vivos* deeds of trust. These could be regarded as the "core" or general conditions or powers which would apply to all but the most simple of trust deeds.

ADDITIONAL POWERS

Additional powers to deal with specific purposes could be added, as in **5–51** the following example:

Special provisions as to business interests	And whereas I am engaged in business as a leather mer- chant and boot-maker's outfitter meantime by myself alone but before this Will comes into operation there may be changes by a partnership or otherwise in that business and I may become engaged in other businesses as a partner or otherwise all which businesses and shares of businesses are herein referred to as "my business interests" I confer upon my trustees the widest possible powers and discretions as to carrying on or not carrying on renewing extending or restricting my business inter- ests entering into partnership or amalgamation arrangements or formation of a joint stock company or companies employing managers accountants and others borrowing money incurring expenses of investigations and flotation or attempted flotation and selling my busi- ness interests on credit or for payment by instalments and with or without security giving time to purchasers taking payment wholly or partly in debentures or deben- ture stock or preference ordinary or deferred shares with or without liability for uncalled capital which they shall hold or sell as they think fit and generally power to act or refrain from acting in regard to my business interests or the extinction thereof as fully and unrestrictedly in all respects as I could have done if in life or as if they were beneficial owners and that all in their uncontrolled dis- cretion and without prejudice to their general right of indemnity against my estate I provide that they shall be entitled to be indemnified by my estate in respect of all liabilities which they may incur with reference to my business interests in the execution or intended or assumed execution of or in reliance on the powers and discretions hereinbefore conferred upon them.

Where the estate is more substantial and involves such assets as farms, mines and the like the following clause may be considered:

Special powers	In the exercise of any of the powers, purposes or condi- tions expressed herein, and without prejudice to any other of said powers, purposes or conditions, it is declared that my Trustees may apply or part or any part of the trust estate in the purchase, development, mainte- nance and management of any real or heritable property, including shooting rights, fishing rights and sporting rights, mines, mineral rights, agricultural land, woodlands and commercial and industrial land, with or without buildings and with or without plant and machinery on in or at any such property; to employ workmen in and enter into partnership with any other person, firm, company or corporation for the management and development thereof; to erect buildings, install plant and machinery, and carry out any other works and provide services which my trustees in their absolute discretion may consider necessary; **DECLARING** that if my trustees exercise this

	power for any of powers, conditions or purposes herein mentioned, they may and shall be free to act in regards to any such property in all respects as if they were absolute owners thereof in general and in particular the trustees shall not be obliged to pay out monies under their charge as trustees with a view to making or realising profit, capital gain or making income or revenue; and further the trustees shall not be personally liable for any loss incurred as a result of them so acting nor for the diminution or depreciation in value of any asset of the trust estate or the capital or income thereof which results from such activities.

It may be prudent to insert the following general clause dealing with the exclusion of benefit to the grantor or truster:

Exclusion of benefit	It is expressly provided and declared that no discretion, condition nor power conferred on the Trustees and that nothing in the foregoing shall operate in such a way as to allow or permit or cause my Trustees to make payable to or apply for the benefit of me, the grantor of these presents, or, during my lifetime any spouse of mine, any part of the income or capital of the trust estate or of any property derived therefrom.

It is often suggested that the key to successful trust drafting is to attempt to achieve as much flexibility as possible while remaining within statutory constraints. It is often appropriate to give powers to trustees **to set up another trust** or to reconstitute itself as another type of trust.

It may also be appropriate to retain power to the truster to appoint further trustees:

> The power to appoint additional trustees shall be vested solely in me in so far as I retain full legal capacity.

It might be that additional indemnity is considered appropriate:

> Notwithstanding any rule of law to the contrary, it is hereby provided that the trustees shall be entitled to hold on to any asset of the trust estate acquired by them from the truster, including, without prejudice to the foregoing generality, the shares of any private company, business and heritable property, notwithstanding that any professional advisors might advise it prudent to sell the same; and, so long as the trustees act in good faith in doing so, no beneficiary hereunder shall have any claim against any trustee who retains any such asset under this power even although, by so doing, a diminution in the trust estate results; should any beneficiary hereunder seek to claim damages of breach of trust because of a loss occurring to the trust estate as a result of the exercise by the trustees of this power in good faith, then any such beneficiary so claiming shall forthwith forfeit any benefit which he or she would otherwise take or has already taken under this deed, to the extent required to indemnify the trustees against such claim.

It might be wished to restrict this as follows:

> to the extent required to indemnify the trustees against any such claim; and
> if benefit has already been taken, the same shall be repayable by the
> beneficiary to the trustees to the same extent.

FORMAT OF TRUST DEED

5–52 The deed in outline would be as follows:

1 Inductive Clause
2 General Purpose
3 Appointment of Trustees
4 Name of Trust
5 Definitions and Powers—General (Schedule)
6 Specific Powers (peculiar to that trust)
7 Testing clause
8 Acceptance by trustees of office

Style

I JASON BOURNE, residing at Three Chalets, Milngavie, hereinafter referred
to as "the truster", considering that I wish to provide for the [*insert general
provisions of trust*] do hereby appoint [*insert the full names addresses and
occupations of the trustees*] as trustees for the purposes after mentioned together
with such other person or persons who may hereafter be appointed or assumed,
and the acceptor or acceptors, survivor or survivors of them as such trustees (the
trustee or trustees for the time being acting hereunder being hereinafter referred
to as "the trustees"); And I direct the trustees to hold and administer all funds,
property and assets of whatever nature which may hereafter at any time and
from time to time be paid, conveyed and made over to the trustees hereunder
the whole funds, property, assets from time to time being held by the trustees,
including accumulation, if any, being hereinafter referred to as "the trust estate"
in trust for the following purposes and subject to the following provisions
videlicet:

1. Name of Trust

This trust should be known as [*insert name of trust*]

2. Definitions

[*Take the definitions from the schedule.*]

3. Powers

I declare that the conditions and powers set out in the Schedule annexed and
signed as relative hereto so far as not inconsistent with any provisions of this
deed, shall apply to the administration of the trust funds.
[*specify them in the deed.*]

4. Specific Powers

[*If any*]

IN WITNESS WHEREOF these presents consisting of this and the preceding
pages are together with said schedule hereto annexed and subscribed by me the
said

[*specify*] at [*specify*]

before the witness hereto subscribing whose designation is appended to their signature.

Place   Date

We, the trustees appointed in the foregoing deed hereby accept office as trustee foresaid.
[*To be signed by all accepting trustees.*]

Chapter Six

PARTICULAR TYPES OF TRUST DEEDS AND PROBLEM SOLVING

"Perish policy and cunning"[1]

How Do We Choose which Type of Trust to Utilise?

6–01 It seems trite to say but this will depend initially upon who the beneficiaries are and how old they are.

Until recently, if the beneficiaries were all under the age of 25 and had a common parent or grandparent, then the accumulation and maintenance trust would have been the obvious choice. Recent legislation would indicate that the full benefits of the accumulation and maintenance trust provisions will be restricted to those attaining the age of 18. The question of capital gains tax holdover relief will be available as regards non-business/agricultural assets. The tax treatment of trusts has been dealt with at Ch.3.

If it is wished to benefit a much wider class of persons such as surviving spouse, the truster himself (although this can lead to fairly complex fiscal rules) and perhaps others as well such as children, then a discretionary trust may have to be chosen. Clearly there may be capital gains tax advantages in a discretionary trust by way of holdover relief or otherwise and if the initial sum paid in does not exceed the nil rate band then a discretionary trust can be created *inter vivos*. If the appropriate powers are included it can later be converted in whole or in part to an accumulation and maintenance trust, thus enabling a move from an initially wide class of beneficiaries to a narrower class without an inheritance tax cost. Alternatively, where the truster has a specific beneficiary or class of beneficiaries in mind whom he wishes to benefit from an income of trust property without recourse to the capital, he may consider a liferent trust.

As wide a discretion as possible is usually to be aimed for. It may be that the truster can produce an informal letter which is not binding as a guide to the existing trustees.

The question of which assets to transfer into the trust is a question which crops up from time to time. Cash, quoted and unquoted shares, heritable property and life insurance can all be transferred. There may be a particular merit in transferring assets which have a low value but which may be expected to appreciate in the future such as the shares in a

---

[1] Church Hymnary 4.

private company. It may be that the increase in value would be free of inheritance tax for the beneficiaries. This would not of course include the truster himself.

The trusts which will be considered are as follows, following the layout in Ch.3:

1. Discretionary Trusts
2. Accumulation and Maintenance Trusts
3. Liferent trusts
4. Disablement Trusts
5. Charitable Trusts
6. Offshore Trusts
7. Bare Trusts
8. "Pilot Trusts"
9. Trusts for a bereaved minor

DISCRETIONARY TRUSTS

General

As previously remarked discretionary trusts are extremely flexible. At **6–02** their essence they are trusts where no one person has a right to receive capital or revenue. They can be used, almost routinely, in many different cases. Perhaps their greatest utility is in wills where a testator cannot make up his mind or is unsure if, e.g. he wishes to use the nil rate band ("NRB") or part of the NRB for the benefit of his children. However, he may be unsure if his widow will have sufficient to live on. Here, he can include her as a potential beneficiary in a discretionary trust along with his issue. It may be that the truster is a young person and is unsure as to what will happen, e.g. if he will marry and have children etc.

The discretionary trust, notwithstanding the harshness of the tax regime, is and will be for many the vehicle of trust to choose. This trend will probably increase given the government's policy of bringing other trusts into line with discretionary trusts as far as tax treatment is concerned. Generally it will be that the deed is drawn in very wide terms.

As stated, possibly the most common type of discretionary trust will be one for the NRB, presently £285,000.[2] This will be mainly an IHT saving measure on the death of the widow or widower of the truster or more usually the testator. Although the NRB cannot be set aside it may that it has to be reduced by:

- lifetime gifts;
- non-exempt legacies in the case of a testamentary provision;
- transfers into *inter vivos* trusts.

The other asset which may cause difficulty, particularly in the NRB context, is the vexed question of the family home which, for a couple of

---

[2] 2006/07.

moderate means, may be the largest asset. It may be that, e.g. the deceased's share of the family home is needed to make up the NRB legacy. However, it is likely that the surviving spouse may wish to continue to occupy the house.

While extremely important from the IHT saving point of view, it is only fair to point out that there are other methods of IHT saving which are not restricted to the use of NRB discretionary trusts. However, many of them refer to life insurance written in trust. This, of course, may not be economic for elderly clients. Another scheme is that based on investment in shares within the Alternative Investment Market ("AIM"). Providing the choice is wisely made these may qualify for full IHT relief if held for two years. Stockbrokers have set up schemes to attempt to minimise the high risk often associated with investments of this kind.

FAMILY HOME

6–03   This often causes difficulty—particularly so where the house is in joint names and the survivor. To have the half share placed into the NRB trust it may be necessary to dismantle the survivorship destination as follows:

Style

We, **ALLAN ALABAMA MONTGOMERY** and **MRS JUNEAU ALASKA ARIZONA** or **MONTGOMERY**, Spouses, both residing at Number One Phoenix Lane, Crowsham, Glasgow G11 1AA, heritable proprietors of the subjects aftermentioned wish to discharge the destination in Disposition by the said Allan Alabama Montgomery in favour of himself and me, the said Mrs Juneau Alaska Arizona or Mongomery dated Twenty first September and recorded in the Division of the General Register of Sasines applicable to the County of Renfrew on the Twenty first October both months in the year Two thousand and CONSIDERING THAT the said Allan Alabama Montgomery in favour of himself and me, the said Mrs Juneau Alaska Arizona or Mongomery are infeft in ALL and WHOLE the dwelling-house subjects known as at Number One Phoenix Lane, Crowsham, Glasgow G11 1AA in the Parish of Renfrew and County of Renfrew being the subjects more particularly described in and disponed by Feu Charter by Henry Adams flock in favour of the said John Anderson dated First and Second and recorded in the Division of the General Register of Sasines applicable to the County of Renfrew on Third March all in the year Nineteen hundred and sixty and **WHEREAS** the said last mentioned Disposition contains a survivorship destination in favour of the survivor of us the said Allan Alabama Montgomery in favour of himself and me, the said Mrs Juneau Alaska Arizona or Mongomery **AND CONSIDERING** that we **HEREBY AGREE** and **CONFIRM** that the said survivorship destination should be evacuated **THEREFORE** We **HEREBY EVACUATE** the aforementioned destination to the effect that the subjects hereinbefore described will be held by us to extent of a one-half share by the said Allan Alabama Montgomery (husband) and the remaining one-half share by me, the said Mrs Juneau Alaska Arizona or Mongomery (wife) and **WE HEREBY AGREE** and **DECLARE** that either of us shall be entitled to dispone and convey our respective one-half share in the subjects by way of *inter vivos* or *mortis causa* Deed; and it is hereby certified that this instrument falls within Category L in the Stamp Duty (Exempt Instruments) Regulations 1987.

This will then enable a one half *pro indiviso* share of the house to be transferred to the trust fund. This may enable it to be sold to the surviving spouse who would purchase it at market value; stamp duty land tax may be due depending on the value of the one half interest, however, the trustees could accept a standard security by the purchasing spouse.

> **Danger Warning !!!**
>
> **Please watch out if the house is in the sole name of one of the spouses who then dies after conveying a one half *pro indiviso* share thereof to the other spouse. On death of the first spouse, the Finance Act 1986, s.103 could operate to reduce the amount of the loan allowable.**

Tustees

While the appointment of trustees is always important it is absolutely **6–04** fundamental, in the case of discretionary trusts, particularly so because of the wide ranging discretion as to which a beneficiary will receive benefit under the trust. Often a husband may wish to appoint his spouse and, say, two or more of his children as trustees. It does not take a great leap of imagination to envisage a situation where there is a clear conflict developing where the children may hold a majority vote. In cases such as these perhaps an impartial, "professional" advisor should be appointed along with a wife and perhaps one child. It is recommended that the trustees under a NRB will trust should be different from the executors.

Beneficiaries

The usual beneficiaries will be spouse and issue including spouses of **6–05** issue. However the beneficiaries can, in the case of a childless couple, range from the issue of the parents of the truster, which obviously includes the truster's brothers and sisters, nephews and nieces, together with their spouses. It will often also be prudent to include in any trust established for the benefit of any one of the class of beneficiaries plus any maintenance fund or charity. This will avoid the trust funds being restored to the truster often with dire consequences. There is usually an open-ended power to pay income or capital to any of the class of beneficiaries or trusts mentioned.

It will generally be prudent to specifically exclude the truster from benefit principally to avoid the income of the trust being treated for tax purposes as his income; there may also be pre-owned assets tax consequences.

As mentioned before, the IHT regime is such that the capital is taxed not only when it is put into the trust and where it comes out of the trust but also every 10 years where it is subject to periodic charge.

Discretionary Trust[3]

The following style is by a childless Truster, who perhaps wishes to make **6–06** provision for nephews and nieces. Provision is made to exclude him as a beneficiary. It is in non-tabular form and relatively short. The powers are

---

[3] These styles are adapted from those formerly included for Diploma Students.

very general and are to be found in the deed, not in a schedule. The emphasis is on brevity.

Style

I, **ROBERT ANDREW CRANE**, Fifty Carpenter's Close, Kirkcaldy with a view to making a trust under the following terms do hereby **APPOINT JOHN GRABBIT and JAMES SUE**, both Solicitors, Ten High Street, Milngavie, to be the original Trustees of this trust (who and any other Trustees who may be assumed to act hereunder are hereinafter referred to as "the Trustees") and **I Do Hereby Assign, Transfer** and make over to the Trustees the sum of **TWENTY POUNDS (£20.00) STERLING** (which sum or property to that value together with such other sums, securities and other property which may from time to time herein be paid, transferred and made over by me or any other person to the Trustees are hereinafter called "the Trust Fund") and the Trustees shall hold the Trust Fund for the following purposes:

Expenses

6–07   (ONE) For payment out of income or capital as the Trustees may decide the expenses of setting up and administering this Trust.

Beneficiaries/discretionary purposes

6–08   (TWO) I direct the Trustees to hold the Trust Fund for such one or more of the following, namely

>   (1)   the issue of each of my parents but always excluding me;
>   [*This could, of course include any children which the truster himself might have.*]
>   (2)   any person who is or was a spouse of any of such issue but always excluding during my lifetime any spouse of mine;
>   [*Sometimes the inclusion of former spouses causes difficulty to trusters. It should be pointed out that the marriage may have ended by death rather than otherwise. This is the first of several times that the truster excludes himself from benefit.*]
>   (3)   any trust established by any person for the benefit (whether of an income a capital or a discretionary nature) of any one or more of the foregoing persons but always excluding a trust of which either I or during my lifetime any spouse of mine is or may be a beneficiary;
>   (4)   any maintenance fund within the meaning of the Inheritance Tax Act 1984 Section 27 or any similar statutory successor established by any person but always excluding a fund of which either I or during my lifetime any spouse of mine is or may be a beneficiary; and
>   (5)   any charity within the meaning of the Income and Corporation Taxes Act 1988 Section 505 or any similar statutory successors, all as the Trustees may in their absolute discretion by minute or minutes at any time or times determine, and that in such shares or proportions if more than one as the Trustees shall decide.

[*It is also useful to have a "fail-safe" provision regarding charity.*]

Declaring:

6–09   (1)   that the Trustees may by such minute or minutes create vested interests in fee, interests in possession or prospective or contingent interests of any kind in the whole or any part or parts of the Trust

Fund and that subject to such provisions, conditions or restrictions, including but without prejudice to the foregoing generality provisions as to the accumulation of income, the vesting of capital in any beneficiary and the granting to any beneficiary of powers to transfer or convey rights to income or capital, as they may in their sole and absolute discretion determine;

(2) that during the period of Twenty-one years from the date hereof, or until the date when any such determination or determinations take effect, the Trustees may accumulate all or any part of the income of the Trust Fund and hold the same as an accretion to the capital thereof, and subject to the capital thereto the Trustees shall distribute the income of the Trust Fund to such one or more of the beneficiaries as they may in their sole and absolute discretion determine;

(3) that there shall be no apportionment of revenue accruing any part of the Trust Fund between income and capital on any occasion, all revenue being deemed to have accrued on the date upon which it is payable.

Beneficiaries not of full capacity

(THREE) If any part of the Trust Fund falls to a beneficiary who has not **6–10** attained full legal capacity, the Trustees shall have full power either to pay or apply the whole or any part of the income or capital falling to such beneficiary for his or her benefit in any manner the Trustees may think proper or to retain the same until full legal capacity is attained accumulating income with capital or to pay over the same to the legal guardian or the person for the time being having the custody of such beneficiary whose receipt shall be a sufficient discharge to the Trustees, and any such part shall be regarded as being part of the Trust Fund for the purposes of the Trustees Powers and Immunities purposes hereof.

[*This could include not only children but also adult beneficiaries who are incapax.*]

Exclusion of Truster

(FOUR) The Trust Fund and the income therefrom at all times be possessed **6–11** and enjoyed to the entire exclusion of my and during my lifetime any spouse of mine and of any benefit to me or during my lifetime to any such spouse by contract or otherwise and no part thereof shall be paid or lent to or applied for my benefit or during my lifetime for the benefit of any such spouse in any circumstances whatever, and in the event of total failure of the trust purposes any funds not disposed of shall be held for the Executors of the last to die of the issue of whatever degree of each of my parents but always excluding me.

Trustees' powers

My Trustees shall have the fullest powers of and in regard to retention, **6–12** realisation, investment, appropriation, transfer of property without realisation and management of my estate as if they were absolute beneficial owners; and shall have power to do everything they may consider necessary or expedient for the administration of the trust; (and in particular and without prejudice to the foregoing generality the Trustees shall have the following powers and under the conditions so far as not inconsistent with the provisions hereof).

[*List here any powers, which are specifically needed. The emphasis here is on brevity. However, it may be that the truster will wish for a more extensive list of powers or even a schedule of powers.*]
IN WITNESS WHEREOF

We the trustees designed in the foregoing Deed of TRUST accept office as trustees hereunder.

[*Please remember to have the trustees sign this as acceptance of the office of trustee. Often in the heat of practice this is overlooked and if challenged at a later stage reference to the trust deed, which may by that time have been registered in the Books of Council and Session, can be quickly and decisively made.*]

TRUSTER WITH CHILDREN

6–13 The next style is appropriate to a **Truster with Children**. It is also non-tabular and is in a longer form.

Style

I, **BENJAMIN LEVI HARRISON**, residing at Number Six Cleveland Drive, Milngavie Being desirous of making provision for my children and their respective issue (all hereinafter referred to as the "beneficiaries") do hereby: **NOMINATE AND APPOINT** as my trustees, (hereinafter referred to as "the trustees") for the purposes aftermentioned, myself, the said Benjamin Levi Harrison, my son, **LEVI MORTON HARRISON** residing at Number Ten Hendricks Place, Forfar, my daughter, **MRS SENGA CHESTER HARRISON or FAIRBANKS**, residing at Number One Garner Avenue, Banff and **JAMES CHEATHAM**, Solicitor, carrying on business at Number One Sherman Drive, Penicuik, and such other persons as may hereafter be appointed or assumed, and the acceptor or acceptors, survivor, or survivors of them as such trustees; of which any two trustees shall constitute a quorum at any meeting of trustees for the transaction of the business of my trust; **CONVEY** and make over to, and in favour of, the said trustees the sum of Five Pounds sterling; **DIRECT AND APPOINT** that the said sum and any property, funds, and assets, of any kind in which my estate may from time to time, and at any time, be invested, together with any further or other property, funds, or assets, which may be conveyed or made over to the trustees by me or any other party, and any income accumulated thereon, (hereinafter referred to as "the trust estate") shall be held and applied by the trustees for the following purposes while I remain alive:

FIRST: To pay the expenses incurred in the execution and administration of the trust hereby created;

SECOND: To pay, apply, allocate, or appoint, to, or for the benefit of, the beneficiaries, the whole or any part of the trust estate whether it be the free income, or the capital, or any combination of them, and any accumulation of income (all of which are hereinafter referred to as the "trust funds"); any or all of which the trustees may do in exercise of the absolute discretion hereby conferred on them: (i) for the benefit of such one or more of the beneficiaries exclusive of the other, or others of them, as the trustees may decide; (ii) in such shares and proportions and in such a manner and subject to such provisions, limitations, conditions, and qualifications as the trustees may think fit; (iii) with, and subject to, the discretionary powers contained herein, all which discretionary powers may be exercised from time to time, and at any time, by the trustees, in whole or in part, as they at their sole discretion may decide; And the trustees may: (i) create liferents, and the accumulation and maintenance settlements; (ii) accumulate for such period during which income may lawfully be accumulated any income not so paid or applied or allocated and add it to capital;

AND I MAKE THE FOLLOWING DECLARATIONS:

(One) Without prejudice to the foregoing generality, the trustees may exercise the powers hereby conferred on them, to settle on such other trustees as the trustees may appoint or select for the purpose, the whole or part of the trust funds, to be held for any one or more of the beneficiaries; and this the trustees may do: (i) subject to such directions, authorities, powers, conditions, limitations, and restrictions, (ii) with such provisions for maintenance, education, support, advancement, and benefit and (iii) subject to such other protective and other trusts exercisable at the discretion of the trustees or any other person or persons, all as may seem appropriate to the trustees, and all interest created by such settlement in favour of any beneficiary shall become absolute and indefeasible;

(Two) The trustees' powers to accumulate income shall be during the period of twenty one years from and after the date of this deed or during my lifetime, whichever is the shorter, and on the expiry of such period the trustees shall pay or apply the whole of the trust funds to, or for the benefit of, one or more of the beneficiaries;

(Three) All income provisions made by the trustees for a beneficiary shall be strictly alimentary and shall thereby not be assignable by the beneficiary, nor be affected by the beneficiary's debts, or anything the beneficiary may do, or by any arrestment or attachment which the beneficiary's creditors purport to impose;

(Four) If the trustees exercise their powers to confer on any of the beneficiaries rights of a continuing nature or to settle funds on them, they may do so expressly and irrevocably, or subject to such powers of cancellation or recall prior to the vesting date of such rights, as they, the trustees, may determine;

(Five) In the event of my death the trustees shall hold the trust funds for the benefit of my said children in the proportion of one-third for each, or in such proportion as they, the trustees, may determine; and may at their discretion pay over all or part of the trust funds to my children in the said proportion to each; and if any of my children predecease me the issue of such children shall take equally among them *per stirpes* the share which otherwise would have gone to the parent; and insofar as the trust funds are not disposed of in terms of the foregoing provisions they shall be made over to the estate of the last to die of my children and their issue absolutely, vesting taking place only when payment falls to be made.

(Six) My Trustees shall have the fullest powers and in regard to retention, realisation, investment, appropriation, transfer of property without realisation and management of my estate as if they were absolute beneficial owners; and shall have power to do everything they may consider necessary or expedient for the administration of the trust; and in particular and without prejudice to the foregoing generality the conditions an powers specified and contained in the Schedule annexed and signed as relative hereto shall apply to the administration of my estate and the trusts herein, in so far as not inconsistent with the provisions hereof. IN WITNESS WHEREOF

We the trustees designed in the foregoing Deed of Trust accept office as trustees hereunder.

DISCRETIONARY TRUST

6–14　A discretionary trust long form with schedule: Fuller style with full powers to appoint.

Under this form of discretionary trust, the trustees are given:

> (1) An absolute discretion as to capital and income for a very long period amongst a large class of beneficiaries.
>
> (2) Powers at any time to authorise trustees to transfer part of the whole fund on accumulation and maintenance trust if that is thought appropriate; and in the past this power has frequently been used in trusts to advantage.
>
> (3) The vesting date of 80 years ahead.

Style

　I, **JOHN LEYTON** residing at Number Seven Mornington Crescent, Petercuilter, (hereinafter termed "the truster"), **CONSIDERING** that I desire to make provision for the beneficiaries aftermentioned **Do Hereby NOMINATE and APPOINT** as trustees for the purposes aftermentioned **JAMES PARK ROYAL** residing at Number Fifteen Piccadilly Circus, Newton Mearns, **DANIEL TOMPKINS** residing at Number Three Quincey Place, Arden and **JOHN CALHOUN** Solicitor, Number Seven Madison Gardens, Balloch TOGETHER with such other person or persons who may be hereafter appointed or assumed and the acceptor or acceptors, survivor or survivors of them as such trustees (the trustee or trustees for the time being acting hereunder being hereinafter referred to as "the trustees"); And I DIRECT the trustees to hold and administer all funds, property and assets of whatsoever nature which may hereafter at any time and from time to time be paid, conveyed and made over to the trustees hereunder, (the whole funds, property and assets from time to time held by the trustees and all (if any) accumulated income thereon being hereinafter referred to as "the trust estate") in trust for the following purposes and subject to the following provisions, videlicet:

1. Name of trust

6–15　This trust shall be known as **THE JOHN LEYTON DISCRETIONARY TRUST**

2. Definitions

6–16　In this deed, the following terms, where the context so admits, have the following meanings:

> (i) subject to the provisions of clauses 5 and 6 hereof, "beneficiaries" and "beneficiary" mean and include all or any one or more of the following persons, namely:
>
>> (1) the issue of each of my parents but always excluding me;
>>
>> (2) the issue of **THOMAS COBLEY** residing at Number Nine Jackson Plaza, Newbattle;
>>
>> (3) the issue of the late **MARTIN VAN BUREN** sometime residing at Number Eleven Harrison Road, Currie;
>>
>> (4) any person who is or was a spouse of any of the foregoing issue but always excluding during my lifetime any spouse of mine;
>>
>> (5) any trust established by any person for the benefit (whether of an income a capital or a discretionary nature) of any one or more of

the foregoing persons but always excluding a trust of which either I or during my lifetime any spouse of mine is or may be a beneficiary;

(6) any maintenance fund within the meaning of the IHT Act 1984 Section 27 or any similar statutory successor established by any person but always excluding a fund of which either I or during my lifetime any spouse of mine is or may be a beneficiary and;

(7) any charity within the meaning of the Income and Corporation Taxes Act 1988 Section 505 or any similar statutory successors, all as the Trustees may in their absolute discretion by minute or minutes at any time or times determine, and that in such shares or proportions if more than one as the Trustees shall decide.

(ii) "vesting date" means July 10, 2086

(iii) the head notes to each clause or sub-clause are for convenient reference only and shall not affect the terms of this deed.

3. Trust powers

Until the vesting date, the trustees shall hold the trust estate on the following **6–17** trusts, but with and subject to the discretionary powers herein contained, all of which discretionary powers may be exercised from time to time and at any time by the trustees in whole or in part as they in their sole discretion may decide, videlicet:

(i) Accumulation of income

To accumulate the income arising from time to time on the trust estate, or on any separate fund as hereinafter provided, for the whole period of 21 years from the last date of execution by the settlor of these presents, or for such lesser period or several periods within the said period of 21 years as the trustees may decide, or such other period during which income may lawfully be accumulated, all such accumulations of income to be added to and thereafter to form part of the capital of the trust estate.

(ii) Payment of income

To pay or apply the income arising from time to time on the trust estate or any part thereof to or for the benefit of any beneficiary to the exclusion of any other beneficiary or beneficiaries, and that at such time and otherwise in such way and manner as the trustees in their uncontrolled discretion may decide.

(iii) Payment of capital

To pay to, or apply for behoof of, any beneficiary, to the exclusion of any other beneficiary or beneficiaries, part or the whole of the capital of the trust estate, notwithstanding that by so doing, they may bring this trust to an end before the vesting date.

(iv) Insurance

To effect in their own name as trustees any policy of insurance upon the life of the settlor or of any beneficiary or upon any other life and to apply income or capital of the trust estate in payment of the premiums thereof, the proceeds of any such policy to be held and applied by the trustees as an accretion to the capital of the trust estate.

(v) Power to transfer and convey

By declaration of trust, executed by the trustees, to convey part or the whole of the capital of the trust estate, notwithstanding that, by so doing, they may bring this trust to an end before the vesting date, as a separate fund to or for the benefit of any beneficiary or beneficiaries, to the exclusion of any other beneficiary or beneficiaries, such beneficiary or beneficiaries to or for whose benefit such appointment is made being referred to in this clause as "the appointee", and in such declaration of trust to make provision for all or any of the purposes following, videlicet:

(a) during and within the said period of 21 years referred to in clause 3(i) hereof, for accumulation of income of the separate fund until a specified date or until the happening of a specified event;

(b) for payment of the income of the separate fund to the appointee: either (1) at the discretion of the trustees with the like powers and discretions as are contained in clause 3(ii) hereof; or (2) for life or for any lesser period ending on a specified date or on the happening of a specified event and, whether for life or any lesser period, terminable at the discretion of the trustees;

(c) for payment of the capital of the separate fund, with all accumulations of income, if any, on a specified date or on the happening of a specified event or at the discretion of the trustees to the appointee or to any one or more of the beneficiary;

(d) for the reverting of the capital of the separate fund (with all accumulations of income if any) to the trust estate at a specified date or on the happening of a specified event or at the discretion of the trustees upon which reversion the purposes of the said declaration of trust shall thereupon forthwith determine and the capital of the separate fund shall revert to and from part of and be held by the trustees as an accretion to the trust estate for the purposes hereof.

(vi) Power to resettle

To make over, by way of resettlement, part or the whole of the capital of the trust estate to the trustees acting under any other settlement, whether created by the settlor or any other person, and whether created in Great Britain or abroad, provided that any one or more of the beneficiaries hereunder is or are amongst the beneficiaries for whose benefit such settlement has been made and that no person other than a beneficiary or beneficiaries hereunder may benefit thereunder but declaring that the rights of the beneficiaries under such settlement may be discretionary or contingent or subject to defeasance at the discretion of the trustees thereunder; and it shall be no objection to the exercise of the power hereby conferred on the trustees that the trustees of such other settlement, or some of them, are resident out of Great Britain, or that the proper law of such other settlement is the law of some country other than Scotland or England provided that under such proper law trusts are recognised and administered as nearly as may be according to rules similar to those which apply to Scottish trusts, and being a proper law under which the other settlement would be recognisable, enforceable, irrevocable and would take effect; and declaring for the avoidance of doubt that the trustees shall not have power to resettle part or the whole of the capital of the trust estate in any manner of way by virtue of which any part of the capital or income which is or has been comprised in the trust estate at any time, nor any property derived therefrom, shall be payable to or applicable for the benefit of the settlor, or during the lifetime of the settlor for any spouse of the settlor.

(vii) Expenses of administration

To pay the expenses of the trust hereby created, including all government and other duties, which may become exigible during the course of administration.

4. Ultimate destination

Subject to the foregoing purposes, the trustees shall hold the trust estate for **6–18** such of the individual beneficiaries as are living at the vesting date to whom the trustees were empowered to make any discretionary payment under clause 3 hereof, or failing all such individual beneficiaries then for the executors of the last of such beneficiaries to have previously died, or if not such individual beneficiary was ever in life or if any one or more of them or the said executors cannot be traced then and to that extent for any charitable institution or charitable institutions to be selected at the discretion of the trustees.

5. Power of beneficiary to renounce

If any beneficiary, being of full age and capax, shall renounce his or her **6–19** interest hereunder by deed of renunciation and discharge in favour of and intimated to the trustees, such beneficiary shall, forthwith upon such intimation, cease thereafter to be included in the meaning of the terms "beneficiaries" or "beneficiary" for the purposes hereof.

6. Power to exclude beneficiary

The trustees shall have power, by deed executed by the trustees at any time **6–20** before the vesting date, to declare that any beneficiary or beneficiaries, either as individuals or as a class, shall, from and after a date to be stated in such deed, cease to be a beneficiary or beneficiaries for all the purposes hereof, whereupon from and after such stated date these presents shall be read and construed as if such beneficiary or beneficiaries were no longer included in the meaning of the term "beneficiary" and "beneficiaries" for all the purposes hereof; but shall not exercise this power in such a way that, following on such exercise, there would be no remaining beneficiary then living who is qualified to benefit hereunder.

7. Administrative powers and indemnities

The Trustees shall have the fullest powers and in regard to retention, **6–21** realisation, investment, appropriation, transfer of property without realisation and management of my estate as if they were absolute beneficial owners; and shall have power to do everything they may consider necessary or expedient for the administration of the trust; and in particular and without prejudice to the foregoing generality the conditions and powers specified and contained in the Schedule annexed and signed as relative hereto shall apply to the administration of my estate and the trusts herein, in so far as not inconsistent with the provisions hereof.

8. Exclusion of truster

It is hereby expressly provided and declared that no discretion nor power **6–22** herein conferred on the trustees shall be exercised, and no provision of these presents shall operate, so as to permit or cause any part of the capital or income of the trust estate, nor any property derived therefrom, to become payable to or applicable for the benefit of the settlor, or during the lifetime of the settlor, for any spouse of the settlor.

9. Irrevocability and proper law

These presents and the trusts hereby created shall be irrevocable, and shall be **6–23** construed, covered by and administered according to the law of Scotland: IN WITNESS WHEREOF

Under this form of discretionary trust, the trustees are given an absolute discretion as to capital and income for a very long period amongst a large class of beneficiaries. The deed also contains powers at any time to appoint part of the whole fund on accumulation and maintenance trust if that is thought appropriate; and in the past, this power has frequently been used in trusts to advantage. If the truster is English, the vesting date should not be more than 75 years ahead. For Scottish trusts, there is no definite limit but 75 years would seem to be appropriate.

Provisions specific to discretionary trusts

6–24   It is of course vital and essential that there is exclusion of benefit as to the truster. In addition, it might be prudent that there should be a general charitable trust provision can be included. This should be drafted so that the trust can be turned into a charitable trust if all the beneficiaries or class of beneficiaries fail. A form of this clause is shown below:

On the occurrence of the death of any such spouse or of the death of issue as herein specified or their predeceasing me I direct my trustees to hold the residue of the trust funds and failing children or issue I direct my trustees, in order to create a trust to be known as the **FRANCK BOWMAN WHITAKER CHARITA-BLE TRUST**, to hold and apply the residue of the trust funds thousand and ninety four hereinafter referred to as "the final date of vesting." I hereby direct my Trustees within six months from the date of final vesting to . . .

It may be that additional specific provisions are required. If, e.g. the truster wished to empower his trustees to erect and develop a super casino in the Kelvinside area of Glasgow.

To employ labour in and enter into partnership for the management and development thereof; to construct buildings, carry out other works and provide suitable services; and generally declaring that, if the trustees exercise this power in *bona fide* for any of the purposes hereinbefore contained, they shall be entitled to act in relation to any such property as freely in all respects as any absolute proprietor thereof and, in particular, the trustees shall not be bound to lay out monies under their charge as trustees with a view to appreciation or to the realisation of profit or the earnings of income or revenue; and the trustees shall not be personally liable for any loss incurred by them in so acting nor for the diminution or depreciation in the value of the estate or in the capital and interest of the trust estate resulting from any such actings.

One problem, which might be faced, is the possibility of the trustees failing to make any distribution at all. It may be that there are good and valid reasons for them not making payments such as:

1. Beneficiary being *incapax* and the necessity to legitimately safeguard benefit from public funds.
2. Divorce of a beneficiary and benefit being deferred until the financial provisions on divorce become clearer.

3. Impending insolvency of beneficiary.
4. Unworthiness of beneficiary, e.g. criminal conviction and imprisonment.
5. Disappearance of beneficiary (this is more common than might be thought!).

As stated, there are many good and valid reasons why trustees should not make payment. However, if this goes on for some considerable time, or if payment is deferred for reasons of caprice, it might be that some should be provided for. This could be dealt with by providing for a "longstop" provision. Thus, it could be provided that if funds have not been distributed at all or if there are funds remaining after, say, a date 90 years hence then funds will vest and provision should be made for such funds as remain to be paid out to the surviving beneficiaries. The date of 90 years is arbitrary. It might allow for funds to be paid to the truster's children and children during their lifetimes.

Trust funds

Some thought should be given to the ultimate amount or nature of **6–25** trust funds, bearing in mind the likelihood of a CGT liability in disposing constituted by the transfer of funds into the trust or the necessity of realising capital to provide funds.

Often it will be helpful to "start off" with a nominal sum, say twenty pounds £20.00 and to provide for future sums or assets to be transferred into the trust.

Where assets may attract business or agricultural relief, it may be considered prudent to include these in a NRB trust. This will be particularly relevant where the relief may be lost if the holder or legatee ceases to qualify for the relief and it may be lost.

An informal private letter stipulating the truster's wishes can be placed with the trust papers. While it does not have the force of the writ, it may give some guidance as to the truster's wishes:

> To my trustees
>   I have set up this trust not because of any wish to disinherit any one but because I wish to make provision for my wife in the event of her not having sufficient to live on. I also wished to make provision for my son Tam who, because of his problems with alcohol. . . .

ACCUMULATION AND MAINTENANCE TRUSTS

Drafting accumulation and maintenance trusts is not for the faint of **6–26** heart. This statement is reinforced by the recent changes in the law relating to the taxation of trusts. Some commentators consider that the changes will sound the death knell of accumulation and maintenance trusts—to be replaced with either discretionary trusts or with trusts for bereaved minors. It is possible that by the time this text comes into being they will be a matter of historic interest only. The more popular view is that they will survive and the truster will accept the relevant property regime which may only be for the period from age 18 to 25. They will accept this rather than have assets in the hands of teenagers.

It is useful to precede this section by yet a further consideration of the former statutory provisions.

Section 71 of IHTA 1984 provides:

71.—(1) Subject to subsection (2) below, this section applies to settled property if—

(a) one or more persons (in this section referred to as beneficiaries) will, on or before attaining a specified age not exceeding twenty-five, become beneficially entitled to it or to an interest in possession in it, and

(b) no interest in possession subsists in it and the income from it is to be accumulated so far as not applied for the maintenance, education or benefit of a beneficiary.

(1A) This section does not apply to settled property at any particular time on or after 22nd March 2006 unless this section—

(a) applied to the settled property immediately before 22nd March 2006, and

(b) has applied to the settled property at all subsequent times up to the particular time.

(1B) This section does not apply to settled property at any particular time on or after 22nd March 2006 if, at that time, section 71A below applies to the settled property.

(2) This section does not apply to settled property unless either—

(a) not more than twenty-five years have elapsed since the commencement of the settlement or, if it was later, since the time (or latest time) when the conditions stated in paragraphs (a) and (b) of subsections (1A) to (1) above became satisfied with respect to the property, or

(b) all the persons who are or have been beneficiaries are or were either—

    (i) grandchildren of a common grandparent, or

    (ii) children, widows or widowers or surviving civil partners of such grandchildren who were themselves beneficiaries but died before the time when, had they survived, they would have become entitled as mentioned in subsection (1)(a) above.

(3) Subject to subsections (4) and (5) below, there shall be a charge to tax under this section—

(a) where settled property ceases to be property to which this section applies, and

(b) in a case in which paragraph (a) above does not apply, where the trustees make a disposition as a result of which the value of settled property to which this section applies is less than it would be but for the disposition.

(4) Tax shall not be charged under this section—

(a) on a beneficiary's becoming beneficially entitled to, or to an interest in possession in, settled property on or before attaining the specified age, or

(b) on the death of a beneficiary before attaining the specified age.

(5) Subsections (3) to (8) and (10) of section 70 above shall apply for the purposes of this section as they apply for the purposes of that section (with the substitution of a reference to subsection (3)(b) above for the reference in section 70(4) to section 70(2)(b).

(6) Where the conditions stated in paragraphs (a) and (b) of subsection (1) above were satisfied on 15th April 1976 with respect to property comprised in a settlement which commenced before that day, subsection (2)(a) above shall have effect with the substitution of a reference to that day for the reference to the commencement of the settlement, and the condition stated in subsection (2)(b) above shall be treated as satisfied if—

(a) it is satisfied in respect of the period beginning with 15th April 1976, or

(b) it is satisfied in respect of the period beginning with 1st April 1977 and either there was no beneficiary living on 15th April 1976 or the beneficiaries on 1st April 1977 included a living beneficiary, or

(c) there is no power under the terms of the settlement whereby it could have become satisfied in respect of the period beginning with 1st April 1977, and the trusts of the settlement have not been varied at any time after 15th April 1976.

(7) In subsection (1) above "persons" includes unborn persons; but the conditions stated in that subsection shall be treated as not satisfied unless there is or has been a living beneficiary.

(8) For the purposes of this section a person's children shall be taken to include his illegitimate children, his adopted children and his stepchildren.

General

Capital transfer tax, the forerunner of IHT, spawned much of our **6–26** present trust practice. One of the most important was the accumulation and maintenance trust. At the outset it should be stated that drafting these trusts requires perhaps the greatest degree of skill of the trust drafter. This is coupled often with the necessity of grafting into the trust provisions for converting the trust to a liferent trust, perhaps, for one or more of the beneficiaries and/or removing one beneficiary from benefit altogether. Failure would probably result in a discretionary trust and the loss of the advantages of an accumulation and maintenance trust. The basic requirements to satisfy IHTA 1984, s.71 to allow this type of trust to be given favourable tax treatment were until recently as follows:

(a) there must be no interest in possession in the trust capital;

(b) one or more persons (the qualifying beneficiaries) will become beneficially entitled to the property, or to an interest in possession in it, by the age of 25; and

(c) in the meantime any income, which is not applied for the maintenance, education or benefit of a qualifying beneficiary, is to be accumulated.

If the trust did not satisfy these requirements it is not an accumulation and maintenance trust within the meaning of IHTA 1984; it is probably a pure discretionary trust, and will be taxed accordingly.

The advantage of being an accumulation and maintenance trust was that when the beneficiary takes either an interest in possession, that is to say, a right to the income, or an absolute right to capital before attaining 25 years of age **there was no charge to IHT**. If the trust was not within the accumulation and maintenance trust there would be a charge. An accumulation and maintenance trust is technically a type of discretionary trust without some of the tax disadvantages of discretionary trusts. As previously remarked, great care is required in framing accumulation and maintenance trusts as otherwise the tax advantages will be lost. Reference is made to Ch.3, which details the tax treatment of accumulation and maintenance trusts. Now to secure the above benefits it is necessary to give the children the trust capital outright at age 18. If the children are left capital on the basis of the former "pre-2006 budget" basis where the children are to receive capital at 25, what is now to happen is that the trusts will become subject **to the "6 per cent charge regime" until the child becomes 18**, that is to say the additional "penalty" to be paid for leaving the capital in trust for seven years after age 18 will be 4.2 per cent (seven tenths of 6 per cent).

Trustees

6–27   As for discretionary trusts (see para.6–04).

Beneficiaries

6–28   The usual beneficiaries will be **Children or Grandchildren** of the truster or the testator. It will generally be absolutely essential to exclude the truster from benefit principally to avoid the income of the trust being treated for tax purposes as his income. It is really to be used for younger children, perhaps aged up to, say, 16 years of age. If there is a child who is older then it would be advisable to make separate provision for that child.

Where large sums are involved it might be appropriate for an accumulation and maintenance trust to be set up under a will. As stated, an accumulation and maintenance settlement is a privileged type of discretionary trust under IHTA 1984, s.71.

If it is made *inter vivos* the privilege existed that transfers to the trust were potentially exempt transfers. There were no 10-year charges levied on the trustees, and there were no exit charges when the property vested in the beneficiaries.

Provisions specific to accumulation and maintenance trusts

6–29   It is of course vital and essential that there is exclusion of benefit as to the truster.

Trust funds

6–30   Some thought should be given to the ultimate amount or nature of trust funds, bearing in mind the likelihood of a CGT liability in disposing constituted by the transfer of funds into the trust or the necessity of realising capital to provide funds.

The trust deed, which follows, is an accumulation and maintenance trust by Mr Odin who wishes to make provision for his grandchildren who live with him and his wife.

1. £20 is being transferred into the trust. Mr Odin wished to set up the trust as soon as possible and this sum is stated as being transferred to the trust to get it started and show "delivery". It might be of a pilot nature. He wishes to make decisions regarding cash or which investments he will transfer/realise to fund the trust. He knows this will take some time so that, e.g. all exemptions can be maximised.

2. Beneficiaries. The beneficiaries at clause (TWO) are the grand-children who are alive plus any other grandchildren who may be born. **It is not possible to set up an irrevocable trust for potential beneficiaries unless there is at least one alive at the time the trust is set up.** It is possible, however, to set up a revocable trust when no grandchildren are alive which becomes irrevocable on the birth of a grandchild. If that single grand-child subsequently dies, the trust would remain in force to cover the possibility of subsequent grandchildren. These considera-tions would also apply to children.

3. Satisfaction of clause "a" and "c" above (see para.6–26). Clause (THREE) plus clauses (SEVEN) and (EIGHT) satisfy the accumulation and maintenance provisions mentioned above at (a) and (c) because no interest in possession exists in the trust fund, i.e. no one has the right to receive the income and the income is either accumulated or paid out for the maintenance, education or benefit of the beneficiaries.

4. Satisfaction of clause "b" above. Clause (FOUR) satisfies the accumulation and maintenance provision) above by giving the beneficiaries a right to receive the income on attaining 21 years of age, i.e. under the minimum age of 25.

5. Capital. Although clause (FIVE) gives the beneficiaries the capital on attaining 30 this is not required to satisfy the accumulation and maintenance provision at (b) above which is satisfied by clause (FOUR). The accumulation and mainte-nance trust finishes as and when each beneficiary attains 21 and a liferent trust (interest in possession trust) exists between 21 and 30.

6. Predeceasing Beneficiaries. Clause (SIX) gives the issue of predeceasing children the same right as their parents would have had had they survived to take an interest.

7. Vesting before attaining 21. Clause (NINE) gives some extra flexibility in that the trustees can assign an interest in posses-sion as their parents would have had had they survived to take an interest in possession in a share of the trust fund to a beneficiary before they attain 21 years of age when they would under the provisions of the deed obtain an interest in posses-sion. This power could be used, e.g. where a two-year old potential beneficiary had purchased a flat and needed a regular income to obtain a mortgage.

8. Exclusion of Trusters. It is prudent to exclude the trusters from any benefit, otherwise, and on the assumption they are over 25, the capital taxes office may maintain that clause (ONE) is not satisfied. There are also the IHT gifts with reservation of benefit rules to consider.

ACCUMULATION AND MAINTENANCE TRUST FOR GRANDCHILDREN

Style 9

6–31   I, **ROLFE JAMES ODIN**, residing at Number Twenty-seven High Street, Glasgow, wishing to make a trust under the terms hereinafter set forth Do Hereby APPOINT myself, my wife **MRS SENGA ANTHEA THOR or ODIN**, residing with me, and **ANDREW JAMES MACPHERSON**, Solicitor, 5 High Road, Kilmarnock, Ayrshire, to be the original Trustees of this trust (who and any other Trustees who may be assumed to act hereunder are hereinafter referred to as "the Trustees") and I DO Hereby Assign, Transfer and make over to the Trustees the sum of **TWENTY POUNDS (£20.00) STERLING** (which sum or property to that value together with such other sums, securities and Other property which may from time to time hereinafter be paid, transferred and made over by me or any other person to the Trustees are hereinafter called "the Trust Fund") and the Trustees shall hold the Trust Fund in Trust for the following purposes:

Expenses

6–32   (ONE) For payment out of income or capital, as the Trustees may decide, the expenses of setting up and administrating the Trust hereby created;

Beneficiaries

6–33   (TWO) For the benefit of my grandchildren, **DAMIAN ODIN and ROWENA ODIN**, residing with me and any other grandchildren of mine ("the said children") contingently on their attaining a vested interest as after provided for.

Accumulation

6–34   (THREE) To accumulate the income arising from the Trust Fund by investing all surplus thereof and the resulting income therefrom in accordance with the powers hereafter conferred until the said children respectively attain the age of Twenty-one years.

Payment of income

6–35   (FOUR) For payment of the income of the share of the Trust Fund, to which any of the said children is prospectively entitled, to such child from the attainment by him or her of the age of Twenty-one until he or she attains a vested interest as provided for in the immediately succeeding purpose.

Payment of capital

6–36   (FIVE) For payment of an equal share of the capital of the Trust Fund and the income accumulated prior to his or her acquiring a vested interest in the income to the said children on their respectively attaining the age of Thirty years and subject as aftermentioned the said capital and accumulated income shall not vest in any of the said children until the date of payment of his or her share, Declaring (1) that when each child attains the age of Thirty years his or her share shall be calculated by reference to the number of children (or issue as representing predeceased children) then in life whose age does not exceed Thirty years and whose shares have not previously been wholly advanced or appointed under purpose (TEN), and the share of such child then vesting in him or her shall be fixed accordingly indefeasibly, (2) that any advances of capital or partial appointments under purpose (TEN), shall be taken into account in such way as the Trustees in their absolute discretion shall determine, and (3) that in the event of any part of the Trust Fund remaining unvested or unappointed under purpose (TEN) when the youngest child then in life (or issue then in life as representing predeceasing children) attains the age of Thirty years, such remaining part then vest in him or her indefeasibly.

Failure

(SIX) If any of the said children fail to attain a vested interest by reason of his or **6–37** her predeceasing leaving issue (including adopted issue), such issue as survive and attain the age of Thirty years shall be entitled to the share original and accresced which his, her or their parent would have taken on survivance: and if any of the said children fail to attain a vested interest as before provided for leaving no issue who survive and attain the age of Thirty, to hold the share of the trust fund and any income accumulated at the date of such failure for behoof of the survivors or survivor of the said children or the issue of any predeceasing child as an accretion to their his or her shares: And any such accrescing share shall be subject to the same trusts as any original share.

Prohibited accumulations

(SEVEN) If any accumulation of income of the Trust Fund is prohibited by law **6–38** by reason of any event the income affected by such prohibition shall be paid or applied to or for the said children or their issue for the time being presumptively entitled to the capital of the Trust Fund or that part thereof from which such income arose.

Advances of income and capital

(EIGHT) The Trustees may apply for the maintenance education or benefit of **6–39** any beneficiary of a share of the Trust Fund (1) the income thereof including accumulated income in whole or in part and (2) the capital thereof in whole or in part, and such advances shall vest on payment or such application.

Power of assignation—income

(NINE) The Trustees may assign revocably or irrevocably at any time or times **6–40** and in whole or in part that the age at which a beneficiary would otherwise become entitled to a share of the capital of the Trust Fund or to a right to the income thereof shall be advanced to such earlier age as they may decide, and if any such assignation is revocable it shall unless earlier revoked become irrevocable when and to the extent that it shall become operative.

Power of assignation—capital

(TEN) The Trustees shall have power, in relation to any part of the Trust Fund **6–41** of which a beneficiary is then entitled to the income, to assign that such part of the Trust Fund or any part or parts of the income or capital thereof shall be held for such trust purposes, together with such limitations, conditions and provisions for accumulation during minority, maintenance, education and advancement, for the benefit of such beneficiary alone or of such beneficiary's issue or the spouses of any of these persons, or of any other person or persons whom such beneficiaries but always excluding me and during my lifetime any spouse of mine), or of him, or her and them, and generally with such powers and Discretions exercisable by the Trustees or by any other person or persons and on such terms as the Trustees shall think fit declaring that on the exercise of such power such part of the Trust Fund or part or parts of the income or capital thereof shall be fixed indefensibly and shall be held wholly in terms of such assignation.

Exclusion of apportionments

6–42 (ELEVEN) There shall be no apportionment as between capital and income on any occasion.

Beneficiary not of full capacity

6–43 (TWELVE) If any part of the Trust Fund falls to a beneficiary who has not attained full legal capacity, the Trustees shall have full power either to pay or apply the whole or any part of the income or capital falling to such beneficiary for his or her behoof in any manner the Trustees may think proper or to retain the same till the said full capacity is attained income with capital or to pay over the same to the legal guardian or the person for the time being having custody of such beneficiary whose receipt shall be a sufficient discharge to the Trustees, and any such part shall be regarded as being part of the Trust fund for the purposes of the Trustees' Powers and Immunities purposes hereof.

Exclusion

6–44 (THIRTEEN) The Trust Fund and the income therefrom shall at all times be possessed and enjoyed to the entire exclusion of me and during my lifetime any spouse of mine and of any benefit to me or during my lifetime to any such spouse by contract or otherwise and no part thereof shall be paid or lent to or applied from my benefit or during my lifetime for the benefit of any such spouse in any circumstances whatever, and in the event of total failure of the purposes (which shall include a time when there are no children or issue of predeceasing children then in life notwithstanding any possibility that such beneficiaries might be born thereafter) any funds not disposed of shall be held for the Executors of the last to die of the beneficiaries.

Powers

6–45 (FOURTEEN) per schedule
IN WITNESS WHEREOF
We THE TRUSTEES designed in the foregoing deed of trust accept office as trustees hereunder.

Trust Deed with Commentary

Style

6–46 I, **ROLFE JAMES ODIN**, residing at Number Twenty-seven High Street, Glasgow, wishing to make a trust under the terms hereinafter set forth Do Hereby **APPOINT** myself, my wife **MRS SENGA ANTHEA THOR or ODIN**, residing with me, and **ANDREW JAMES MACPHERSON**, Solicitor, 5 High Road, Kilmarnock, Ayrshire, to be the original Trustees of this trust (who and any other Trustees who may be assumed to act hereunder are hereinafter referred to as "the Trustees") and I DO Hereby Assign, Transfer and make over to the Trustees the sum of **TWENTY POUNDS (£20.00) STERLING** (which sum or property to that value together with such other sums, securities and Other property which may from time to time hereinafter be paid, transferred and made over by me or any other person to the Trustees are hereinafter called "the Trust Fund") and the Trustees shall hold the Trust Fund in Trust for the following purposes:

[It is considered bad practice to set up any trust with the trusters appointing only themselves as trustees. The main reason for this stems from the requirement that to validly set up a trust there must be delivery. Moreover, it will be apparent that proof of "delivery" between trusters and trustees who happen to be the same people would be difficult. It may be vital that HMRC and indeed other official bodies will require to be satisfied. It is absolutely paramount that clients should always be advised to appoint an additional trustee to themselves where they are the trusters of a trust. Lord Reid said in Allan's Trustees v Inland Revenue, *1971 S.L.T. 62:*

> *"think that we can now accept the position as a reasonable develop-ment of the law, that a person can make himself a Trustee of his own property provided that he also does something equal to delivery or transfer of the Trust Fund".*

The trust deed narrates that £20 is stated as being transferred to the trust. This is a way of actually starting the trust and showing "delivery". It is important that £20 is actually transferred into a trust bank account or similar. The relevant form 41G should be completed and sent to the appropriate tax office, usually this will be HMRC Inland Revenue Trusts, Meldrum House, 15 Drumsheugh Gardens, Edinburgh EH3 7UB; DX IR Trusts Edinburgh: 542000—Edinburgh 14.]

Expenses

(ONE) For payment out of income or capital as the Trustees may decide the **6–47** expenses of setting up and administering the Trust hereby created;

[This is fairly straightforward but useful provision putting the vexed question beyond doubt in the decision of the trustees.]

Beneficiaries

(TWO) For the benefit of my grandchildren DAMIAN and ROWENA BURNS **6–48** residing with me and any other grandchildren of mine the said children") contingently on their attaining a vested interest as after provided for.

[The beneficiaries are the grandchildren alive at the date of the trust deed and any other children who may be born. As with liferent trustees it is not possible to set up an irrevocable trust for potential beneficiaries unless there is at least one in life at the time the trust is set up. It is not feasible, however, to set up a revocable trust when no children are in life, which becomes irrevocable on the birth of a child. If that single child subsequently dies the trust would remain in force to cover the possibility of subsequent children.]

Accumulation

(THREE) To accumulate the income arising from the Trust Fund by investing **6–49** all surplus thereof and the resulting income there from in accordance with the powers hereafter conferred until the said children respectively attain the age of Twenty-one years.

[This provision along with (SEVEN) and (EIGHT) are necessary to satisfy the accumulation and maintenance provisions in the statute. No interest in possession exists in the trust fund, no one has the right to receive the income and the income is either accumulated or paid out for the maintenance, education or benefit of the beneficiaries.]

Payment of income

6–50 (FOUR) For payment of the income of the share of the Trust Fund to which any of the said children is prospectively entitled to such child from the attainment by him or her of the age of Twenty-one until he or she attains a vested interest as provided for in the immediately succeeding purpose.

[This clause satisfies the accumulation and maintenance by giving the beneficiaries a right to receive the actual income when they become 21 years of age, although under the minimum age of 25.]

Payment of capital

6–51 (FIVE) For payment of an equal share of the capital of the Trust Fund and the income accumulated prior to his or her acquiring a vested interest in the income to the said children on their respectively attaining the age of Thirty years and, subject as after mentioned, the said capital and accumulated income shall not vest in any of the said children until the date of payment of his or her share, Declaring (1) that when each child attains the age of Thirty years, his or her share shall be calculated by reference to the number of children (or issue as representing predeceased children) then in life whose age does not exceed Thirty years and whose shares have not previously been wholly advanced or appointed under purpose (TEN), and the share of such child then vesting in him or her shall be fixed accordingly indefeasibly, (2) that any advances of capital or partial appointments under purpose (TEN), shall be taken into account in such way as the Trustees in their absolute discretion shall determine, and (3) that in the event of any part of the Trust Fund remaining unvested or unassigned under purpose (TEN) when the youngest child then in life (or issue then in life as representing predeceasing children) attains the age of Thirty years, such remaining part then vest in him or her indefeasibly.

[While (FIVE) gives the beneficiaries the capital on attaining 30, this is not required to obtemper *the accumulation and maintenance provision, which are actually satisfied by (FOUR). The accumulation and maintenance part of the trust ends as and when each beneficiary attains 21; thereafter and a liferent trust exists between 21 and 30.]*

Failure

6–52 (SIX) If any of the said children fail to attain a vested interest by reason of his or her predeceasing leaving issue (including adopted issue), such issue as survive and attain the age of Thirty years shall be entitled to the share original and accresced which his, her or their parent would have taken on survivance: And if any of the said children fail to attain a vested interest as before provided for leaving no issue who survive and attain the age of Thirty, to hold the share of the trust fund and any income accumulated at the date of such failure for behoof of the survivors or survivor of the said children or the issue of any predeceasing child as an accretion to their his or her shares: And any such accrescing share shall be subject to the same trusts as any original share.

[*(SIX) gives the issue of predeceasing children the same right as their parents would have had had they survived to take an interest.*]

Prohibited accumulations

(SEVEN) if any accumulation of income of the Trust Fund is prohibited by law **6–53** by reason of any event the income affected by such prohibition shall be paid or applied to or for the said children or their issue for the time being presumptively entitles to the capital of the Trust Fund or that part thereof from which such income arose.

Advances of income and capital

(EIGHT) The Trustees may apply for the maintenance education or benefit of **6–54** any beneficiary of a share of the Trust Fund (1) the income thereof including accumulated income in whole or in part and (2) the capital thereof in whole or in part, and such advances shall vest on payment or such application.

Power of transfer—income

(NINE) The Trustees may assign revocably or irrevocably at any time or times **6–55** and in whole or in part that the age at which a beneficiary would otherwise become entitled to a share of the capital of the Trust Fund or to a right to the income thereof shall be advanced to such earlier age as they may decide, and if any such appointment is revocable it shall unless earlier revoked become irrevocable when and to the extent that it shall become operative.

[*Vesting before attaining 21. Clause (NINE) gives some extra flexibility in that the trustees can appoint an interest in possession as their parents would have had had they survived to take an interest in possession in a share of the trust fund to a beneficiary before they attain 21 years of age when they would under the provisions of the deed obtained an interest in possession. This power could be used, for example where a two-year old potential beneficiary had purchased a flat and needed a regular income to obtain a mortgage.*]

Power of assignation—capital

(TEN) The Trustees shall have power, in relation to any part of the Trust Fund **6–56** of which a beneficiary is then entitled to the income, to assign that such part of the Trust Fund or any part or parts of the income or capital thereof shall be held for such trust purposes, together with such limitations, conditions and provisions for accumulation during minority, maintenance, education and advancement, for the benefit of such beneficiary alone or of such beneficiary's issue or the spouses of any of these persons, or of any other person or persons whom such beneficiaries but always excluding me and during my lifetime any spouse of mine, or of him, or her and them, and generally with such powers and. Discretions exercisable by the Trustees or by any other person or persons and on such terms as the Trustees shall think fit declaring that on the exercise of such power such part of the Trust Fund or part or parts of the income or capital thereof shall be fixed indefensibly and shall be held wholly in terms of such appointment.

Exclusion of apportionments

6–57 (ELEVEN) There shall be no apportionment as between capital and income on any occasion.

Beneficiary not of full capacity

6–58 (TWELVE) If any part of the Trust Fund falls to a beneficiary who has not attained full legal capacity the Trustees shall have full power either to pay or apply the whole or any part of the income or capital falling to such beneficiary for his or her behoof in any manner the Trustees may think proper or to retain the same till the said full capacity is attained income with capital or to pay over the same to the legal guardian or the person for the time being having custody of such beneficiary whose receipt shall be a sufficient discharge to the Trustees, and any such part shall be regarded as being part of the Trust fund for the purposes of the Trustees' Powers and Immunities purposes hereof.

Exclusion

6–59 (THIRTEEN) The Trust Fund and the income therefrom shall at all times be possessed and enjoyed to the entire exclusion of me and during my lifetime any spouse of mine and of any benefit to me or during my lifetime to any such spouse by contract or otherwise and no part thereof shall be paid or lent to or applied from my benefit or during my lifetime for the benefit of any such spouse in any circumstances whatever, and in the event of total failure of the purposes (which shall include a time when there are no children or issue of predeceasing children then in life notwithstanding any possibility that such beneficiaries might be born thereafter) any funds not disposed of shall be held for the Executors of the last to die of the beneficiaries.

[*Exclusion of Trusters. It is prudent to exclude from any benefit the trusters, otherwise, and on the assumption they are over 25 the capital taxes office may maintain that clause (ONE) is not satisfied. There are also the IHT gift with reservation of benefit rules to consider.*]

Powers

6–60 (FOURTEEN) per schedule

IN WITNESS WHEREOF

We THE TRUSTEES designed in the foregoing deed of trust accept office as trustees hereunder.

LIFERENT TRUSTS

General

6–61 These trusts in their essence provide for one beneficiary to receive the income or revenue of the trust funds and for other beneficiaries to receive the capital or fee of the trust funds. They may be over trust funds or over a specific asset, e.g. a dwelling-house. Traditionally these were used and were extremely common until the advent of capital transfer tax for liferent to wife, fee to children. As previously stated, it is important for the truster to be clear as to whether he is giving a liferent or a right of occupancy. In the latter the trustees would pay expenses apart from those relating to actual occupance, e.g. council tax. In the former, the liferentor would be obliged to undertake more of the obligations incumbent on an owner and would be entitled to lease the premises, carry out repairs, pay repairs, etc.

They may be of use with a second spouse where the truster wishes to safeguard the interests of the children of his first or previous marriage.

Alimentary liferents are those which are not capable of being attached, e.g. by diligence. These are not so common as formerly. They are referred to south of the border and in tax legislation as "interest in possession trusts" sometimes abbreviated to "IIP Trusts" to differentiate between discretionary trusts where there is no interest in possession.

Cautionary note on liferent trusts

It is extremely important that clear drafting takes place with liferent **6–62** trusts vis à vis discretionary trusts. The inheritance tax consequences of a badly drafted discretionary trust giving a liferent or being deemed to give a liferent (or interest in possession) can be disastrous. In a recent case highlighted by Alan Barr in course materials relating to *Judge and Another* [2005] (S.P.C.506) Mr and Mrs W had lived in the matrimonial home, which Mr W owned, for some years when Mr W died in 2000.

> I give free of tax and of any money secured thereon by way of legal charge or otherwise to my trustees all that my interest in the property known as and situated at 30 Perrymead Street, London SW6 0R, the property in which I am at my death ordinarily resident or in which I have been last ordinarily resident **UPON TRUST** with the consent in writing of my wife during her lifetime to sell the same with full **power to postpone sale for so long as they shall in their absolute discretion think** fit and to hold the net proceeds of sale and other monies applicable as capital and the net rent and profits until upon the trusts and with and subject to the powers and provisions of my Residuary Fund (as hereinafter defined) as an accretion thereto **AND I DECLARE my Trustees during the lifetime of my wife to permit her to have the use and enjoyment of the said property for such period or periods as they shall in their absolute discretion think fit pending postponement of sale she paying the rates, taxes and other outgoings and keeping the same in good repair and insured against fire to the full value thereof in some office of repute nominated by my Trustees in the names of my Trustees.**

This case turned on the wording of the terms of the will. In fact, the Revenue failed in their attempt to have this held as a liferent. The main point, however, is that the lack of accuracy in drafting could be extremely expensive from the point of view of inheritance tax.

A further use of liferent trusts might be to transfer properties occupied by old former employees and thus to remove the value of the assets which would not otherwise qualify for business property relief, or agricultural property relief, from the estate. The aggregation of the liferent estate with the estate of the former employee will probably not lead to a large increase in IHT as the estate of the former employee is unlikely to cause a problem, since the aggregate of the value of the property in the liferent trust, and the free estate of the former employee is unlikely to exceed the NRB.

On the death of the former employee the liferent trust funds will pass to the fiar, and will obtain the benefit of a free uplift for CGT purposes to date of death values.

As these liferents are effectively rights of occupancy it is not necessary for the former employees to die before the property can be passed to the ultimate intended beneficiary. If they decide to move to either sheltered accommodation or a nursing home the right of occupancy/liferent will terminate, but as the property is the principal private residence of a beneficiary entitled to occupy the property in terms of the settlement, principal private residence exemption will be available.[4]

The trustees who make any disposals after December 2003 must make a claim for principal private residence relief.

Generally, however, a testator will leave a liferent of his estate to the wife. Obviously this creates a trust and she received the income arising, less trust management expenses.

Generally the will states that this is for the rest of her life or it could cover a shorter period, e.g. until she remarries. Thereafter, the estate will go to the children when she dies. Obviously, the widow and her children each have legal rights; she can give up the liferent and claim one third of the net moveable estate; the children can between them claim one third of the net moveable estate. If the widow claims her legal rights, the trustees must decide the date when the children become entitled to their share of the estate. The trust deed will generally be drafted on the basis that it will not vest until the residue becomes available. If the trust deed is silent then earlier vesting will be presumed, i.e. on the death of testator. It is important not to create a cap, e.g. by providing that the fee will not vest until the date of death of the liferentrix who may by this time have given up the liferent. It may be that the income requires to be accumulated under the Income and Corporation Tax Act 1988, s.686.

It should be stressed that where a liferent trust is set up under a deed of variation that early vesting is provided. It should also be remembered that the liferent cannot be created for persons unborn at the date of death of the liferentor. Thus, if a grandfather created a liferent trust for his grandchildren and then for his great grandchildren, the bequest would become potentially void for the beneficiary who had not been born when the trust was set up became entitled to the liferent.

Liferent of property

6-63   It is important if a truster wishes to give a liferent of say, a house, that you know what is being given. Is it a liferent or is it a right of occupation?

Merely to give it by name may not be sufficient. It should be spelled out in detail what is being given. Thus, is the liferentor to be entitled to rent out the property, or merely to occupy it during her lifetime? If it is sold, are the funds to be invested and the interest made available? Is there a duty on the liferentor to carry out all repairs or only mainte-

---

[4] This may be under review by HMRC.

nance? And if not are funds being left in the hands of the trustees to do this, who is to pay for insurance? The traditional rule is that it is shared equally between the interest of the liferentor and the fiar, but it may be wished for the liferentor to pay all the insurance. Should the trustees have the right to pay insurance premiums on default by the liferentor and carry out repairs? Often these matters will be irrelevant if the house is part of the liferented fund. However, it may be as well to spend a bit of time going over the options with the truster or testator.

It may be useful if the trustees have power to terminate the liferent in whole or in part or so that where a surviving spouse is elderly, indecisive or even *incapax*, the liferent can be brought to an end, thus effectively triggering a potentially exempt transfer by the surviving spouse, which could be effective for IHT planning in their estate.

Trustees

The appointment of trustees is important. Traditionally the spouse will **6–64** be one of the trustees (representing the liferent interest) along with one of the children (representing the fee) and an independent and impartial "professional" adviser. If discretionary powers are involved, other considerations would apply as for discretionary trustees.

Beneficiaries

The usual beneficiaries are: **6–65**

1. Spouse or second spouse. They appear to be making something of a comeback where a truster marries for a second time, with children from an earlier marriage. Civil Partners and cohabitees;
2. a child who is *incapax* (as below);
3. a beneficiary who is impecunious or spendthrift;
4. a beneficiary who suffers from some form of addiction although a discretionary trust might also be considered;
5. family servants or retainers may be given the liferent of a "tied" house.

Provisions specific to liferent trusts

Perhaps the first consideration is for the truster to decide when the **6–66** liferent is to terminate. If set up by will and the liferentor predeceases the testator then the liferent will fall on death of the testator. Generally, it will be ended by the death of the liferentor. However, it may be provided that the trustees may end the liferent by using their powers to advance the entire capital or the liferentor may renounce the liferent in whole or in part.

As with other trusts it is, of course, vital and essential that there is exclusion of benefit as to the truster. In addition, it might be that there should be a general charitable trust provision. This should be drafted so that the trust can be turned into a charitable trust if all the beneficiaries or class of beneficiaries fail. A form of this clause is included in the style which follows.

The trend nowadays is for a certain flexibility to be introduced into drafting. There may be power to advance capital. It is easy to envisage a situation where the revenue is insufficient to provide for the widow. In this situation the trustees may be given power to advance capital. Care is needed here since technically the whole capital could be advanced thereby defeating the rights of children. Once again, the selection of trustees is paramount in this type of case. Alternately, there may be power to advance capital to a fiar. Usually this will be fenced in with a consent being required from the liferentor or it may be permitted without her consent if, in the opinion of the trustees it is required. However, this may have unforeseen consequences in that the liferentor may be transmogrified into a trustee.

Style

There follows a style of such clause:

DECLARING that notwithstanding any provision to the contrary the trust funds, as hereinbefore defined, shall vest on the Thirty-first day of December in the year Two Thousand capacity this may mean that any income arising as a result will be aggregated with that of the liferent/trustee!

Although the power to renounce a liferent exists some thought might be given to including a power to the liferentor to renounce in whole or in part and actually including this *in gremio* the deed.
In certain cases, the liferentor may be given power to appoint the fiars.
Finally, in the event of a spouse/liferentor it may be that the truster may wish the liferent to terminate in the event of the spouse remarrying. It may not be far off for legislation will extend this to civil partnership or entering to a common law relationship.

Danger Warning!!!

The recent alteration to trust tax law which leaves a liferent to the surviving spouse but includes a power to advance capital to the surviving spouse could mean that the surviving spouse exemption is excluded!

Vesting

6–67   The general rule is that vesting should take place only when assets are transferred to a beneficiary. However, it is probably more sensible to make vesting on the earlier of the death of the liferentor or the termination of the liferent.
The one exception to this rule is where a trust is set up by deed of variation. Here it will be appropriate, other considerations being neutral, to make vesting as at the date of death of the testator. In any event, it is always better to specify the date of vesting so that there is no ambiguity.
There may be some merit in deferring the vesting until under age fiar beneficiaries attain full legal capacity or a stated age, e.g. 21 years of age although this latter may give rise to other trusts being deemed to have been set.

Liferent of a specific asset

If the liferent is to be over a house, is the liferentor entitled to liferent **6–68** the cash if it is sold or does the trust provide for another house to be purchased? Please consider, particularly in the case of a liferent set up by will, not to extend the liferent over corporeal movables. It is difficult to provide for the capital value of tea towels to be preserved. In addition, it should be spelled out exactly who is responsible for repairs, insurance and for the trustees to deal with these matters in the event of default subject to being reimbursed by the liferentor or from the proceeds of sale. Power to charge the property may be given if thought necessary.

SON WHO IS *INCAPAX*

A tabular format has been used for some of the styles. This facilitates the **6–69** use of marginal headings.

Style

I, **FRANCIS BOWMAN WHITAKER**, residing at One hundred and Twelve Heaven Lane, Inverness, being desirous of making provision for my son, **DAVID WHITAKER**, residing with me at One hundred and Twelve Heaven Lane, aforesaid (hereinafter referred to as "my son") and any wife and family he may have or otherwise as hereinafter described provide as follows:

Trustees	I appoint as my trustees under this Deed of Trust, **WILLIAM RAYMOND**, Solicitor, Fifteen Blythswood Square, Glasgow G2 4AH, **JOHN DEAGEN TALLMAN**, Accountant, residing at Thirty six Mexico Gardens, Paisley G52 3PG and **DIEGO RIVERA**, Stockbroker, residing at Forty seven Hadynn Crescent, Stonehaven (hereinafter referred to as "my trustees").
Trust fund	(FIRST) I direct my trustees (1) to hold such sums of money, investments, securities and others of whatever kind whatsoever and wherever situated which I may by Assignation, Disposition, Transfer or otherwise convey or cause to be conveyed to them, all which sums of money, investments, securities, funds and others which shall be transferred to my trustees from time to time are hereinafter referred to as "the trust funds", in trust always for the following purposes:
Expenses	(2) to make payment of the expenses of the formation and execution of the trust hereby created;
Liferent	(3) to pay or make over to my son or for his behoof the whole free net income of the trust funds in each year and that by instalments paid quarterly or at such time or times in each year as may be most convenient to my trustees;

Capital advances	(4) to hold and retain the free capital of the trust funds or investments from time to time representing the same with power to them, but always subject to their sole and absolute discretion, notwithstanding the liferent provision conceived in favour of my son as aforesaid, to make payments to my son or on his instructions of such amounts of capital or even the whole capital at any time or from time to time as they may think fit to be used or expended for any specific purposes such as buying and furnishing a house, setting up in business, educating any children he may have, taking out Life, Endowment Annuity or other Policies of Assurance or Bonds for the benefit of him or others or for setting up and providing funds for any trust he may make hereafter for the benefit of any wife and children he may have and without prejudice to the said generality for any other purposes of whatever nature which my trustees in their sole and absolute discretion may consider beneficial or expedient and in the event of my trustees refusing to make any such payments of capital they shall not be bound to give any reasons for such refusal and
Death of son	(5) that on the death of my son the residue of the trust funds shall be held and made over and applied as follows:
Spouse and children of son	(SECOND) in the event of the death of my son being survived by a widow, I direct my trustees to hold the residue of the trust funds then remaining after meeting all Government Duties and Taxes and any other duty, taxes or other charges for behoof subject as aftermentioned of such widow in liferent and to pay the whole net income therefrom to her during her lifetime at such time or times as may be mutually convenient to the trustees and her, with power to my trustees if they think fit to make payments of capital to such widow at such time or times or such amount and for such purposes as the trustees in their sole and absolute discretion may deem expedient or proper; And I further empower my trustees to make advances of capital to or for behoof of any children or issue my son may have out of said liferented funds of such amounts and for such purposes relating to their education, advancement in life, setting up in business or otherwise as my trustees shall in their sole and absolute discretion consider to be beneficial and proper providing and declaring (a) any capital sum or sums advanced or paid to my son's children or issue in terms of any of the provisions hereunder shall be treated as payments to account of the shares of the trust funds provided for or following in terms of these presents to the children or issue so benefited or their representatives and shall be brought in to the accounting accordingly and (b) that the foregoing provisions in favour of any widow who may survive my son, shall be deemed and taken to be in full satisfaction of any legal or prior rights in his estate to

which she may be entitled on her death; In the event of her claiming any such rights she shall forfeit all benefit under these presents and the foregoing provisions in her favour shall be terminated and cancelled;

(THIRD) on the occurrence of the death of any such widow or of her claiming her prior or legal rights in my son's estate as aforesaid or on his death should he not be survived by a widow I direct the trustees to hold the residue of the trust funds subject as aftermentioned in the case of beneficiaries who have not yet reached full legal capacity, for payment and division equally to and among any surviving children he may have jointly with the issue *per stirpes* of any child who may have predeceased such relative occurrence leaving issue, such issue taking equally between them or among them *per stirpes* the share to which their parent would have taken had he or she survived and failing children or issue I direct my trustees, in order to create a trust to be known as the **FRANCK BOWMAN WHITAKER CHARITABLE TRUST** and to hold and apply the residue of the trust funds
(1) for payment of the expenses of administering the said FRANCK BOWMAN WHITAKER CHARITABLE TRUST (hereinafter referred to as the "charitable trust") and (2) for payment of the whole or such part of the free income and the whole or such part of the capital of the trust funds as my Trustees may from time to time consider desirable for such charitable purposes or to such charitable institutions, societies, foundations or funds as my Trustees may in their absolute discretion select.

(FOURTH), I declare that the conditions and powers set out in the Schedule so far as not inconsistent with any provisions of this deed, shall apply to the administration of the trust funds.

(FIFTH) I declare that this deed shall be irrevocable: IN WITNESS WHEREOF

Commentary

Although the son is incapable of handling money and dealing with **6–70** property, it may be that he is capable of a wide range of "normal" activities, e.g. working. Often the preference here will be for a discretionary trust but in this instance, the truster, the father, elected for the liferent trust because he felt "more comfortable" with it. It does give the trustees discretion to advance capital.

DEED OF TRUST FOR CHILD IN LIFERENT AND GRANDCHILDREN IN FEE

Son who is imprudent with money or facing divorce or other difficulty.

Style

I, **SVEN NORDIIN ELLING**, residing at Twenty-seven High Street, Dumfries **6–71** being desirous of making a trust under the terms hereinafter set forth Do Hereby Appoint myself and **CHETHAM, STEELE & CO (TRUSTEES) LIMITED,** incorporated under the Companies Act 1948 and having its Registered Office at Seventy five Taransay Terrace, Edinburgh, to be the original Trustees of this trust (who and any other Trustees who may be assumed to act hereunder are hereinafter referred to as "the Trustees") and I Do Hereby Assign, Transfer and make over to the Trustees the sum of Ten Pounds (which sum or property to that value together with such other sums, securities and other property which may from time to time hereinafter be paid, transferred and made over by me or any other person to the Trustees are hereinafter called "the Trust Fund") and the Trustees hold the Trust Fund in Trust for the following purposes:

Expenses of setting up and administering the trust hereby created

6–72 (FIRST) For payment out of income or capital as the Trustees may decide expenses

Liferent

6–73 (SECOND) I direct the Trustees to pay to my son **PER CHRISTIAN ELLING** residing with me during all the days of his life the free annual income of the Trust fund, but declaring that there shall be no apportionment as between capital and income at the commencement of, during or at the termination of the said liferent either as regards income received or on realisation or purchase of any part of the liferented estate, all income being deemed to have accrued at the date upon which it is payable.

Termination of liferent

6–74 (THIRD) On the failure or termination in whole or part of the foregoing liferent, I direct the Trustees to convey and make over the said or such balance thereof as may then remain to my grandchildren in equal shares subject to the following conditions: if any of the said grandchildren shall have predeceased the date or dates of vesting aftermentioned leaving issue surviving, such issue shall take equally among them *per stirpes* the share which their parent would have taken if he or she had survived and upon the same conditions;

Declaring that in the event of any share of the said Trust Fund becoming payable to any beneficiary who has not attained full legal capacity my Trustee shall have full power either to pay or apply the whole or any part of the income of capital falling to such beneficiary for his or her behoof in any manner the Trustees may think proper or to retain the same till the said age of full capacity is attained accumulating income with capital or to pay over the same to the legal guardian or the person for the time being having the custody of such beneficiary whose discharge shall be sufficient exoneration; and in every case vesting shall be postponed until the date of dates of failure or termination of the foregoing liferent.

Death of grandchildren

6–75 (FOURTH) In the event of all my grandchildren and their issue (if any) dying before the whole of the Trust Fund has vested in terms of Purpose THIRD hereof, I direct the Trustees subject to the liferent provisions contained at Purpose SECOND hereof to convey and make over the same or such balance thereof as may remain to the Executors of the last of such grandchildren and their issue to die.

Power to make advances

6–76 (FIFTH) The Trustees shall have power in their sole and uncontrolled discretion to make advances out of the capital of the Trust Fund to any beneficiary provided;

(Primo) that any such advances made to my said son shall not be compellable by him;

(Secundo) that any such advances made to any grandchild or remoter issue shall not be made without the consent of my said son if in life; and any advances made to or for behoof of my said grandchildren or their issue shall be taken into account in arriving at the ultimate shares payable to them.

Exclusion of benefit

(SIXTH) Save as hereinbefore expressly provided the Trust Fund and income **6–77** Exclusion from benefit therefrom shall at all times be possessed and enjoyed to the entire exclusion of me and of any benefit to me by contract or otherwise and no part thereof shall be paid or lent to or applied for my benefit in any circumstances whatever.

Trustees' powers

(SEVENTH) The Trustees shall be regarded as gratuitous Trustees and shall **6–78** have all the powers, privileges, rights and immunities conferred by Statute or enjoyed at Common Law by gratuitous Trustees in Scotland including the power to resign office and the Trustees shall have the fullest powers of retention, realisation, investment, administration and division of the Trust as if they were beneficial owners; and in particular and without prejudice to these general powers I empower the Trustees:

(ONE) to retain the investments and property, which I or either of us may transfer to them;

(TWO) to invest the whole or any part of the Trust Fund and estate at their sole and uncontrolled discretion and heritable and leasehold property investments securities insurance Policies and other assets of whatever description and whether producing income or not which do not fall within the class of investments authorised for trust funds;

(THREE) to hold on deposit of whatever nature the Trustees think fit any cash forming part of the Trust Fund;

(FOUR) to allow any investments or other assets of the trust estate to be registered in the names of or held or the documents of title to be held by any persons, firm, corporation or other body as nominees of the Trustees;

(FIVE) to borrow on the security of the estate or any part thereof on such terms and conditions as the Trustees may think proper;

(SIX) to set apart and appropriate specification investments or assets to represent the whole or part of the shares, prospective or otherwise, of any beneficiary at such valuation as the Trustees may determine, so that thereafter the particular share or shares shall have the full benefit and the whole risk of the appropriated investments or assets;

(SEVEN) to settle with any beneficiary, whether entitled to a fixed sum of money or a share of residue, by conveying to him or her in satisfaction of his or her rights either specific investments or money, or partly one and partly the other, as to the Trustees shall seem proper and at such valuation as they shall think fit and to require and compel acceptance accordingly;

(EIGHT) to apply the whole or any part or parts of the capital or of the income of the Trust Fund in effecting or maintaining any policy or Policies of assurance for the benefit of any beneficiary but always without prejudice to the foregoing trust purposes;

(NINE) to lend or allow to be occupied the whole or any part of the Trust Fund at such rate of interest or rent as they may consider appropriate, or free of interest or rent, to or by any person who is for the time being entitled to the income of the Trust Fund or part at the time question;

(TEN) to appoint any one of their own number or any other person to be factor, accountant or solicitor in the execution of this settlement and to allow him the same professional remuneration to which he would have been entitled if not a Trustee; and

(ELEVEN) to renounce for themselves and their successors in Office the power to exercise any of the foregoing powers in this purpose as if the same were vested in them beneficially and note as Trustees.

Trustees' immunities

6–79   (EIGHTH) I DECLARE that the Trustees shall not be liable for depreciation in the Immunities value of investments of whatever from nor for omissions nor errors in judgement nor neglect in management nor for the insolvency of debtors, nor for the acts, omissions, neglect or defaults of each other or of any banker, factor, solicitor or agent, but each for his own actual Intromissions only; AND I DECLARE this settlement to be irrevocable by me: AND I consent to registration hereof for preservation: IN WITNESS WHEREOF:

Commentary

6–80   *This style has been set out in a non-tabular style but using bold type and block capitals. If the layout from the point of view of understanding of the tabular form is easier then it should be preferred, since our object in drafting should always be to comply with the prime requirement to make the sentence or paragraph understandable at one reading. The difficulty of achieving this objective should not be ignored. If by a simple alteration of the style or format of the deed this easiness to read once and understand can be achieved then it should be grasped with both hands. In this style, a solicitor's trustee company has been appointed as one of the trustees. This has the advantage that the death of a partner does not bring the trusteeship to an end in the way that the death of a truster as the other trustee would bring that trusteeship to an end. Clause SECOND gives the liferent of the trust to the truster's son, Per Christian. Clause THIRD states that on the termination of the liferent the grandchildren take equally between them the capital of the trust fund and there follow various provisions as to whether any of the grandchildren have predeceased the date of vesting of the capital with or without issue and before or after attaining the age of 18 years. Finally the question of when the capital vests is put beyond doubt by the statement that it is postponed until the date of termination of the liferent. Clause FOURTH is a backstop so that the intestate "heirs" of the last grandchild or their issue to die takes the trust fund.*

As with the previous style, clause FIFTH allows advances to be made to any beneficiary bearing in mind that for taxation purposes a payment to the liferentor is merely an enlargement of his entitlement which is to an interest in possession and therefore there is no charge to IHT whereas an advance to a grandchildren or their issue is the termination for an interest in possession which does give rise to a charge to tax within the liferentor's accumulative totals. The Exclusion from Benefit has been inserted and it is probably worth utilising. The Powers of Trustees and Immunities are shown in the deed as opposed to in a Schedule.

STYLE OF WILL LEAVING LIFERENT TO SECOND WIFE

6–81   This style shows the trust being set up *mortis causa*.

Style

I, BENJAMIN FRANKLIN MARCO, Retired Army Officer, Fourteen North Avenue, Johnstone, in order to settle the succession to my estate after my death provide as follows:

Revocation

(ONE) I revoke all prior wills and testamentary writings and I direct and **6–82** instruct my solicitors, **GRABBIT & RUNNE**, Solicitors, Arran House, One hundred Frederik Street, Glasgow, G1 4CC, to destroy all wills and testamentary writings held by them for my behoof dated prior to the date of these presents.

Executors and trustees

(TWO) I appoint my solicitor, **RAYMOND SHAW**, Solicitor, Bute House, One **6–83** hundred and thirty Fredrick Street aforesaid, and my sons, **ANDREW MARCO**, residing at One Lembeck Street, Paisley, and **THOMAS MARCO**, residing at Twelve Gertrude Place, Thurso, to be my Executors and Trustees (who along with any other persons who may be appointed or assumed are referred to as "my Trustees").

Informal writings

(THREE) I direct my Trustees to give effect to any future writings subscribed **6–84** by me however informal the same may be provided that in the opinion of my Trustees they clearly express my intentions.

Legacies

(FOUR) Unless otherwise specified any legacy granted by any writing shall be **6–85** paid or made over as soon as my Trustees consider practicable after my death free of government Duties in respect of my death and of delivery expenses but without interest.

Legacy to mother

(FIVE) I direct my Trustees to pay to my mother, **MRS HELEN MARCO**, **6–86** residing at Eleven D'Arcy Chambers Greenock, the sum of **TWO THOUSAND POUNDS (£2,000.00) STERLING**.

Liferent of house

(SIX) I direct my Trustees to hold the house owned by me at Fourteen North **6–87** Avenue, Johnstone or such other house owned and occupied by me at date of my death, or the property representing such house following a sale after my death in liferent for **MRS EUGENE ROSE or ISELIN or MARCO**, residing with me at Fourteen North Avenue, aforesaid (Primo) that the provisions of clause (FOUR) shall apply to this bequest and (Secundo) the said liferent shall be subject to payment by the said Mrs Eugene Rose or Iselin or Marco of all burdens, debentures, rates, insurance premiums as arranged by my Trustees, as also for all necessary repairs and renewals to the same, as to the amount, necessity and sufficiency of which repairs and renewals my Trustees shall be the sole judges; And further declaring that the said liferent is granted for the personal use of the said Mrs Eugene Rose or Iselin or Marco who shall not be entitled to let the same or any; part thereof without the prior consent in writing of my Trustees.

Personal effects

(SEVEN) I direct my Trustees to make over as convenient to my Trustees to **6–88** the said Mrs Eugene Rose or Iselin or Marco as her own absolute property, all furniture and plenishings belonging to me at my death.

Residue

6–89   (EIGHT) I direct my Trustees to divide the residue of my estate into three equal parts or shares and to make over (Primo) one of said shares to the said Mrs Eugene Rose or Iselin or Marco whom failing to such of my children, the said Andrew Marco and Thomas Marco, as shall survive me; equally between them and (Secundo) two of said shares to such of my children, the said Andrew Marco and Thomas Marco as shall survive me; equally between them declaring that should either of my children predecease me leaving issue (including adopted issue) who shall survive me each member of a generation of issue of such predeceasing child shall share equally in the part of my estate, both original and accresced, which would have fallen to its parent if in life.

Termination of liferent

6–90   (NINE) Subject to the foregoing liferent, I direct my Trustees to make over the parts of my estate which were or would have been liferented to such of my children, the said Andrew Marco and Thomas Marco, as shall surviving me, declaring that should either of my children predecease me leaving issue (including adopted issue) who shall survive me each member of a generation of issue of such predeceasing child shall share equally in the part of my estate, both original and accresced, which would have fallen to its parent if in life; Declaring that to prevent doubts vesting as regards this bequest shall only take place when and to the extent that the same may from time to time be actually paid and conveyed.

No apportionments

6–91   (TEN) There shall be no apportionment as between capital and income on any occasion.

Beneficiaries without full legal capacity

6–92   (ELEVEN) If any part of my estate falls to a beneficiary who lacks full legal capacity my Trustees shall have full power either to pay or apply the whole or any part of the income or capital falling to such beneficiary for his or her behoof in any manner my Trustees may think proper, or to retain the same until such capacity is attained accumulating income with capital, or to pay over the same to the legal guardian or the person for the time being having the custody of such beneficiary whose receipt shall be a sufficient discharge to my Trustees.

Renunciation

6–93   (TWELVE) In the event of any benefit conferred by this will being renounced in whole or in part, the benefit or such part or parts shall pass to the beneficiary or beneficiaries who would have been entitled and on the terms and conditions, which would have applied, had the beneficiary so renouncing predeceased me.

Trustees' powers

6–94   USUAL CLAUSES or reference to schedule.

DISABLEMENT TRUSTS

6–95 Trusts can be extremely useful in making provision for disabled persons whether mentally or physically. Clearly, if circumstances permit, funds should not be transferred to an *incapax*. The provisions and practice under the Adults with Incapacity (Scotland) Act 2000 relating to appointment of guardians are so complex and Byzantine that if they can be avoided by use of trust or "power of appointment" (if this is appropriate) they should be wherever possible.

Welfare benefits

Welfare law and practice is also complex and the scope of it is well **6–96** beyond this modest work. However, some regard should be had to the impact of these on trust provisions. Clearly if a person receives capital or income then this will have and impact on any means tested benefits and rightly so. Income from public funds is likely to be reduced if income is received directly from other sources, e.g. trust income. This would tend to militate against liferent trusts where the liferentor receives the income of the trust each year.

The tax provisions for a disabled person's trust are similar to a liferent trust. However, there are certain advantages, which accrue to the disabled person's trust. This is one of the few matters to remain intact after Budget Day 2006.

In his book *"Drafting Trusts and Wills Trust"*, James Kessler suggest one way of dealing with the problem is to split the funds of the trust, one fund to deal with the strict interpretation of the statute; the balance can be "held on whatever trusts may seem appropriate".

Generally speaking, it will be best if a discretionary trust vehicle is utilised. For various reasons, therefore, these disablement trusts are rarely used. It might be worth considering if it was envisaged that the trust being set up was likely to have capital gains on a regular basis.

A further alternative would be for a discretionary trust to be set up to include the disabled person as a potential beneficiary initially but thereafter to provide that:

> **DECLARING** that my trustees shall:
> **(FIRST)** apply half the capital of the trust fund for the benefit of my son, the said Charles Dawes and
> **(SECOND)** that where income is not accumulate but paid out one half of the income shall be paid to or for my son, the said Charles Dawes.

It may be that additional provisions could be added to specifically address the problems of caring for an *incapax*. The normal provisions may not go far enough to deal with this in general and in particular the question of making provision for carers. Something along the following lines might cover most aspects of this.

Additional Powers suitable perhaps for child or beneficiary who is incapax

1. To invest the whole or any part of the capital of the trust fund in **6–97** the purchase or improvement of any dwelling-house or flatted dwelling-house (whether owned or leased) and to permit the same to be used as residence for any beneficiary whether alone or jointly with any other person or persons without being required to insist upon on payment by any other person (whether or not a joint occupier thereof) of a market rent; and the trustees shall have completed discretion as to the terms which they permit such dwelling-house or flatted dwelling-house to be occupied.

2. To purchase or invest in moveable items for the use of any beneficiary notwithstanding that the value of the trust fund may thereby become depleted or exhausted and to permit the said beneficiary to have the use and enjoyment of any such moveable item forming part of the trust fund in such a manner and subject to such conditions (if any) as the trustees consider reasonable and without being liable to account for any consequential loss.

3. To apply or any part of the capital or income of the trust as the trustees may in their absolute discretion think fit in or towards any investment or plan which may provide a degree of security and protection for any beneficiary during their life.

4. To raise capital out of the trust fund and lend it on such terms as to interest repayment etc as the trustees may think fit or to any person to whom or to any charitable body to which they consider that it would in the interests of any beneficiary to make a loan and that the trustees will not be liable for any consequential loss of capital.

5. The trustees shall also be entitled to meet the cost of altering any dwelling-house in the ownership of any person for a more convenient occupation of any beneficiary and for purchasing domestic appliances or assistance for any beneficiary or for any person or persons with whom any beneficiary may from time to time reside; to purchase a caravan or motor car and to adapt same appropriate to the needs of any beneficiary and/or the person or all or any of the persons with whom the said beneficiary may from time to time reside; to provide a holiday for the said beneficiary or the expenses incurred by any suitable person or persons to enable a carer to accompany the said beneficiary on holiday or the provision of a holiday unaccompanied; finally to reimburse any person who bears the daily burden of caring for any beneficiary provided that such person does not do so for reward.

Additional Miscellaneous Powers suitable perhaps for the carer or carers of a child or beneficiary who is incapax

6–98   6. My trustees may apply any part of the trust fund to the purchase of a holiday for any beneficiary and for any person who may require to accompany any beneficiary on holiday.

And finally

7. My trustees may apply any part of the trust fund towards the cost of a funeral or cremation of any beneficiary.

CHARITABLE TRUSTS

6–99 As previously mentioned this has been the subject of extensive legislation in recent years culminating recently in the Charities and Trustee Investment (Scotland) Act 2005. Not all of the legislation has been helpful and in many cases has occasioned considerable additional expense not only to charitable trustees but also to those responsible for running charities. The executive and those in authority seem to be affected by a mistaken belief that they can legislate against and thus prevent criminal activity. It is likely that the next few years will prove them wrong.

Trustees

As always, the appointment of trustees is important. It is likely that **6–100** because of the statutory regulations that charities will be obliged to recruit trustees from amongst professionals perhaps in the legal and financial professions.

Purposes

Generally speaking, the testator will wish to keep the powers wide. **6–101** This clearly runs counter to the current legislation and perhaps under- lines the failing of the executive to address the position of small charitable trusts. The current position is that the trust should identify one or more of the statutory criteria.

At the root of matters is the charity test.

A charitable trust will only meet the charity test if its purposes consist of one or more the charitable purposes; it provides public benefit and is independent.

Charitable purposes—The Act 2005 expands the four existing defini- tions, which date back to 1601: the relief of poverty, advancement of education, advancement of religion and any other purposes beneficial to the community. These have been replaced with 13 new twenty-first century definitions of charity, compatible with the English and Welsh definitions.

The test of the 13 charitable activities is:

1. Prevention of relief or poverty.
2. Advancement of education.
3. Advancement of religion.
4. Advancement of health;
5. Advancement of civic responsibility/citizenship is the word used in England or community development.
6. Advancement of the arts heritage (culture) or science.
7. Advancement of amateur sport.
8. Advancement of human rights, conflict resolution or reconciliation.
9. Advancement of environmental protection or improvement.
10. Provision of accommodation to those in need of it by reason of age, ill health, disability, financial hardship or other disadvantage.
11. Provision of care to the aged, people with disability, young people or children.
    (The alternative for England: Relief of those in need by reason of youth, age, ill health, disability, financial hardship or other disadvantage.)
12. Advancement of animal welfare.
13. Any other purpose that may reasonably be regarded as an analogist to any of the preceding purposes.

(The alternative for England: Any purposes not within the headings listed above but already recognised as charitable or that may reasonably be regarded as analogist to those headings or to purposes already recognised as charitable under existing law.)

It is suggested that the trust deed should be framed in as wide terms as possible. Failure to do this can be fatal and result in expensive *cy près* scheme.

In the past, something along the following lines was quite sufficient.

STYLE OF CHARITABLE TRUST

Style

6–102 **I MRS JEAN BROWN BLACK or WHITE** residing at Hope House, Sin, Milngavie, Fifty Queen Street, Helensburgh in order to create a trust to be known as the **JEAN BROWN WHITE CHARITABLE TRUST** (the Trust")

(ONE) appoint as trustees me, the said Mrs Jean Brown Black or White and **JOHN DIABLO**, residing at Seventeen Vermin Avenue, North Mount Vernon, Glasgow (who and their successors are referred to as "the Trustees

(TWO) pay the sum of ONE HUNDRED POUNDS to the Trustees who shall hold, apply the said sum together with such other funds and assets, if any, as I or any other person may from time to time transfer to them as Trustees (the Trust Estate") for the following purposes:

(1) for payment of the expenses of administering the Trust
(2) for payment of the whole or such part of the free income and the whole or such part of the capital of the Trust Estate as the Trustees may from time to time consider desirable for such charitable purposes or to such charitable institutions, societies, foundations or funds as the Trustees may in their absolute discretion select (and without prejudice to the discretion of the Trustees it is my wish that the Trust Estate be used in supporting charitable bodies with the primary purpose of care and treatment of cancer patients)

(THREE) declare that the conditions and powers set out in the schedule so far as not inconsistent with any provisions of this Deed, shall apply to the administration of the Trust Estate;

(FOUR) declare that this deed shall be irrevocable: IN WITNESS WHEREOF

Comment

6–103 It might now be worthwhile expanding the trust purposes as follows: for payment of the whole or such part of the free income and the whole or such part of the capital of the trust estate as the trustees may from time to time consider desirable for such charitable purposes or to such charitable institutions, societies, foundations or funds as the trustees may in their absolute discretion select and without prejudice to the discretion of the trustees it is my wish that the trust estate be in supporting charitable bodies with the primary purpose of care and treatment of cancer patients and without prejudice thereto for the following additional purposes:

1. Prevention of relief or poverty.
2. Advancement of education.
3. Advancement of religion.
4. Advancement of health.

5. The saving of lives.
6. Advancement of citizenship or community development.
7. Advancement of the arts heritage (culture) or science.
8. Advancement of public participation in sport.
9. Provision of recreational facilities etc.
10. Advancement of human rights, conflict resolution or reconciliation.
11. Promotion of racial harmony.
12. Advancement of environmental protection or improvement.
13. Relief of those in need of it by reason of age, ill health, disability, financial hardship or other disadvantage. (The alternative in England: relief of those in need by reason of youth, age, ill health, disability, financial hardship or other disadvantage.)
14. Advancement of animal welfare.
15. Any other purpose that may reasonably be regarded as an analogist to any of the preceding purposes. (The alternative for England: any purposes not within the headings listed above but already recognised as charitable or that may reasonably be regarded as analogous to those headings or to purposes already recognised as charitable under existing law.)

The truster could select which should be excluded. This may seem a bit stupid but it may be worth doing to avoid possible loss of tax relief etc.

OFFSHORE TRUSTS

These, by definition, are non-UK based trusts. Generally, they will be **6–104** based in the Channel Islands. While a detailed scope of the tax is outwith the scope of this text it is suggested that the provisions regarding exporting the trust and appointing non-UK trustees in the general conditions would cover most commonly required instances. It is suggested, however, that detailed advice be obtained from legal advisers in the jurisdiction concerned. The general provisions in the conditions will be sufficient to export the trust should this be of advantage if there occurred a truly punitive tax regime in this country.

BARE TRUSTS

In a bare trust, the trustees hold the trust funds absolutely for the **6–105** beneficiary or beneficiaries. Sometimes these are referred to as trusts for administration.

General

The HMRC accept that when a trust for administration is set up and **6–106** the assets are transferred into the names of the trustees there is no beneficial change of ownership and therefore no transfer for tax purposes.

Income and capital

6–107   Clauses (THIRD) and (FOURTH) of the style on p.163 direct the income to be paid to the truster and the capital to be held for the truster, reaffirming what is said above that no beneficial change in ownership has taken place.

Following on the recent increase in Trust Rate Tax to 40 per cent, and the restricted tax benefits for liferent and accumulation and maintenance trusts, bare trusts are likely to become more popular. Where beneficiaries under 18 are involved there is nothing to prevent a testator leaving the estate in the hands of the trustees, as bare trustees for the individual beneficiaries. The trustees will be acting as nominees for the individuals. Any gains made by the trustees will utilise the individual beneficiary's CGT exemption of and as the testator has died, the income will be the income of the beneficiaries, even if the testator was their parent.

Stocks and shares can be held by the trustees as bare trustees. Depending on the nature of the asset held, it may be that the individual beneficiary will be entitled to a repayment of income tax on the income deemed to be theirs by virtue of the bare trust.

On attaining 18, the individual beneficiaries are entitled to the capital held for them under the bare trust, but as the trustees are merely holding as nominees for the beneficiary, there is no disposal for CGT purposes by the trustees at that time.

If the beneficiary is happy for the bare trust to continue beyond 18, a private arrangement between the beneficiary and the trustees can be entered into, usually without difficulty.

STYLE OF TRUST FOR ADMINISTRATION

Style

6–108   **I, PEREGRINE JOHN MACDONALD**, Fifteen Park Place, Edinburgh **CONSIDERING** that I wish to establish a trust for the administration of my affairs DO therefore **APPOINT ALFRED JOHN COOMBS**, Writer to the Signet, One Atholl Place, Edinburgh, and **DENNY & CO. (TRUSTEES) LIMITED**, One Atholl Place, Edinburgh Trustees for the purposes hereinafter set forth and I ASSIGN, DISPONE and CONVEY to them and to such other person or persons who may be assumed into the Trust hereby created, and to the acceptors or acceptor, survivors and survivor of them as Trustees and Trustee, a majority of said Trustees being a quorum and the Trustees acting for the time being throughout the remainder of these presents denominated "my Trustees", the sum of TEN POUNDS (£10.00) STERLING or property to that value and also such Properties, cash, securities or investments as I or any other person may hereafter convey or transfer to my Trustees to be held for the purposes hereof; And the said sums now given with Such further properties, cash, securities or investments which may hereafter be conveyed or transferred as aforesaid or the balance thereof or the cash, securities, investments or other property from time to time representing the same are hereinafter called "the Trust Estate": BUT these presents are granted in trust only for the purpose and subject to the declarations set forth in the clauses following:

Expenses	(FIRST). For payment of the expenses of the setting up and administration of the Trust hereby created.
Debts	(SECOND). For payment of all my just and lawful debts now due or to become due in any manner of way.
Income	(THIRD). For payment to me of the free annual income of the Trust Estate.
Capital	(FOURTH). To hold the capital of the Trust Estate from and insofar as not disposed of at my death to convey and make over the same to my Executor as if it were held in my own name as an individual.
Powers	(FIFTH). My Trustees shall be regarded as gratuitous Trustees and shall have all the powers, privileges, rights and immunities conferred by Statute or enjoyed at Common Law by gratuitous Trustees in Scotland including the power to resign office and the Trustees shall have the fullest powers of retention, realisation, investment and administration of the Trust as if they were beneficial owners; and in particular and without prejudice to these general powers I empower my Trustees: (ONE) to retain the investments and property which may be transferred to them; (TWO) to invest the whole or any part of the Trust Fund and estate at their sole and uncontrolled discretion in heritable and leasehold property investments securities insurance Policies and other assets of whatever description and whether producing income or not and whether or not falling within the class of investments authorised for trust funds; (THREE) to hold on deposit of whatever nature the Trustees think fit any cash forming part forming Trust Fund; (FOUR) to allow any investments or other assets of the trust estate to be registered in the names of or held or the documents of title to be held by any persons, firm, corporation or other body as nominees of the Trustees; (FIVE) to borrow on the security of the estate or any part thereof on such terms and condition as the Trustees may think proper; (SIX) to apply the whole or any part or parts of the capital or of the income of the Trust Fund in effecting or maintaining any policy or Policies of assurance for the benefit of any beneficiary but always without prejudice to the foregoing trust purposes; (SEVEN) to lend or allow to be occupied the whole or any part of the Trust Fund at such rate of interest or rent as they may consider appropriate, or free of interest or rent, to or by any person who is for the time being entitled thereto at the time in question; and (EIGHT) to appoint any one of their own number or any other person to be factor, accountant or solicitor in the execution of this trust and to allow him the same Professional remuneration to which he would have been entitled if not a Trustee.

Immunities	(SIXTH) I DECLARE that my Trustees shall not be liable for depreciation in the value of investments made by them or made by me or any other person and retained by them nor for omissions nor errors in judgement nor neglect in management nor for the insolvency of debtors, nor for the acts, Omissions, neglect or defaults of each other or of any banker, factor, solicitor or agent, but each for his own actual Intromissions only; and persons paying money to my Trustees shall have no concern with the application thereof and shall not be answerable or accountable for any loss, misapplication or non-application of the same, but shall be fully exonered by the receipts and discharges of my Trustees or of their factors, solicitors or others: IN WITNESS WHEREOF

A more complete version for a wealthy truster with extensive estates

Style

6–109   I, **MONTMORENCY ARTEMIS PYTHON**, residing at Cranley House, Cleghorn, Lanark ML11 7SN, **CONSIDERING** that I wish to establish a trust for administration of my affairs, **DO THEREFORE APPOINT CHARLES MANN FLEMING EWING**, residing at Windyshields, Cranley, Cleghorn, Lanark ML11 7SN, **JAMES STEVENSON-HAMILTON**, residing at Fairholm, Larkhall ML9 2UQ and **HARRY LUDWIK LUCAS** residing at "The Old Schoolhouse", Drumelzier, Biggar ML12 6HQ as trustees for the purposes hereinafter set forth and I **ASSIGN, DISPONE and CONVEY** to them and to such other person or persons who may be assumed into the Trust hereby created, and to the acceptors or acceptor, survivors and survivor of them as Trustees and Trustee, a majority of the said Trustees being a *quorum* and the Trustees acting for the time being throughout the remainder of these presents denominated "my Trustees", the sum of **TEN POUNDS (£10.00) STERLING** or property to that value and also such properties, cash, securities or investments as I or any other person may hereafter convey or transfer to my Trustees to be held for the purposes hereof; And the said sums now given with such further properties, cash, securities or investments which may hereafter be conveyed or transferred as aforesaid or the balance thereof or the cash, securities, investments or other property from time to time representing the same, are hereinafter called "the Trust Estate": BUT these presents are granted in trust only for the purpose and subject to the declarations set forth in the Clauses following:

Expenses

6–110   (1) For payment of the expenses of the setting up and administration of the Trust hereby created.

Debts

6–111   (2) For payment of all my just and lawful debts now due or to become due in any manner of way.

Income

6–112   (3) For payment to me of the free annual income of the Trust Estate.

Capital

6–113   (4) To hold the capital of the Trust Estate for me and insofar as not disposed of at my death to convey and make over the same to my Executor as if it were held in my own name as an individual.

Powers

(5) My Trustees shall be regarded as gratuitous Trustees and shall have all the **6–114** powers, privileges, rights and immunities conferred by Statute or enjoyed at Common Law by gratuitous Trustees in Scotland including the power to resign office and the Trustee shall have the fullest powers of retention, realisation, investment and administration of the Trust as if they were beneficial owners; and in particular and without prejudice to these general powers I empower my Trustees:

(ONE) to retain the investments and property which may be transferred to them;

(TWO) to invest the whole or any part of the Trust Fund and estate at their sole and uncontrolled discretion in heritable and leasehold property investments, securities, insurance policies and other assets of whatever description and whether producing income or not and whether or not falling within the class of investments authorised for trust funds and, without prejudice to the foregoing generality, to invest in corporeal moveables, notwithstanding that the value of the Trust Fund may become depleted and to permit me to have the use and enjoyment of any corporal moveables in such manner and subject to such conditions as my Trustees may consider reasonable without being liable to account for any consequential loss.;

(THREE) to hold on deposit of whatever nature the Trustees think fit any cash forming part of the Trust Fund;

(FOUR) to allow any investments or other assets of the trust estate to be registered in the names of or held or the documents of title to be held by any persons, firm, corporation or other body as nominees of the Trustees;

(FIVE) to borrow on the security of the estate or any part thereof on such terms and conditions as the Trustees may think proper;

(SIX) to apply the whole or any part or parts of the capital or of the income of the Trust fund in effecting or maintaining any policy or policies of assurance for the benefit of any beneficiary but always without prejudice to the foregoing trust purposes.

(SEVEN) to lend or allow to be occupied the whole or any part of the Trust fund at such rate of interest or rent as they may consider appropriate, or free of interest or rent, to or by any person who is for the time being entitled thereto at the time in question; and

(EIGHT) to appoint any one of their own number or any other person to be factor, accountant or solicitor in the execution of this trust and in carrying out the functions herein mentioned, including, without prejudice to this generality, brokers, managers, land agents staff of all necessary kinds and type, as well as contractors, and to allow him or them the same professional remuneration to which he would have been entitled if not a Trustee;

(NINE) to administer and manage any heritable or real property forming part of the estate, including, without prejudice to the foregoing generality any quarries, peat bogs, farms and agricultural holdings, golf courses and forests and areas of growing timber; to repair, maintain, renew and improve the same and to erect additional buildings and structures; to grant, vary and terminate leases and rights of tenancy or occupancy; to plant, thin and cut down timber; to work or let minerals; all as my Trustees may think proper and as if they were absolute owners of the estate;

(TEN) to continue or to commence any business, whether alone or in partnership with any other persons, or through any companies, for such period as my Trustees may think proper; to appoint or employ any trustee or any other person in any capacity in relation to such business and to pay them suitable remuneration for such services, including pension provisions for any employees or their dependants; and to delegate or entrust to any persons the control and management of such business to such extent as my Trustees may think fit; and my Trustees:

   (a)   may employ for the purposes of such business such part of the income or capital as they think proper;
   (b)   shall exercise only such control or supervision of such business as they think fit;
   (c)   shall be entitled to be relieved from the estate from all personal responsibility for any loss arising from such business operations; and
   (d)   shall be entitled to retain personally any remuneration for their services;

(ELEVEN) to borrow or lend with or without security; and to grant or continue any guarantee or indemnity for the benefit of any beneficiary actual or prospective and to raise capital out of the Trust Fund and to lend it on such terms as to interest security and repayment or otherwise as they think fit to any person to whom or charitable or other body to which they consider it would be in my interests to make a loan without being liable for any consequent loss of capital, to apply any part or parts of the capital of the Trust Fund for the cost of meeting the cost of altering or adapting any residence or accommodation in the ownership of any person or body for the more convenient occupation thereof as a whole, purchasing any domestic appliances or procuring domestic assistance for any of the Family Beneficiaries or persons with whom they reside from time to time, purchasing caravans or motor cars appropriate to the needs of any Family Beneficiaries and the person or persons with whom they from time to time reside, holidays for me or the expenses incurred by any person or persons to enable them to accompany any beneficiary on holiday or the provision of holidays unaccompanied by them for any person who bears the daily burden of caring for them and to accepting the receipt of any person caring or having financial responsibility for any of the Family Beneficiaries as a full and sufficient Discharge for any money intended to be paid to them FURTHER to claim any social security or other benefits to which I may be entitled and to demand, sue for and recover all debts, claims and sums of money or property due or which may become due to me or be exigible by me on any account or in any manner or way and to give time for payment of any debt or claim and to grant receipts or discharges therefore;

(TWELVE) to lend or allow to be used the whole or any part of the estate at such rate of interest or rent as they may consider appropriate, or free of interest or rent, to or by me or any person who is for the time being entitled to payment of a share of the income of the estate or to whom or for whose benefit the income may be paid or applied in the exercise of a discretion then available to my Trustees;

(THIRTEEN) to allow the estate or any part thereof to be registered in the names of or held or the documents of title to be held by any person, firm, corporation or other body as nominee of my Trustees;

(FOURTEEN) revocably to delegate any power or powers of making, managing, realising or otherwise dealing with any investment or deposit comprised in the estate to any person or persons upon such terms as to remuneration or otherwise as my Trustees may think fit and no trustee shall be responsible for the default of any such agent if the trustee in question employed him in good faith;

(FIFTEEN) to accept as an addition to my estate any other property which may be made over to them;

(SIXTEEN) to decide what is capital and what is income and the proportion in which expenses are to be charged against capital and income respectively

(SEVENTEEN) to set apart and appropriate specific property of any description to represent the whole or part of the share, prospective or otherwise, of any beneficiary at such valuation as my Trustees shall determine, so that thereafter the particular share or part shall have the full benefit and the whole risk of the appropriated investments or assets;

(EIGHTEEN) to settle with any beneficiary entitled to any part of the estate by conveying to him or her in satisfaction thereof either specific property or money, or partly one and partly the other, as to my Trustees shall seem proper and at such valuation as they shall determine and to compel acceptance accordingly;

(NINETEEN) to enter into any transaction or do any other act otherwise authorised by law or by this deed notwithstanding that any trustee is or might be acting as *auctor in rem suam* or with a conflict of interest between such trustee and himself as an individual or as a trustee of any other trust or any partnership which a trustee is a partner or any company of which a trustee is a shareholder or director or in relation to any combination of these capacities provided that the trustee or trustees with whom there is or may be any such conflict are not the sole trustee or trustees;

(TWENTY) to participate in the exercise of any discretion granted to my Trustees notwithstanding that a trustee is or may be the sole beneficiary in whose favour the discretion is then exercised provided that there is at least one trustee not so favoured;

(TWENTY-ONE) to resign office notwithstanding any benefit hereunder;

(TWENTY-TWO) to appoint one or more of their own number to act as solicitor or agent, accountant, financial advisor, surveyor, manager factor or any other capacity and to allow him or them the same remuneration to which he or they would have been entitled if not a trustee or trustees;

(TWENTY-THREE) to appoint any one or more trustees resident out of the UK and themselves to resign office;

(TWENTY-FOUR) to carry on the administration of the trust hereby created in some place out of the UK;

(TWENTY-FIVE) to renounce for themselves and their successors in office the power to exercise any of the foregoing powers in this purpose as if the same were vested in them beneficially and not as trustees;

(TWENTY-SIX) to apply for and carry out all applications for grants, loans and other subvention whether from government or otherwise;

(TWENTY-SEVEN) to deal with all government bodies whether local, central or otherwise, all quangos and similar;

(TWENTY-EIGHT) to pay for any nursing, medical residential and/or care costs.

Immunities

6–115   **I DECLARE** that my Trustees shall not be liable for depreciation in the value of investments made by them or made by me or any other person and retained by them nor for any omissions nor errors in judgement nor neglect in management nor for the insolvency of debtors, nor for the acts, omissions, neglect or defaults of each other or of any other banker, factor, solicitor or agent, but each for his own actual intromissions only; and persons paying money to my Trustees shall have no concern with the application thereof and shall not be answerable or accountable for any loss, misapplication or non-application of the same, but shall be fully exonered by the receipts and discharges of my trustees or of their factors, solicitors or others: and I consent to registration hereof for preservation: IN WITNESS WHEREOF

Pilot Trusts

6–116   These are not really a separate form of trust. In the football analogy, they would be on the substitutes' bench. They exist to possibly circumvent the related settlements clause. Thus, a prospective testator might set up a pilot discretionary trust in his lifetime and provide in his will that the nil rate band legacy be transferred to it. Any of the discretionary trusts would be suitable. To minimise cost it should be set up with a non-interest bearing account with a nominal sum, say £20. The use of non-taxable national savings product might be considered. It would only be when the truster/testator passed away that the pilot trust would come off the bench on to the field of play.

It should be noted that there is no obligation to report the trust to HMRC unless there is to be taxable income or capital gains.

Trusts for a Bereaved Minor

6–117   It looks as if under current proposals the status and exemptions which previously effeired to accumulation and maintenance trusts will be changed to the more restricted class of trusts known as "a trust for a bereaved minor". The assets of this trust will be exempt from inheritance tax and no charges will apply if the beneficiary dies or assets are transferred from the trust.

This will be an exemption from the proposed new "mainstream" rules.

To qualify as a trust for a bereaved minor the following requirements are necessary:

- The beneficiary of the trust must be under 18 years of age.
- At least one parent must be dead.

The trust requires to be set up under intestacy or the criminal injuries compensation scheme or the will of a deceased parent. It is this last one with which we will be principally concerned in this text.

The beneficiary must become absolutely and fully entitled to the assets at the age of 18. Reference has already been made to transitional arrangements for accumulation and maintenance trusts but for the pure trust for a bereaved minor it is necessary that he is entitled to benefit from the assets at this age.

This will be somewhat of a disappointment to many testators who will consider that the age is far too young for children to have assets. It is not so much the fact that they, themselves, may not be mature enough. It is that they may be subject to pressure from other parties!

Until the beneficiary reaches 18 the trust fund may only be applied for the benefit of the beneficiary.

The trust income may be either applied for the benefit of the minor, given directly to them or accumulated. As stated there will be a partial exemption up until the age of 25. What is likely to happen is that the trust assets will become relevant property when the beneficiary reaches the age of 18. There will be no inheritance tax charge then but there will be an exit charge at the age of 25.

Style

Clause in Will

6–118

Residuary bene-ficiaries under 18	I direct my Trustees to hold any part of the residue of my estate for a beneficiary under the age of Eighteen years which is referred to as "the Trust Fund" for the following trust purposes:
	(1) For behoof of such children contingently on their attaining a vested interest as after provided for.
	(2) To accumulate the income arising from the Trust Fund by investing all surplus thereof and the resulting income therefrom in accordance with the powers hereafter conferred until such children respectively attain the age of eighteen years.
	(3) For payment of an equal share of the capital of the Trust Fund and the income accumulated prior to his or her acquiring a vested interest in the income to such children on their respectively attaining the age of eighteen years and subject as aftermentioned the said capital and accumulated income shall not vest in any of such children until the date of payment of his or her share.
	(4) If any of such children fail to attain a vested interest by reason of his or her predeceasing leaving issue, such issue as survive and attain the age of eighteen years shall be entitled to the share original and accresced which his, her or their parent would have taken on survivance: And if any of such children fail to attain a vested interest as before provided for leaving no issue who survive

and attain the age of Eighteen, to hold the share of the Trust Fund and any income accumulated at the date of such failure for behoof of the beneficiaries who would have been entitled if such child had never existed.

(5) My Trustees may apply for the maintenance education or benefit of any beneficiary the income including accumulated income in whole or in part and any part up to the whole of the share of the capital of the Trust Fund of any child of any child presumptively entitled to such share of the capital of the Trust Fund and such advances shall vest on payment.

(6) My Trustees may create in favour of any beneficiary presumptively entitled to a share of the capital of the Trust Fund a right to the income of the whole or part of such share prior to such beneficiary attaining the age of eighteen years at which age such right shall terminate.

(7) There shall be no apportionment as between capital and income on any occasion.

Chapter Seven

TRUST ADMINISTRATION

RUNNING THE TRUST

This aspect of the trust will take on more significance for the future. It 7–01 will be absolutely paramount for the trust to be run in a proper manner **and** for it to be demonstrated to be run in a proper manner. Otherwise, there may be serious consequences. For example in a mini-discretionary trust set up under a deed of variation HMRC may take the view that this is merely a sham for the purpose of avoiding IHT and what we have is in effect a liferent trust.

Proper meetings should be held, decisions taken about exercise of discretion, accounts produced and minutes taken and recorded in a Sederunt Book or similar. The writer recalls as an apprentice spending many happy hours engrossing, that is to say, handwriting minutes etc. into the many trust sederunt books. It is hoped that these may now be able to be engrossed on word-processed documents and stored electronically.

MINUTES OF MEETINGS

It will be essential that minutes of meetings are kept along the lines of 7–02 the following:

> **MINUTE OF FIRST MEETING** of the Trustees appointed by and acting under Will of the late **JAMES IGNATIOUS BROWN**, 10 Weeple Drive, Inchinnan, Glasgow G3 3AB (who died on 1st November 2005) dated 1st January 2004 held at the Chambers of Messrs Cheatham & Steele, Solicitors, Glasgow at 134 James Street, Glasgow on Friday 13th March 2006.

Present: Mrs Winifred Jamieson Black or Brown, Donald Cheatham, Solicitor and Frederick Steele, Solicitor, Trustees.

In Attendance: Miss Adele Cheadle, Solicitor and Mr James Bond, Stockbroker, Glasgow

Apology

An apology was intimated from Miss Jennifer Brown, one of the Trustees, nominated under the Will, who was unable to attend owing to ill health. The best wishes of those present were expressed and the hope that she would soon be restored to full health.

Acceptance of Trustees

The Will incorporating the deed of variation setting up the trust deed having been read over and submitted, the Trustees present, Mrs Winifred Jamieson Black or Brown, Donald Cheatham and Frederick Steele, accepted the office of Trustee conferred on them as is evidenced by their signatures endorsed on the deed and hereto.

Appointment of Factors

The Trustees appointed Messrs Cheatham & Steele, Solicitors, Glasgow to be the Law Agents and Factors to the Trust.

Factors Report

The Factors reported that the funds of £20,000 and the share certificates, stock transfers and dividend mandates, which had been prepared in advance were to hand. Following a report by the stockbroker.

The Law Agents were instructed as follows:

1. To register the stock transfers, lodge the dividend mandates and which were duly signed.
2. To have the Deed of Trust registered in the Books of Council and Session and to obtain an Extract.
3. To pay the expenses of creating the Trust and investments.
4. To lodge the form 41G (Trust) with HMRC.
5. The Trustees fully discussed the question of investing the capital of the Trust and instructed the Factors to arrange for the purchase of the following additional stocks and shares.

   £2,000 3% Funding Stock
   £2,000 4% Consolidated Stock
   £1,000 Diageo plc ordinary stock.
   £2,000 Imperial Chemical Industries plc ordinary stock.

10 Weeple Drive, Inchinnan, Glasgow G3 3AB

Following on a report from the factors the trustees resolved to sell the one-half *pro indiviso* share in the above property to Mrs Brown at a price of £110,000, which the trustees were assured, was the market value of half share. Mrs Brown was to be offered a loan to be secured by standard security over the property by Mrs Brown in favour of the Trustees. The terms of the loan were that no interest would be charged until the date of sale or on Mrs Brown passing away. Mrs Brown declared an interest in this aspect of the matter and took no part in the discussion.

The Revenue of the Trust

The Factors were instructed to collect the revenue from the investment and to lodge this in credit of the clients' account with Messrs Cheatham & Steele.

Date of next Meeting

Resolved that it should be left to the Factors to arrange a suitable time for all parties as and when Miss Brown had fully recovered.

MINUTE OF SECOND MEETING by the Trustees appointed by and acting under Will of the late **JAMES IGNATIOUS BROWN**, 10 Weeple Drive, Inchinnan, Glasgow, dated 1st January 2006 held at the Chambers of Messrs Cheatham & Steele, Solicitors, Glasgow at 134 James Street, Glasgow on 1st July 2006

Present: Miss Jennifer Brown, Donald Cheatham, Solicitor and Frederick Steele, Solicitor, Trustees.

In Attendance: Miss Adele Cheadle, Solicitor.

Reports

The Trustees record with regret the death of their co-Trustee, Mrs Brown which occurred on 31st March 2006

Accounts of the Trustees

The Factors submitted the Accounts of the Trust, which had previously been circulated. It was noted that these closed with a balance at credit of capital of £300,000. The investments as per the valuation were as follows:

The balance at credit of Revenue was £3,400. The Accounts of Charge and Discharge was approved. Resolved to make no payment under their discretionary powers at present but to review the position in six months when the tax position had been clarified.

Tax Matters

The factors or the trustees will require to submit forms   **7–03**

41G (Trust)	Intimation to HMRC of existence of trust
64–8	Agent's authority
SA900	Trust Tax return
R185 (Trust Income)	Form to advise the beneficiaries of their income.

DEEDS OF ASSUMPTION

Style

We, **MRS MARGARET FRANKLIN**, residing at Number One hundred **7–04** Kennedy Street, Helensburgh G12 12DQ and **DAVID ANDREW CARTER**, Chartered Accountant, residing at Number Five Hancock Avenue, Milngavie, the present Trustees originally appointed by and acting under (FIRST) Trust Disposition and Settlement of the late **MRS MARGARET CLINTON**, Number Five Nixon Court, Allander, Stirlingshire dated Thirty-first May Nineteen hundred and ninety-nine and recorded in The Sheriff Court Books of the

Commissariot of Tayside, Central and Fife on Twelfth September in the year Two thousand, as varied by Deed of variation and (SECOND) Minute of Resignation by **GERALD FORD**, Solicitor, Number One hundred Washington Road, Bearsden dated Seventh and Thirty-first January and Twenty-fourth February registered in the Books of Council and Session on Twenty First March all in the year Two thousand and five; WHEREAS we have decided to assume **JOHN ADAMS**, Surveyor, residing at Madison House, Monroe Road, Glasgow as Trustee under the said Trust Disposition and Settlement, THEREFORE, We, the said Mrs Margaret Franklin and David Andrew Carter, as Trustees foresaid, DO HEREBY ASSUME the said John Adams, as Trustee under the said Trust Disposition and Settlement, and we dispone and convey to ourselves, the said Mrs Margaret Frances McArthur and David Andrew Carter and to the said John Adams, as Trustees foresaid, and the survivors and survivor and to the Executor of the last survivor **ALL AND SUNDRY** the whole trust estate and effects, heritable and moveable, real and personal of every description and wherever situated at present belonging to us or under our control as Trustees foresaid; together with the whole vouchers, titles and instructions thereof; And I, the said David Andrew Carter, do hereby resign the office of Trustee under the said Trust Disposition and Settlement; and the said John Adams hereby accepts office, as Trustee foresaid; and we, the said Mrs Margaret Frances McArthur and John Adams, hereby accept intimation of the said resignation of the said David Andrew Carter as aforesaid; and we all hereby certify that this Instrument falls within category (A) in the Schedule to the Stamp Duty (Exempt Instruments) Regulations 1987 IN WITNESS WHEREOF

Alternative methods of laying these out, i.e. in columns can be found in the Greens Practice styles.

A form of discharge is also shown in the appendix. These should always be obtained from beneficiaries after approval of accounts of charge and discharge have been submitted.

Chapter Eight

CURRENT TRENDS IN POST DEATH PLANNING OR DEEDS OF VARIATION

INTRODUCTION

While not specifically a matter for trust drafting it is necessary for the **8–01** drafter to be fully aware of the opportunities and pitfalls after death. There has, in recent years, been a burgeoning interest in utilising deeds of variation to set up trusts.

There is a window of opportunity after death for making sometimes quite spectacular savings in tax. This chapter will address methods of identifying and maximising this opportunity.

In England and Wales claims against practitioners for failure to exploit and/or advise on this are now common. With the nil rate band ("NRB") now[1] at £285,000 a claim could amount to £114,000.

A deed of variation can thus present a major tax planning opportunity. It should be considered in virtually all executries. For example, a surviving spouse may wish to redirect part of his or her inheritance to the children in order to take advantage of the NRB of IHT for the estate. Alternatively, a beneficiary may be able to set up a discretionary trust arrangement from which he or she can be eligible to benefit but which should escape IHT on his or her eventual death. Other taxes need to be considered.

The popular notion that it is possible to rewrite/vary the Will itself (or the law of intestacy or the doctrine of survivorship) is a misconception since the Will itself cannot be varied after the testator has died. It is, however, possible for an original beneficiary to sign a Deed of variation in order to make some sort of gift and to redirect all or part of an inheritance. By means of a statutory fiction, the HMRC will, if required, treat the gift as having been made by the deceased person and not by the original beneficiary for IHT purposes and/or for most CGT purposes but (apart from certain income tax redirection) not for any other purpose.

Arguably, one of the most popular tax saving provisions of all time, the Inheritance Tax Act 1984, s.142 (and the Taxation of Chargeable Gains Act 1992, s.62) has expanded in a most spectacular manner and, somewhat surprisingly, has survived successive Labour governments. Broadly stated, it allows a two-year period after death in which to "rewrite" a deceased's will or to alter the destination of property on intestacy.

---

[1] 2006/07.

It is, and should be, one of the first matters addressed by executry and trust practitioners after death. Traditionally, as above mentioned, it is utilised where a spouse dies leaving everything to the surviving spouse "whom failing" to their children by directing part or all of the estate to children. The benefit of the NRB is saved and at current rates of IHT the saving, on the second death, can be as much as a staggering £114,000[2] in IHT in even relatively modest estates.

It can be an extremely valuable source of income for executry practitioners. **The other side of the coin is that if the practitioner fails to advise and indicate the possibility it is likely to be a source of, at the least, complaint to the Law Society and, at worst, a claim for profes-sional negligence!**

On the subject of negligence, it is important to remember who your client in deeds of variations is. It is, of course, the beneficiary making the deed of variation (not the executors); and therefore the costs incurred are not an expense of the estate. For the estate or legatees to pay the cost could constitute "consideration" preventing s.142 (or, for CGT, TCGA 1992, s.62) from applying. While it may be that the beneficiary is also the residuary beneficiary and is in effect "paying" the fees from residue, it might be prudent to include a notation in the account of charge and discharge to this effect.

Its utility is not restricted to IHT saving. Its "sister" provision, the Taxation of Chargeable Gains Act 1992, s.62(6) for CGT must also be considered. The effect of income tax and other taxes such as stamp duty have also to be measured. Each of these must be considered separately and together. Particular consideration must be given to their impact and how they may interact. In this chapter we will cover the current IHT, CGT and income tax provisions and in particular how these three taxes interact. Finally, some possible future trends will be identified.

It may be that a scheme is set up whereby a discretionary trust sells a one-half *pro indiviso* share in the family home to the surviving spouse. If this is above the threshold for stamp duty land tax, this possibility should be identified and an estimate of the duty involved given.

Stamp Duty Land Tax Rates from March 23, 2006

Rate	Land in disadvantaged areas—Residential	All other land in the UK—Residential
Nil	£0–£150,000	£0–£125,000
1%	Over £150,000–£250,000	Over £125,000–£250,000
3%	Over £250,000–£500,000	Over £250,000–£500,000
4%	Over £500,000	Over £500,000

Thus, it might be that a one-half share of a substantial house could amount to £270,000 on which the duty would be £8,100!

---

[2] 40 per cent of £285,000.

It is, of course, important to ascertain if the area comes within a "disadvantaged area".

Incidentally, these writs are sometimes called Deeds of Family Arrangement but this is a technical English law term. Generally, they will be referred to as "Deeds of Variation".[3]

Consideration by practitioners and/or the executors of variations and/ or discharges (discharges/discharge/disclaimers)[4] under IHTA 1984, s.142 should be standard practice. Executors and their advisors will be required to pay much more attention to the possible savings to be made. Failure to have regard to this could give rise to a negligence claim by the beneficiaries and rightly so. The executors and beneficiaries should be advised of the potential saving **at the first available opportunity**. Thereafter, it should be mentioned at every reasonable opportunity. At the earliest opportunity this should be conveyed to them in writing; they should be encouraged to pass the information on to their professional advisors. It is not necessary to reiterate that this advice should be fully minuted and signed by them if possible. The two-year deadline should be mentioned **IN BLOCK CAPITALS in the letter of engagement** also confirming that this is the final date when it should be completed, that is to say:

> "we will require time say several months to have the deed drafted, advice taken from other professionals, approved executed and submitted if necessary. To achieve all this it will be necessary to put the matter in hand, preferably, some months before the two-year deadline".

VARIATIONS AND DISCLAIMERS GENERALLY

If a beneficiary receives a bequest under a will or under the rules of intestacy, he or she is under no legal obligation to accept the bequest and may instead refuse or decline to accept. If the bequest is refused by the way of a formal discharge/disclaimer, the asset thereafter passes, in the absence of a substitution, to the person entitled to the residue under the will; on intestacy if the asset is disclaimed, it vests under the rules of intestacy. However, a discharge/disclaimer cannot be made **if the original beneficiary has already received some benefit from the property being disclaimed**, e.g. if an individual is left shares under a will and has received some dividend income on those shares, no formal discharge/ disclaimer can be made in respect of that property.

If a beneficiary does not wish to accept a gift but instead wishes the property to pass to a nominated person, this can only really be achieved by deed of variation, which differs from a discharge/disclaimer in that the person making the variation, will stipulate the new recipient within the deed. Only persons relinquishing an interest in an estate may make a variation. In practice, deeds of variation are more commonly used than disclaimers.

8–02

---

[3] HMRC refers to Instruments of Variation.
[4] Generally these will be referred to as disclaimers.

It should be noted that s.142 has effect as if the variation has been effected by the deceased and/or, as the case may be, the disclaimed benefit had never been conferred. Without making use of these rules, any variation or disclaimer made by the original recipient would be a transfer of value, and therefore potentially liable to an IHT charge as a PET, possibly requiring the donor to survive seven years before escaping an IHT charge.

The equivalent provision for capitals gains tax purposes is TCGA 1992, s.62. An election under that section works in a similar way to IHTA 1984, s.142 in that it disregards the original disposal at the date of the variation or disclaimer. Without making use of this section, any variation or discharge/disclaimer made by the original recipient would be treated as a disposal at the market value for CGT purposes, and could leave him or her with CGT liability.

In view of the usefulness of these provisions, practitioners sometimes take the view that there is little need to update wills because any adjustments can be done in appropriate variations. The writer does not share this view for two main reasons. First, anti-avoidance legislation may prevent these plans. Secondly, the beneficiary under the will may, for various reasons, be unwilling or unable to enter into the variation. The correct practice must therefore be to prepare the will correctly initially, and keep it under regular review.

The use of these deeds is something to be kept in reserve, a safety net at second best. Norman Lamont, a Conservative Chancellor of the Exchequer, nearly abolished variations in 1989. However, in the context of the new pre-owned assets income tax charge, the use of variations can have special significance. These provisions are extremely useful planning tools and can be used to save substantial amounts of tax.

VARIATIONS AND DISCHARGES/DISCHARGE/DISCLAIMERS CONTRASTED

8–03 The following general distinctions should be borne in mind.

In case of a variation, the original beneficiary re-directs the destination of the disposition as he chooses. In the case of a discharge/disclaimer, he has no choice and the discharge/disclaimer merely accelerates the subsequent interest, e.g. a disclaimed legacy may fall into residue. To overcome this, the will could provide that any disclaimed interest should fall into a trust with wide powers of appointment and advancement or a discretionary trust.

On a variation, part of a specific bequest or share of residue can be redirected, whereas it is sometimes suggested that with a discharge/disclaimer the whole interest must be disclaimed. However, it is considered that partial discharges/discharge/disclaimers (e.g. of a partial interest in a property) are permissible **provided that they are authorised by the will**.

With deeds of variation, it does not matter that the original beneficiary may earlier have received some benefit or indeed the whole estate has been wound up and distributed to the beneficiary. In the case of a discharge/disclaimer, however, it is a condition that before the discharge/disclaimer the original beneficiary has received no benefits (e.g. rent from property, dividends from shares). A variation can benefit anyone, not merely another beneficiary or a member of the family. It will be uncommon for a discharge to be used. We are principally concerned with deeds of variation setting up trusts but other aspects will be considered.

INHERITANCE TAX

IHTA 1984, s.142 is as follows: **8–04**

142.—(1) Where within the period of two years after a person's death—

(a) any of the dispositions (whether effected by will, under the law relating to intestacy or otherwise) of the property comprised in his estate immediately before his death are varied, or

(b) the benefit conferred by any of those dispositions is disclaimed,

by an instrument in writing made by the persons or any of the persons who benefit or would benefit under the dispositions, this Act shall apply as if the variation had been effected by the deceased or, as the case may be, the disclaimed benefit had never been conferred.

(2) Subsection (1) above shall not apply to a variation unless the instrument contains a statement, made by all the relevant persons, to the effect that they intend the subsection to apply to the variation.

(2A) For the purposes of subsection (2) above the relevant persons are—

(a) the person or persons making the instrument, and

(b) where the variation results in additional tax being payable, the personal representatives.

Personal representatives may decline to make a statement under subsection (2) above only if no, or no sufficient, assets are held by them in that capacity for discharging the additional tax.

(3) Subsection (1) above shall not apply to a variation or disclaimer made for any consideration in money or money's worth other than consideration consisting of the making; in respect of another of the dispositions, of a variation or disclaimer to which that subsection applies.

(4) Where a variation to which subsection (1) above applies results in property being held in trust for a person for a period which ends not more than two years after the death, this Act shall apply as if the disposition of the property that takes effect at the end of the period had had effect from the beginning of the period; but this subsection shall not affect the application of this Act in relation to any distribution or application of property occurring before that disposition takes effect.

(5) For the purposes of subsection (1) above the property comprised in a person's estate includes any excluded property but not any property to which he is treated as entitled by virtue of section 49(1) above or section 102 of the Finance Act 1986.

(6) Subsection (1) above applies whether or not the administration of the estate is complete or the property concerned has been distributed in accordance with the original dispositions.

(7) In the application of subsection (4) above to Scotland, property which is subject to a proper liferent shall be deemed to be held in trust for the liferenter.

From the taxpayer's point of view, IHTA 1984, s.142 has been, and continues to be, one of the most useful and popular sections in the IHT legislation, because it allows a **two-year breathing space** in which to "re-write" the provisions of the deceased's will or the passing of property on intestacy.

It is indeed useful, but it needs approaching with care.

To summarise IHTA 1984, s.142 operates where:
- Within a period of two years after the individual's death the destination of any of the assets of his estate (excluding assets charged under the reservation of benefit rules) passing by will, intestacy or "otherwise";
- Is varied/altered or the benefits are disclaimed, by a deed in writing made by the original beneficiary (i.e.) irrevocably; and
- For variations (but not discharges/discharge/disclaimers), as from August 1, 2002 the deed of variation contains a "statement" that the deed of variation is to apply for IHT.
- For all practical purposes, the "variation" must be carried by the way of a deed. This is not essential, but is helpful as it ensures that the variation is binding as between the original beneficiary and the legatee.
- The deed of variation must clearly indicate the subject of the legacy or bequest which it seeks to vary, and vary their destination as laid down by the deceased's will or under the law relating to intestate estate or otherwise.
- Practitioners should refer to the useful HMRC checklist on deeds of variation[5];
- Intestacy arrangements can be subject to a variation by, in effect, incorporating a deemed will and also a trust.
- Although it is a little unusual nowadays a beneficiary can also vary a valid nomination in their favour of National Savings;
- Under s.142(6) a variation can apply even though the administration of the estate has been completed and the assets advanced to the beneficiary in accordance with the original disposition, provided of course that it is within the two-year limit.
- A variation or discharge/disclaimer must not be for a consideration in money or money's worth (unless the consideration is another variation or discharge/disclaimer). Under no circumstances should the original beneficiary effecting the variation be reimbursed for expenses of the variation, income tax liabilities

---

[5] IOV2. HMRC refer to it as an Instrument of Variation.

or have a mortgage or other liabilities paid. In this context please do not lose sight of the fact that your client is the beneficiary making the deed of variation and not the executors, although they may be the same person; and so the costs incurred are not an expense of the estate. For the estate or legatees to pay the cost, could constitute "consideration" preventing s.142 (or, for CGT, TCGA 1992, s.62) from applying.

- It is vital that if the variation results in more IHT or CGT being payable, the executors or executors must make the statement. They may decline to do so if there are insufficient assets in the estate to cover the extra IHT (s.142(2A)).
- The executors must, **within six months**, notify the HMRC of the amount additional IHT payable and send a copy of the variation to them.
- **It should be noted that the HMRC has no discretion to extend the two-year period in IHTA 1984, s.142.**
- For both IHT and CGT, a variation requires a disposition, conveyance or assignation and not mere "administration" arrangements.[6] Thus, where a will lacks appropriate administration powers, **a variation cannot merely include such powers**. There must be some substantive matter. Take the common example of a husband, Delano, leaving his estate, including his house "Garner Place" to his wife, Eleanor. Eleanor can enter into a variation whereby the late Delano is deemed to have left a NRB discretionary will trust, including a half share in Garner Place. As it is "intended" that Eleanor will grant a security over part of the home left to her to make up some of the NRB legacy, these powers can be included in the variation arrangements. These powers could not be included if Delano had created such a NRB discretionary will trust, but omitted the powers to charge the home. This cannot be remedied by a variation just including the powers. This would not be classed as a disposition.
- From August 1, 2002 a "statement" must be made in the variation document and notice given to the HMRC if additional tax becomes payable as a result of the variation. The clause in the deed of variation can be adapted to apply to IHT, CGT or both.
- There is nothing to require that a "statement" must be made for both taxes, i.e. IHT and CGT. As the "statement" is written within the deed itself, it can be made clear specifically that it is to operate for one tax only; e.g. for IHT alone under s.142(2) or for CGT alone under TCGA 1992, s.62(6).We should watch out carefully for what is described in some offices as the "word processor's revenge", **that we do not inadvertently elect for both taxes** when that is not in the interest of the taxpayer making the variation or the deceased's estate. For example, it may well be advantageous to elect for IHT but not for capital gains tax.

---

[6] s.142(6).

- The deed effecting the variation should include a "statement" (no longer strictly an "election") made by all "the relevant persons" if IHTA 1984, s.142 and/or TCGA 1992, s.62 is to apply. It is no longer possible to make the election/statement outside the deed.
- For CGT there is normally an exemption on death, in addition to the market-value uplift. The motive for a variation is therefore usually to mitigate IHT and not necessarily CGT.

CAPITAL GAINS TAX

Introduction

8–05 Section 62 of the TCGA 1992 contains a similar power to alter bequests on death for CGT purposes.

The principle is that the new beneficiaries are treated as if they acquired the assets from the deceased **at the date of death** and at the values agreed on the death (TCGA 1992, s.62(6)). Such a CGT statement, therefore, is usually made unless:

(a) there are assets with losses; or
(b) it is wished to use up the small gains exemption; or
(c) non-residency is involved; or
(d) the principal residence has risen in value since death (if it has fallen do include the statement so that the beneficiaries take the higher death value).

Danger Warning!!!

Since the rate of CGT increased to 40 per cent the same as for IHT there may be some advantage in having the gain assessed as a capital gain rather than an increase in IHT since allowances and exemptions may be available.

TCGA 1992, s.62 requirements

8–06 The requirements under TCGA 1992, s.62 are almost identical to those under IHTA 1984, s.142.

Trusts

8–07

Danger Warning!!!

For CGT, where the deed of variation involves the setting up of a trust, following the *Marshall v Kerr*, 1994 S.T.C. 638, it is the original beneficiary, not the deceased testator, who is treated as the truster. Contrast this with the IHT treatment (the wording of IHTA 1984, s.142 and TCGA 1992, s.62 differ somewhat, usually to the taxpayer's disadvantage for CGT).

Marshall v Kerr has particular application to offshore trusts (e.g. TCGA 1992, ss.86 and 87) but can also affect UK trusts. An example of this is where the beneficiary making the variation is also a beneficiary of the recipient trust (or that beneficiary's spouse is a beneficiary). In that case, under TCGA 1992, s.77, the trust gains are taxable on the beneficiary/truster. Note also that, for income tax purposes, the truster of the trust is the original beneficiary who made the deed of variation.

OTHER TAXES

Income tax

There are no income tax provisions corresponding to IHTA 1984, s.14, **8–08** but that does not mean that there are no income tax consequences of making a discharge/disclaimer or deed of variation. Practitioners should consider the following:

- Any income due to, and received by, the original beneficiary who made the deed of variation will be that person's income.
- Where a deed of variation is executed in favour of a charity, it should therefore be done as soon as possible after death. This is because the charity, unlike the original beneficiary, will be exempt from income tax (ICTA 1988, s.505).
- The original beneficiary who made a deed of variation creating a trust **is the truster for income tax purposes**. Therefore, if under the trusts of that settlement that person retains a possibility of benefit, the income of that settled property will be taxed on that person (ICTA 1988, s.660A). In addition, if it is a settlement in favour of the minor children of the maker of the deed, the rules whereby payment to or for the benefit of the minor children of the truster may be taxed as the income of the truster (ICTA 1988, s.660) can apply.

Stamp duty and stamp duty land tax

Variations are exempt from stamp duty provided an appropriate **8–09** certificate is given under the Stamp Duty (Exempt Instruments) Regulations 1987 (SI 1987/516). Discharges/discharge/disclaimers are also exempt from stamp duty. The writer considers category "L" is the correct category, unless there is consideration in the form of a reciprocal variation. If this reciprocity does exist, category "M" is strictly correct, but it seems that the HMRC will then accept either category.

Under Stamp Duty Land Tax, such certification is no longer essential because SDLT is self-assessed.

SUGGESTED USE OF DEEDS OF VARIATIONS/DISCHARGES/DISCHARGE/
DISCLAIMERS

Variations and discharges/discharge/disclaimers can cover a wide range **8–10** of circumstances and uses. Of course, when making a variation, one should take account of the identity of the property and the needs of variation beneficiaries. For example, a widow is likely to need to own the dwelling-house and liquid assets, but may not need or even want(!) shares in the family company. At the outset it should also be considered allocating assets likely to appreciate (e.g. heritable property) to younger individuals and assets likely to depreciate (e.g. moveable assets) to older individuals.

There are many instances of uses. A full treatment of these is outwith the scope of this text. Reference in more detail will be made to those which have direct impact on trusts

Using the IHT nil rate band

8–11   A gift which includes the IHT NRB to an exempt person (such as a surviving spouse or charity) wastes the NRB. In other words, the NRB is not actually used. The usual case of this is when the surviving spouse inherits the whole residuary estate (as happens all too often).

Even if the estate was well in excess of the nil rate and the surviving spouse did not need it all, it would normally still only be worth using a deed of variation for the NRB (plus possibly business and agriculture property for IHT). This is the "classic" form of use of added variation.

An alternative method is for discretionary trusts to be used to enable a surviving spouse to enjoy the benefit of a fund without the penalty of wasting the NRB. Under this method a discretionary trust of the NRB could be used, the distributions from which to the surviving spouse would only be used in cases of need.

Using the IHT NRB on the first to die of spouses/civil partners

8–12   Richard Nixon and his wife Millie each have an estate of £600,000, and Richard wishes his widow to be his residuary beneficiary. The usual procedure would be for Richard to leave his entire estate to his spouse. This ensures that he leaves estate of £600,000 outright or in liferent and that no IHT was payable on his death. On Millie's death, IHT would be payable on an estate of £1.2m (IHT £285,000 for 2006/07). What Richard could do would be to leave Millie only £300,000 and put the sum of £300,000 (the 2007/08 NRB) into a discretionary trust, with informal directions to the trustees to treat Millie as the principle beneficiary. If she needed funds, she could have a capital distribution or a loan which should be a deduction from her estate on her death[7] or she could receive income distributions.

In that case the IHT at 2007/08 on Millie's death would be reduced to £240,000 (i.e. on the widow's estate of £900,000)

If this were not done and Millie left an estate of £1,200,000, the IHT would be £360,000

There would be an IHT saving under this alternative of £120,000 (£360,000 – £240,000).

An further gain is that, after the death of the surviving spouse, further tax benefits can be obtained by skipping a generation, e.g. to grandchildren.

---

[7] FA 1986, s.103.

Danger Warning!!!

The trustees must "act" so there can be no "sham trusts".
HMRC have recently warned practitioners and trustees that it is not
sufficient just to have a well-drawn trust deed. The trustees must be
seen to consider and, as appropriate, exercise their discretion and not
just leave the widow(er) in, say, indefinite favourable occupation. In
particular, the trustees require to meet regularly, e.g. twice a year,
and minute the exercise of their discretion in a proper manner. If the
trustees do nothing, the whole arrangement can be attacked as a
sham. The HMRC is likely to call for the professional advisor's letter
setting up the arrangement; practitioners should exercise caution
here, and must word any such letter carefully!

A surviving spouse might renounce or assign their liferent under deed of
variation.

The executors/trustees might revoke liferent by powers in the will.

This would constitute a PET of the widow's interest, i.e. the s.142
procedure is not adopted. Section 142 used to apply even if the widow
had died in the two-year period. This HMRC view has received some
approval in the Special Commissioner's decision in *Soutter's Executry v
IRC*, 2002 S.T.C. (SCD) 385, where Scottish Law applied. In essence, the
decision was to the effect that once a liferent has ceased with the
liferentor's death, s.142 cannot be applied. The case has been criticised
because, although logical, s.142 is, in essence, a deeming provision and
retrospective to the testator's i.e. the first death. Clearly, s.142 can only
rearrange interests under a trust created under the will in question, e.g.
not under a lifetime trust.

Use of a s.144 discretionary trust

This is dealt with elsewhere.   8–13

Tax-free legacies to become subject-to-tax legacies

Converting "tax free" legacies, where the IHT is paid from the residue   8–14
to "subject to tax" legacies where the beneficiary pays the IHT without
grossing up.

Posthumous increases

It should be possible to pass on free of IHT the benefit of certain   8–15
posthumous increases in the value of an estate within the two-year
period. This depends upon the trustees or those advising them to have
up-to-date valuations of the executry estate. If the value of an estate
increases drastically in the two years after death because of shares going
up in value, a surviving spouse may enter into a deed of variation
whereby she takes a legacy of the original value of the residue with
residue going to a trust. The value of the deceased's total estate
immediately before death would be the same and would all be attributa-
ble to the surviving spouse exemption. However, the increase in value
would now go to the trust.

DESTINATIONS

Joint names or joint names and the survivor

8–16   Reference is made to Ch.23 of Gretton and Reid *"Conveyancing"* (Third edition) which specifically deals with special destinations.

There have of course been further developments in the law of destinations and these are dealt with in Reid/Gretton *"Conveyancing 2005"*.[8]

Reference is made also to this in connection with the section on discretionary trusts.

It relates to a matter which has been covered earlier in this text. It is extremely common in the West of Scotland and elsewhere for survivorship destinations to be included in the titles for heritable properties particularly where these are owned by husband and wife or son and daughter or elsewhere. Clearly, this is a matter which has given a certain amount of trouble over the years as evidenced by the various cases. These cases have stemmed mainly from the disposition by an inexperienced practitioner of a one-half *pro indiviso* share where the original title is affected by a survivorship destination.

If there is a survivorship destination then this may affect parties' ability to deal directly with their own one-half share since this will be affected by the survivorship.

It is possible for survivorship destination to be evacuated or cancelled by *mortis causa* deed.

It is also competent for the survivorship destination to be evacuated by deed of variation and the style of this is included together with a style of conveyance to the discretionary trust and the sale by the discretionary trustees of the one-half share to the surviving spouse. In addition there is also a form of standard security which may be of assistance also.

GIFT WITH RESERVATION

8–17   Where a testator has died and a beneficiary of the estate effects a variation, e.g. by varying an outright gift to that beneficiary into a discretionary trust, the fact that the beneficiary is capable of benefiting from the varied gift (e.g. by being included as a discretionary object) should not constitute a reservation of benefit by the beneficiary. This is because, for IHT purposes, it is the deceased who is deemed to have created the varied gift (e.g. the discretionary trust).

CHARITIES

8–18   Charities can benefit under the post-death variation provision in s.142. As such variations do not operate for income tax purposes in respect of distributed income, the deed of variation should be executed as soon as

---

[8] (2006), p72 (update series).

possible after the death in order to benefit the charity as to any income accruing tax-free.

REVALUATION RELIEF FOR QUOTED SHARES

This relief (in IHTA 1984, s.179) only applies if there is a sale or **8–19** cancellation or suspension of the shares within 12 months of the death. Quite frequently the shares in question may become valueless or virtually so after that 12-month period. In that case, consider a DEED OF VARIATION within two years of the death under s.142 in favour of an exempt party such as a surviving spouse or charity. This should prevent a high unrealisable value being assessed to IHT on the death as the asset valued at death will be exempt.

DISCRETIONARY TRUSTS

Where a testator's bequests are varied into a discretionary trust, the **8–20** settlement is considered to commence from the date of the testator's death for the purposes of IHTA 1984 including s.60 the "ten year anniversary" date.[9]

USING VARIATIONS TO CLARIFY WILLS AND TRUSTS

Variations can clarify the terms of a poorly drafted, ambiguous will. This **8–21** entails all the adult beneficiaries agreeing to a basis set up in the deed and thereby overcoming doubts and ambiguities. This may avoid expensive legal fees.

Variations are exempt from stamp duty and adjustment requirements provided an appropriate certificate is given under the Stamp Duty (Exempt Instruments) Regulations 1987 (SI 1987/516). Discharges/ discharge/disclaimers are also exempt from stamp duty. As stated above, the writer considers category "L" is the correct category, unless there is consideration in the form of a reciprocal variation, which is not the type of consideration which invalidates a deed of variation. If this reciprocity does exist, category "M" is strictly correct, but it seems that the HMRC will then accept either category.

Under Stamp Duty Land Tax, such certification is no longer essential because SDLT is self-assessed.

Redirection of bequest

A son or daughter of a deceased who stands to inherit estate from his/ **8–22** her parent may not require the legacy and may prefer to direct it to his own family or to a trust, such as an accumulation and maintenance or discretionary trust to his/her own family as a means of reducing the

---

[9] IHTA 1984, s.83.

eventual IHT in his/her own estate. This will usually have no impact on the IHT (if any) on the deceased parents' estate which may in any event be below the threshold for IHT. There may be no point in an already wealthy person inheriting, say, £100,000 from his own parent when that will just increase their own eventual IHT and the opportunity may be used to direct it elsewhere. This may be done by way of discharge/disclaimer or assignation by the wealthy son or daughter.

A variation of certain assets may be executed into a s.144 two-year discretionary trust. The assets can then be redirected out of the discretionary trust without further IHT within the two-year period (or up to 10 years if the assets are within the NRB). One additional benefit here is that it avoids the problem in excluding or reducing the interest of an underage beneficiary as he is only a discretionary object.

Capital gains tax

8–23 The statutory provisions are as follows:

Section 62 (Taxation of Chargeable Gains Act 1992) general provisions:

> **62.**—(1) For the purposes of this Act the assets of which a deceased person was competent to dispose—
>
> (a) shall be deemed to be acquired on his death by the personal representatives or other person on whom they devolve for a consideration equal to their market value at the date of the death, but
> (b) shall not be deemed to be disposed of by him on his death (whether or not they were the subject of a testamentary disposition).
>
> (2) Allowable losses sustained by an individual in the year of assessment in which he dies may, so far as they cannot be deducted from chargeable gains accruing in that year, be deducted from chargeable gains accruing to the deceased in the 3 years of assessment preceding the year of assessment in which the death occurs, taking chargeable gains accruing in a later year before those accruing in an earlier year.
>
> (3) In relation to property forming part of the estate of a deceased person the personal representatives shall for the purposes of this Act be treated as being a single and continuing body of persons (distinct from the persons who may from time to time be the personal representatives), and that body shall be treated as having the deceased's residence, ordinary residence, and domicile at the date of death.
>
> (4) On a person acquiring any asset as legatee (as defined in section 64)—
>
> (a) no chargeable gain shall accrue to the personal representatives, and
> (b) the legatee shall be treated as if the personal representatives' acquisition of the asset had been his acquisition of it.

(5) Notwithstanding section 17(1) no chargeable gain shall accrue to any person on his making a disposal by way of donatio mortis causa.

(6) Subject to subsections (7) and (8) below, where within the period of 2 years after a person's death any of the dispositions (whether effected by will, under the law relating to intestacy or otherwise) of the property of which he was competent to dispose are varied, or the benefit conferred by any of those dispositions is disclaimed, by an instrument in writing made by the persons or any of the persons who benefit or would benefit under the dispositions—

(a) **the variation or disclaimer shall not constitute a disposal for the purposes of this Act, and**
(b) **this section shall apply as if the variation had been effected by the deceased or, as the case may be, the disclaimed benefit had never been conferred.**

(7) Subsection (6) above does not apply to a variation unless the person or persons making the instrument so elect by notice given to the Board within 6 months after the date of the instrument or such longer time as the Board may allow.

(8) Subsection (6) above does not apply to a variation or disclaimer made for any consideration in money or money's worth other than consideration consisting of the making of a variation or disclaimer in respect of another of the dispositions.

(9) Subsection (6) above applies whether or not the administration of the estate is complete or the property has been distributed in accordance with the original dispositions.

(10) In this section references to assets of which a deceased person was competent to dispose are references to assets of the deceased which (otherwise than in right of a power of appointment or of the testamentary power conferred by statute to dispose of entailed interests) he could, if of full age and capacity, have disposed of by his will, assuming that all the assets were situated in England and, if he was not domiciled in the United Kingdom, that he was domiciled in England, and include references to his severable share in any assets to which, immediately before his death, he was beneficially entitled as a joint tenant.

The main areas of use for this legislation is the situation where the variation was to effect, in the case of a widow receiving all her husband's estate by his will, an additional bequest superimposed on the will that their son should receive certain shares, there is no CGT on the variation but the son is deemed to acquire at date of death value (if they elect for s.62(6)(a) to apply). Otherwise there would be a disposal by the widow as grantor of the variation and CGT on her gift of shares to the son based on the rise in value from death to variation.

> **Danger Warning!!!**
>
> **Sometimes it may be appropriate to elect that a s.142 exemption for IHT applies to the variation, but not for CGT purposes, e.g. where the variation applies to specific assets which then show a loss compared with their value at the date of death; or where the executors' annual exemption is available to utilise and cover the gain; or where the whole estate is in cash and there will not be a liability to CGT. In theory it is possible to elect for CGT but not IHT, but that is rare in practice.**
>
> **No election should be inserted in the deed if the variation only refers to assets that are not subject to CGT, e.g. cash or government securities or National Savings products.**

Please note that all beneficiaries acquiring assets under a will or on intestacy are defined in s.64 as "legatees", including beneficiaries who take assets in satisfaction of pecuniary legacies and trustees for beneficiaries. The definition is not restricted to beneficiaries who receive legacies from the estate.

A legatee takes over an asset from the executors at their acquisition cost irrespective of the date of transfer to him and the value of the asset at that date. His entitlement to taper relief therefore starts at death. There is no disposal on the transfer by the executors to the legatee.

The date of the legatee's acquisition is the same as the executors' (date of death or subsequent purchase) for calculation of the taper relief but business assets will not qualify for business taper relief unless the executors **and** the beneficiary qualify for relief. The executors may be unable to satisfy the qualifying conditions, which apply to the beneficiary. If the executors do not qualify for relief at the business rate but the beneficiary does qualify, the beneficiary will only be entitled to taper relief at the non-business rate during the executors' administration. They should therefore transfer the business asset to the beneficiary as soon as possible so that his taper relief at the business rate may commence.

If there is no election, the original beneficiary who acquired the investment at its date of death value (provided it has been transferred to him) will make a disposal for CGT at the date of the deed of variation and the new beneficiary will acquire the investment at its value on the same date.

If there is an election under s.62, the new beneficiary will take over the investment at its date of death value and there will be no disposal by the original beneficiary. The new beneficiary's taper relief will run from the date of death if there is an election or from the date of the deed of variation if there is no election.

The decision whether to elect will therefore depend on the respective values at death and variation. The values are likely to be more important than the commencing dates of the taper relief. There may be a conflict of interest between the beneficiaries, but that should not be a problem, because they are usually related. A higher acquisition value will help the new beneficiary for future CGT.

If the higher value is at the date of variation, an election should **not** be made, provided (1) the asset has been transferred to the beneficiary and (2) the gain on the disposal by the original beneficiary is within his exemption. The beneficiary has no acquisition cost until the asset has been transferred to him. If the death value is the higher, an election should be made so that the new beneficiary will take over the investment at death.

Notice of the election has to be given to the HMRC within six months after the date of the deed. The notice is given to the tax district dealing with the executry income.

Income tax

The statutory provisions are as follows: **8–24**

Section 698 of Income and Corporation Taxes Act 1988 provides:

> **698.**—(1) Where the personal representatives of a deceased person have as such a right in relation to the estate of another deceased person such that, if that right were vested in them for their own benefit, they would have an absolute or limited interest in the residue of that estate or in a part of that residue, they shall be deemed to have that interest notwithstanding that that right is not vested in them for their own benefit, and any amount deemed to be paid to them as income by virtue of this Part shall be treated as part of the aggregate income of the estate of the person whose personal representatives they are.
>
> (1A) Subsection (1B) below applies where—
>
> (a) successively during the administration period there are different persons with interests in the residue of the estate of a deceased person or in parts of such a residue;
>
> (b) the later interest or, as the case may be, each of the later interests arises or is created on the cessation otherwise than by death of the interest that precedes it; and
>
> (c) the earlier or, as the case may be, earliest interest is a limited interest.
>
> (1B) Where this subsection applies, this Part shall have effect in relation to any payment made in respect of any of the interests referred to in subsection (1A) above—
>
> (a) as if all those interests were the same interest so that none of them is to be treated as having ceased on being succeeded by any of the others;
>
> (b) as if (subject to paragraph (c) below) the interest which is deemed to exist by virtue of paragraph (a) above ('the deemed single interest') were an interest of—
>
> > (i) except in a case to which sub-paragraph (ii) below applies, the person in respect of whose interest or previous interest the payment is made;
> >
> > (ii) in a case where the person entitled to receive the payment is any other person who has or has had an interest which is deemed to be comprised in the deemed single interest, that other person; and
>
> (c) in so far as any of the later interests is an absolute interest as if, for the purposes of section 696(3A) to (5)—

(i) the earlier interest or interests had never existed and the absolute interest had always existed;

(ii) the sums (if any) which were deemed in relation to the earlier interest or interests to have been paid as income for any accounting period to any of the persons entitled thereto were sums previously paid during the administration period in respect of the absolute interest; and

(iii) those sums were sums falling to be treated as sums paid as income to the person entitled to the absolute interest.

(2) Where successively during the administration period there are different persons with absolute interests in the residue of the estate of a deceased person or in parts of such a residue, the aggregate payments and aggregated income entitlement referred to in subsections (3A) and (3B) of section 696 shall be computed for the purposes of that section in relation to an absolute interest subsisting at any time ('the subsequent interest')—

(a) as if the subsequent interest and any previous absolute interest corresponding to the subsequent interest, or relating to any part of the residue to which the subsequent interest relates, were the same interest; and

(b) as if the residuary income for any accounting period of the person entitled to the previous interest were residuary income of the person entitled to the subsequent interest and any amount deemed to be paid as income to the person entitled to the previous interest were an amount deemed to have been paid to the person entitled to the subsequent interest.

(3) Where, upon the exercise of a discretion, any of the income of the residue of the estate of a deceased person for any period (being the administration period or a part of the administration period) would, if the residue had been ascertained at the commencement of that period, be properly payable to any person, or to another in his right, for his benefit, whether directly by the personal representatives or indirectly through a trustee or other person—

(a) the amount of any sum paid pursuant to an exercise of the discretion in favour of that person shall be deemed for corporation tax purposes to have been paid to that person as income for the accounting period in which it was paid; and

(b) sections 695(4) to (6) shall have effect in relation to an amount which is deemed to have been paid as income by virtue of paragraph (a) above.

(4) Subsection (5) applies in any case where—

(a) successively during the administration period there are different persons with absolute interests in the residue of the estate of a deceased person, or in parts of such a residue, and

(b) some, but not all are companies liable to corporation tax in respect of income within this Part.

(5) References in this section—

(a) to sums deemed to be paid as income for an accounting period to a person who is not such a company,
(b) to the residuary income for any accounting period of such a person, or
(c) to amounts deemed to be paid to such a person as income,
  are references to sums that would be so deemed, to the income that would be such residuary income or, as the case may be, to the amounts that would be so deemed if the assumptions in subsection (6) were made.

  (6) The assumptions are—

(a) that each of the persons who is not a company liable to corporation tax in respect of income within this Part is such a company, and
(b) that in the case of each person who is not a company, the person's accounting periods correspond with years of assessment.

What does this mean in practice?

Notwithstanding that for IHT and CGT purposes a deed of variation **8–25** may be retrospective to the date of death, it is not retrospective to the date of death for income tax purposes and is only effective from the date of its execution. However, an element of retrospection for income tax purposes has been introduced by the back door because of new rules which were introduced for payments made on or after April 6, 1995. This arose because of, and in preparation for, self-assessment for executors and beneficiaries of estates. The practical effect of these rules is that deeds of variation can now have some retrospective effect for income tax purposes if the deed of variation relates to the residue of an estate **which is still in the course of administration when the variation is made**. The retrospective effect is simply the effect of the rules, including statutory provisions for successive interests in residue. If, for instance, payments had been made to the original beneficiary before the execution of the deed of variation, the HMRC would **not** accept that the deed retrospectively changed any income tax liabilities based on such payments. Under self-assessment a beneficiary with an absolute interest in residue is liable to income tax on payments made to him or her during the administration period in respect of his or her absolute interest. Any such payments are treated as income for the year of payment. It should, however, be noted that any such payments will only be treated as income to the extent that they do not exceed the aggregated income entitlement of the beneficiary at the time the payment is made. The aggregated income entitlement is the cumulative share of the estate income, for all years up to and including the year of payment, to which the beneficiary is entitled whether or not that share has actually been paid out. For example, if a testator dies on June 1, 2002 and if his widow signs a deed of variation on December 1, 2002 redirecting the whole of the residuary estate to her adult son, no part of the income will be assessed on the widow unless the executors have previously paid any sum to her in respect of her absolute interest.

Danger Warning!!!

Consideration by you and/or the executors of variations and/or discharges (discharges/discharge/disclaimers) under IHTA 1984, s.142 will be standard practice. Until April 6, 1995 there were no statutory provisions which made variations or discharges (discharges/ discharge/disclaimers) retrospective for income tax purposes. This could be compared with TCGA 1992, s.62 for capital gains. Obviously a discharge is only available where no income or interest has been accepted by the beneficiary. When the bequest is a pecuniary legacy which has interest and it is disclaimed the beneficiary will not be liable to income tax on the interest. In the case of a variation of residue or a share thereof the original beneficiary was liable to income tax for the period from the date of death until the date of variation or discharge/disclaimer, although the executor was assessed initially. The new beneficiary was assessed thereafter. It might have been appropriate in the deed of variation to allow the disclaiming beneficiary some interest, if only to pay the tax levied. Clearly if there is to be a variation then it is best to be made as soon as possible. If not a situation could arise where a higher earning beneficiary who does not vary timeously could be assessed on tax at the higher rate on income he has not received.

  In future executors will be required to pay much more attention to the distribution of estates and its impact upon the beneficiaries' tax position. Failure to have regard to this could give rise to a negligence claim by the beneficiaries. Information must be made available to the beneficiaries as soon after the end of the tax year so that they can comply with the new time limits regarding self-assessment and avoid surcharges, interest and penalties. The beneficiary has a statutory right to receive a statement of income.

Executries becoming continuing trusts

A trust set up under a will does not start until the executors have made over the trust fund (e.g. a legacy) to the trustees, who will probably be themselves acting in a different capacity.

  If the trust fund is part of the residue of the estate, the trust will not start until the residue is established at the end of the administration period. If the trust is discretionary (e.g. an accumulation and maintenance trust) the income tax liability at the trust rates will not start until the trust starts.

  If the executors pay income into the discretionary trust from the executry the trustees will have to pay additional income tax at the trust rates on the income they receive from the executry at 40 per cent (32.4 per cent on non-tax recoverable tax dividends). If the executors pay the income direct to the trust beneficiaries during the executry administration, there is no liability for the additional income tax.

  The trustees' CGT exemption is half the executors' rate. The change of exemption applies from the start of the trust. The executors may have the full exemption in the same year as the trustees' half exemption starts. Both exemptions may be used to minimise the CGT. Executors and trustees are all liable for CGT at the trust rate of 40 per cent.

Stamp duty

As regards non-heritable subjects all deeds executed after May 1, 1987 **8–26** are exempt subject to the appropriate certificate appearing on the Deed (Stamp Duty (Exempt Instruments) Regulations 1987, Schedule Category M or Category L).

As regards heritable subjects the Stamp Duty Land Tax regime applies. The SDLT60 "certification that no Land Transaction Return is required for a land transaction" form is used for this (the first box, i.e. transfer or conveyance of freehold interest in land (in Scotland, ownership . . .) for no chargeable consideration, is "ticked").

Form of deeds

There is no statutory style or form. The May 1985 Press Release **8–27** approach would be taken by the HMRC provided the deed identifies the deceased's estate which is being varied and does vary it.

There can be:

    (a) an Assignation by one or more persons of their rights another (including in Scotland a partial assignation);

    (b) a Discharge/disclaimer where rights are given up or renounced by a beneficiary (including in Scotland a partial discharge/disclaimer);

    (c) a Variation where there are several people involved;

    (d) a Variation by Court of Session under the Trusts (Scotland) Act 1961.

More than one deed?

See HMRC Press Release (May 1985)—one deed to be regarded as **8–28** irrevocable and amending deeds will not usually be accepted (*Russell v IRC*, 1988 S.T.C. 195).

Notice to the HMRC

As indicated above, in appropriate cases, i.e. where there is immediate **8–29** effect on tax this requires to be given within six months from the date of the deed effecting the deed of variation.

OTHER RELEVANT STATUTORY PROVISIONS

Section 93 of the IHTA 1984—discharge/disclaimer of settled property

A discharge/disclaimer of an interest such as a reversionary interest in a **8–30** trust will not be a transfer of value for IHT. This does not extend to a variation. There is no time limit in the section however, apart from s.93, the variation provisions of s.142 do not apply to trust property even if the deceased had power of appointment or a liferent. (Section 142(5): Equivalent provision to s.93 in the TCGA 1992, s.76(1)).

ALIMENTARY LIFERENTS

8–31 General law provides that if an alimentary liferent is accepted it cannot be renounced or varied but if it has not been accepted then any benefit can be disclaimed (*Douglas-Hamilton v Hamilton's Trustees*, 1961 S.C. 205). It is important to ensure therefore that no benefit is conferred if there is any prospect of variation to have a court petition under the 1961 Act. The legislation is complex but the idea is that income should be taxed on the person receiving the income in the year of assessment it is received (ICTA 1988, ss.698(IA), (1B),(2), 695(3) and 696(5)).

POSTPONED VESTING AND CONTINGENT RIGHTS

8–32 Difficulties may crop up in the type of situation where, e.g. the liferent is being renounced and yet vesting of fee is postponed until termination of the liferent; as the fee is *in pendente*, it may not be clear who will actually take the fee, e.g. a Will gives a widow liferent with fee "to such of my issue as survive my wife". Strictly speaking, e.g. that will require a petition to the court under the Trusts (Scotland) Act 1961, because of the possibility of unborn beneficiaries. In practice the HMRC may accept the position if the variation provides for unborn issue by an actuarial division and contingency insurance provides for a fund for such issue. Apart from the IHT aspect, if the trustees proceed without a court petition then it should be remembered that under general principles they may be at risk. It may be advisable to have indemnities from the beneficiaries against any future unborn issue claiming that there has been a breach of trust. If there is a postponed vesting and intermediate income as in *Collie and Buyers*, 1981 S.L.T. 191, interests in possession may be unexpectedly created by operation of law in some cases with consequent possible charge. **It may, in fact, be better practice now to draft liferent wills so that there is no postponed vesting and the fee vests on the testator's death rather than the termination of the liferent**. Strictly speaking, however, in general law, a variation by consent is only possible when all parties are of full age and capacity and all consent to it and in any other circumstances the executors are at risk.

LEGAL RIGHTS

8–33 General treatment: This is related to the question of post death arrangements as the HMRC's view is that legal rights may be deemed claimed unless positively disclaimed within two years of the death, i.e. the provisions of s.142 of the IHTA and s.62(6) of the TCGA can apply to legal rights.

> **Danger Warning!!!**
>
> Attention is drawn to s.3(3) of the IHTA 1984, in terms of which a deliberate omission to assert legal rights may be treated as a transfer of value if gratuitous and made outwith two years of the death.

EXAMPLE DEED OF VARIATION

Style

DEED OF VARIATION
Relative to estate of the late
**ARTHUR DAIRSIE
REDGAUNTLET**

late of Johnston House, Maryhill,
Glasgow
(hereinafter referred to as "the
said deceased")
by

(FIRST) **MRS JEAN DEANS** or
REDGAUNTLET
residing at Johnston House, aforesaid
("Mrs Redgauntlet")
and

(SECOND) **RODERICK
McGREGOR REDGAUNTLET**
residing Waverly House, Galashiels.
and

(THIRD) Mrs Redgauntlet
as Executor of the said deceased
said deceased ("the Executor")

WHEREAS

(PRIMO)	The parties to this deed are as designed above. The said deceased died on 1997 leaving a Settlement dated 1st May and registered in the Sheriff Court, Books of the Commissariot of Glasgow & Strathkelvin on 1st July 2005. A copy thereof is annexed and signed as relative hereto.
(SECUNDO)	Mrs Redgauntlet was appointed executor in terms of the deceased's settlement, conform to Confirmation granted by the Sheriff of Glasgow & Strathkelvin on 2nd July 2005 1995.
(TERTIO)	The deceased was survived by Mrs Redgauntlet, his wife and by Mr Redgauntlet his only son and only child who are the only persons who have legal rights against the estate. Mrs Redgauntlet is the residuary beneficiary and there were no other legacies.
(QUARTO)	Both Mrs Redgauntlet and Mr Redgauntlet are of full legal capacity and the only persons whose rights are, in terms of the settlement, being varied herewith. The parties, having read the Settlement of the said deceased and being of age and sound mind and having been advised that they are entitled to seek independent legal advice

	have elected not to do so and wish to vary the distribution of the estate laid down by the Settlement by Deed of variation under Section 142 of the Inheritance Act 1984 and Section 62 (7) Taxation of Chargeable Gains Act 1992 as follows: **NOW THEREFORE THE PARTIES AGREE**:

The Settlement of the said deceased is hereby varied by the insertion of the following clause:

Trustees	(FIRST) "I appoint my wife, the said Mrs Jean Deans or Redgauntlet, and my son, **RODERICK McGREGOR REDGAUNTLET**, residing at Waverley House, Galashiels, to be my Trustees and I direct my Trustees to hold such sum or property to such value as will exhaust the Nil Rate band of IHT set out in Schedule 1 to the IHT Act 1984 or any similar statutory successor, after taking into account
	lifetime gifts made by me which are for IHT purposes aggregable with or deemed to be part of my executry estate
	legacies other than those exempt from IHT
	funds in Trusts which are aggregable for IHT purposes with my executry estate other than those exempt from IHT and
	any claims to legitim except claims discharged without consideration after my death, as to all of which my Trustees shall be the sole judges (which sum or property is referred to as "the Discretionary Fund") for such (One) or more of my wife, the said Mrs Jean Deans or Redgauntlet, (Two) my issue, including adopted issue (Three) any person who is or was a spouse of any such issue and (Four) any Trust established by any person for the benefit (whether an income or a capital or a discretionary nature of any one or more of the foregoing persons (all of whom are referred to as "the beneficiaries") and in such share or shares in proportions as my Trustees may by Minute or Minutes at any time or times within two years my wife's death, determine, Declaring that my Trustees may by such minute or minutes grant legacies, shares of residue, interests in income or prospective or contingent interests of any kind in the whole or any part or parts of the Discretionary Fund subject to such provisions as they may determine, including but without prejudice to the foregoing generality provisions as to the accumulation of income, the vesting of capital in any beneficiary, the granting to any beneficiary or any other person of powers to appoint rights to income or capital, and the continuation of their discretionary powers;
	that my Trustees may renounce for themselves and their successors in office the power to exercise any of the foregoing powers as if the same were vested in them beneficially and not as trustees;

	that until the expiry of the period of two years from the date of my wife's death, or until the date or dates when any such determination or determinations take effect or the power to make a determination is renounced by them, my Trustees shall pay and apply the whole of the income of the Discretionary Fund without any apportionment being made to or for behoof of any or more of the beneficiaries in such shares or proportions and in such manner as they may determine with power during the said period or until the said date or dates to accumulate the income for twenty one years; and that in the event of my Trustees having failed to make a determination taking effect in relation to the whole or any part of the residue before the expiry of two years from the date of my wife's death or having renounced the power to make such a determination they shall on and from the expiry of the said period or the date of such renunciation hold the whole or such part of the Discretionary Fund as part of the residue of my estate as if my wife had predeceased me.
Powers	My Trustees shall have the fullest powers of and in regard to retention, realisation, investment, appropriation, transfer of property without realisation, and management of my estate as if they were absolute beneficial owners; and shall have power to do everything they may consider necessary or expedient for the administration of the trust; and in particular and without prejudice to these general powers my Trustees shall have power; to retain, sell, purchase, lease or hire the estate or any part thereof;
	OTHER USUAL POWERS OR REFERENCE TO SCHEDULE
Immunities	My Trustees shall not be liable for depreciation in value of the property in my estate, nor for omissions or errors in judgement, nor for neglect in management, nor for insolvency of debtors, nor for the acts, omissions, neglects or defaults of each other or of any agent employed by them."
	(SECOND) Mrs Redgauntlet and Mr Redgauntlet thereby renounce all legal rights competent to them in respect of *jus relictae legitim* or otherwise and accept the terms set out in the will and in this Deed of variation.
	(THIRD) None of the expenses of these presents shall be paid from the said deceased's estate.
	(FOURTH) The executor consents to and concurs in the provisions hereof which are hereby declared irrevocable.
	(FIFTH) The parties hereto elect and give written notice to the Board of HMRC in terms of Section 142(2) of the said IHT Act 1984 that Section 142(1) shall retrospectively apply to these presents and the parties hereto do hereby give notice to the HMRC of their intention to

	have the foregoing variation treated as if it had been effected by the said deceased. The parties also give notice in terms of Section 62(7) Taxation of Chargeable Gains Act 1992 that Section 62(6) of said last-mentioned Act shall respectively apply to these presents to this will of the said deceased.
	(SIXTH) The parties hereto certify that the transfer in respect of which this transaction is made is one which falls within Category L or Category M of the Schedule to the Stamp Duty (Exempt Instruments) Regulations 1987: IN WITNESS WHEREOF

Chapter Nine

THE FUTURE AND CONCLUSION

"There may be trouble ahead, but. . ."[1]

CHILD TRUST FUND

AS mentioned the Government has recognised the advantages and **9–01** underlined the use of trusts under The Child Trust Fund. Ostensibly an initiative for ingraining the habit of saving, it is a new savings and investment account for children born on or after September 1, 2002 if child benefit has been awarded to the child's parents and they live in the UK. There is no need for parents to claim the Child Trust Fund ("CTF")—once a child benefit award has been made and eligibility for the CTF accepted, a voucher worth £250 for the initial Government payment will be sent to the child benefit claimant, who will usually be the parent. A person with parental responsibility for the child can then use the voucher to open a CTF account for that child. An additional £250 will be paid into the CTF accounts of children in families eligible for full Child Tax Credit ("CTC") with household income at or below the CTC income threshold (currently £13,480). Parents receive an information pack giving them details of what they need to do, and information is available on a dedicated website and from a CTF helpline. There will be a range of CTF accounts to suit everyone's needs. All providers have made available a stakeholder CTF account. Charges for this account are kept low and the account is designed to give good returns over 18 years by investing in the stock market. The risks are controlled by making sure that there is a mix of investments and that they are less risky as the child nears the age of 18. If an account is not opened before the voucher expires (usually 12 months from issue) the HMRC will open a stakeholder CTF account for that child. Special arrangements have been made for "looked after" children (as child benefit cannot be claimed for these children) to ensure that they do not miss out on a CTF account. Parents, family and friends will be able to contribute up to a total of £1,200 a year to a CTF account. Income arising on the money and investments in a CTF account is exempt from tax.

The money in a child's CTF account can only be taken out by the child on reaching the age of 18. There is no access to the money until then. The account and the money in it belongs to the child, although it is managed by a person with parental responsibility until the child is 16.

---

[1] Irving Berlin, Follow the Fleet.

When children reach 16 they will manage their own CTF accounts. When a child reaches the age of 18 there will be no restriction on how they use the money in their CTF account. Financial education is a key part of the CTF and all children will receive financial education to help them manage their money with future needs in mind. Information will be available for parents, teachers and children over the lifetime of a child's CTF account. The CTF account and the income and gains from that account will not affect family benefit and tax credits during the time the CTF account is open.

However, of more relevance to trust practitioners was the new reform of charities powers and related matters in the Charities and Trustee Investment (Scotland) Act 2005. The Act was in four parts of which only Part 3 (and to a lesser extent Part 1) are of interest to us.

> Part 1 – Charities
> Part 2 – Fundraising for benevolent bodies
> Part 3 – Investment powers of trustees
> Part 4 – General and supplementary

CHARITIES AND TRUSTEE INVESTMENT (SCOTLAND) ACT 2005

Part 3: Investment powers of trustees

9–02 Some of these have been referred to in chapter five under the section Powers of Trustees. **Sections 92 to 94** provide an extension to the investment powers of trustees (of all trusts, whether charities or not). The Trusts (Scotland) Act 1921 is amended by adding a provision (s.92(2)) allowing a trustee to make any kind of investment of the trust estate (including an investment in heritable property). The effect is that trustees will generally have the same powers of investment as if they were the beneficial owners of the trust estate. Subsection (2) also provides a new wide power for trustees to acquire heritable property for any other reason. These wider powers are subject to any restriction or exclusion imposed by the trust deed.

Part 1, Chapter 2: Scottish charity register, s.122.

9–03 This chapter sets out a new definition of charity, removes the previous presumption of public benefit and creates a publicly accessible register of all bodies eligible to operate as charities in Scotland. It is possible that there may be additional non-charitable organisations which will seek charity status when the new definition is enacted and some current charities may either lose their charitable status or voluntarily seek to surrender it. As the new definition is largely in keeping with the existing definition, the executors do not however anticipate any significant change to either the size or growth of the charity sector as a result of this.

Earlier this year HMRC published proposed legislation under the heading of "Modernising the tax system for trusts". This was on the web at *www.hmrc.gov.uk/trusts/mod-tax-system-trusts.htm*. The legislation was, with alterations and precious few concessions, incorporated in the

Finance Act 2006. It is likely that there will be more difficulties in the reviews of tax. John Riches, Chair of STEP Technical Committee indicated one major problem regarding passing on business assets to the next generation. An accidental consequence (of the changes to the trust tax law) could be:

> "to restrict the ability for individuals to give business property standing at a gain to their dependent children under age eighteen. The proposals give rise to a bizarre situation where an individual can give business property standing at a gain to his or her children without capital gains tax if they are over eighteen or under eighteen so they become absolutely entitled to it on their eighteenth birthday, but not if the individual wants to put in place more sophisticated trusts which are designed to protect children over eighteen from having access to significant funds at an unduly early age."

On November 18, 2004, Royal Assent was given to the Civil Partnership Act 2004. This bewildering Act introduces into the UK (not just Scotland) a new domestic vehicle, known as the civil partnership. This is designed to allow same sex couples a conduit to the rights and liabilities attaching to opposite sex couples whose relationship is recognised by the state as marriage. In all fairness the Westminster Parliament, and the Scottish Executive, were at pains to emphasise that the Civil Partnership Act does not create a "gay marriage". Instead it produces a new type of institution: although Parliament and our "user friendly" Scottish Executive proclaim that civil partnership shall be limited to same sex couples while marriage remains limited to opposite sex couples, nevertheless marriage legislation is the model followed in the Civil Partnership Act; much of the legislation for marriages is used for civil partners. However it is blatantly obvious that the two institutions are dissimilar and various marriage rules have either not been extended to civil partnership or have been applied in more or less modified form. On February 7, 2005 the Scottish Executive published the Family Law (Scotland) Bill, which incorporated various amendments to the Civil Partnership Act, but differences between opposite sex and same sex couples will subsist and will require to be factored into drafting of wills and trusts.

WHAT ARE THE SCOTTISH LAW COMMISSION DOING ABOUT TRUSTS?

In a very helpful article "The Scottish Law Commission's Trust Law **9–04** Review", by David Nichols,[2] Dr Nichols gives his opinion that trusts are very useful to the commercial and the private client lawyer, but the relevant law in Scotland is in need of reform. He gave an overview of what the Commission had achieved in the year 2003:

> "In September 2003 the Scottish Law Commission issued the first two discussion papers in its review of trust law. The review focused

---

[2] Nichols, D. 2003. "The Scottish Law Commission's trust law review", J.L.S.S. 48(11), 30–31.

on those areas causing difficulty in practice. The Law Society, the Society of Trust and Estate Practitioners, our Advisory Group and many other bodies and individuals had helped the Commission to identify the problem areas. The first paper, Breach of Trust (No 123) dealt with breach of trust, the standard of care expected of lay and professional trustees, and relief from liability via immunity clauses or the courts. The second, Apportionment of Trust Receipts and Outgoings (No 124) looked at the more technical area of apportionment and allocation of trust receipts and outgoings between different classes of beneficiaries, such as liferentors and fiars. They and other papers may be downloaded from the Commission's website (*www.scotlawcom.gov.uk*) or bought from The Stationery Office. The consultation period lasted until the end of that year. A third discussion paper is to be published early next year, completing the first phase of the review. It will examine trustees' powers in administering the trust estate (apart from investment powers), the appointment and removal of trustees and the role of the courts in the administration of trusts. Trustees' powers to invest and to buy land have already been the subject of a report, Trustees' Powers and Duties, issued jointly with the Law Commission in 1999. The English recommendations were speedily implemented by the Trustee Act 2000, but the Scottish recommendations have not been acted on. Next year the Commission intends to move on to the second phase of the review and look at trusts and whether they should have legal personality, accumulation of income and the remedies of beneficiaries."

The Scottish Law Commission, in its published Seventh Programme (2005-09) has included a review of trusts in its programme of work. It lists trusts as one of its current projects. The project is under the direction of Professor Joe Thomson and Mr Colin Tyre Q.C. (who is to have special responsibility for variation and termination of trusts).

Two discussion papers are in the course of preparation on the nature and constituion of trusts and the second is to examine the dual parimony theory of "trustees' ownership of trust property" and allied subjects. A discussion paper on the variation and termination of trusts was published in December 2005.[3] Other papers on beneficiaries' remedies are also planned along with a study of excessive accumulations.

It seems reasonable to expect a flow of legislative reform which will bring Scottish trust in line and up to date with other jurisdictions.

As Eccles put it:

"It is unlikely that the constitution and administration of modern trusts will be greatly affected by the extension and clarification of trustees powers and duties. It may operate as a useful reminder to trustees and advisers to review portfolios, clearly communicate and consider decisions that are being made. Nevertheless, rather than provide a set of provisions that proactively develop the law, the 2005

---

[3] DP129.

Act's intentions appear to be more modest: to ensure that the default law of trusts keeps apace with contemporary investment practice and provides parity to less modern trust deeds while ensuring trustees are aware of their overarching duties to consider the trust fund's performance. The Scottish Law Commission is currently undertaking a comprehensive review with the aim of providing a more appropriate, responsive and coherent default law of trusts. The overhaul of the 1921 Act and a coherent updating is required, especially as the law of trusts operates in a more complex investment climate and has a greater exposure to commercial and corporate transactions."

The Future—Trusts Being Set by Attorneys

Commenting on the case of *T, Applicant*, Eccles and Miller underline the **9–05** problems for the profession:

". . . Sheriff Baird[4] helpfully sets out the potential effect on the decision to future applications. It is apparent that this was designed to highlight the need for practitioners to take proactive steps to consider whether or not an application should be made under the 2000 Act. An underlying issue is whether or not practitioners are required to make (or at least to advise potential applicants to make) an application under the 2000 Act to authorise the taking of actions which accord with past and previous wishes and which benefit the adult (analysed purposively, objectively and holistically). Every situation must be considered on its own merits and the area of incapable adults is not one where precedent, it is submitted, should be required to be strictly adhered to. However, it is clear that *T, Applicant* confirms that though the 2000 Act must be considered carefully, it offers many solutions and opportunities.

As Sheriff Baird alludes to, the decision may place greater responsibilities on practitioners to actively consider advising applicants on the uses of the orders available under the 2000 Act. Whilst it may be extending the law of negligence too far to argue that solicitors may be held liable to 'disappointed potential applicants' (especially when the effect of *Robertson v Fleming* (1861) 4 Macq 167 has not been completely removed in respect of disappointed beneficiaries, notwithstanding the decision in *Holmes v Bank of Scotland*, 2002 S.L.T. 544), Sheriff Baird's comments crystallise the need to consider proactively and also enthusiastically the options available under the 2000 Act. It is of note that Sheriff Baird rehearsed the approval given in *B, Applicant*, 2005 S.L.T. (Sh Ct) 95, of the comments in Adult Incapacity that 'advisers are likely to be under a professional duty to test [the limits of when an order will be granted]'"(para 10–34). Therefore, practitioners must be aware of the rise of the 2000 Act to carry out actions connected with tax,

---

[4] *T, Applicant*, Alan W. Eccles. Lisa Miller. S.L.T. 2006, 1, 1–7.

financial and property matters such as to execute testamentary writings and dispositions and, as referred to above discharge legal rights.

Practitioners should also review files of clients whom they are aware have lost capacity and consider whether steps should be taken under the 2000 Act. It is probable, of course, that when capacity is lost, practitioners will be making applications for full guardianship orders. However, the terms of the powers sought should be carefully considered. *T, Applicant* raises the prospect that 'standard' management powers will not be sufficient and other powers should be sought depending on the circumstances. Further powers, tailored to the needs of the adult, may also be required to be applied for as the guardianship develops and circumstances change. Full information gathering is also essential."

TAX

It may be that the introduction of a much stiffer regime for IHT for, say, liferent trust will presage a similar tax treatment for income tax purposes.

FINALLY

9–06 As Dr Nichols puts it:

"Trust law is not glamorous or vote-catching. Nevertheless it is important that Scots trust law is modernised and kept up to date. Trusts play a substantial role in wealth creation, wealth retention and wealth distribution. They are a very useful piece of legal machinery in the commercial and private client fields. If Scotland cannot provide a trust law that meets the demands of the 21st century then people and their money will go elsewhere to a more progressive and forward-looking country."[5]

---

[5] "The Scottish Law Commission's Trust Law Review" by David Nichols *The Journal*, November 2003, page 30.

INDEX TO APPENDIX OF STYLES

A.1	Checklist/questionnaire	211
A.2	Letter of engagement	215
A.3	Deed of trust	218
A.4	Backletter	219
A.5	Deed of variation	220
A.6	Deed of variation incorporating discharge of destination	227
A.7	Style of disposition incorporating sale of one-half share of house by trustees to surviving spouse	231
A.8	Style of standard security over one-half pro-indiviso share by surviving spouse	235
A.9	Old fashioned trust disposition	236
A.10	Deed of assumption	239
A.11	Discharge by beneficiary	240
A.12	Discretionary trust	241
A.13	Deed of assumption and conveyance	246
A.14	Deed of assumption and conveyance incorporating Resignation	247
A.15	Style of informal letter to trustees	248

A.1 CHECKLIST/QUESTIONNAIRE

Instructions for trusts	
LEDGER A/C NO:	
PARTNER:	
FEE EARNER:	
DATE:	
DATE REQUIRED:	
Personal Details	
CLIENT	**CLIENT'S SPOUSE/ PARTNER**
NAME:	**NAME:**
ADDRESS:	**ADDRESS:**
POSTCODE: **TEL NO:** **DATE OF BIRTH:**	**POSTCODE:** **TEL NO:** **DATE OF BIRTH:**
Has terms of engagement letter been sent out Y/N	
Has terms of engagement letter been acknowledged? Y/N	
Has proof of identity been obtained? Y/N	
Family/Financial Information	
IS CLIENT MARRIED? **HAS CLIENT ENTERED INTO A CIVIL PARTNERSHIP?** **IS CLIENT IN A COHABITATION?**	
CHILDREN [*brief details—number and age*]	
GRANDCHILDREN [*brief details—number and age*]	
NEAREST RELATIVE IF NO SPOUSE/CHILDREN **CURRENT VALUE OF ESTATE (TO NEAREST £10K)** **House:** Owned/Rented?	

Title Joint & Survivor

Savings: Sole £	Spouse £	Joint £
(Bank, B.Soc. NSCs, etc)		

Stock Exchange:

Life Policies etc:

IS LIFETIME NIL RATE BAND AVAILABLE?

PLANNING REQUIREMENTS?

WHAT DOES CLIENT WANT TO ACHIEVE BY TRUST?
    Tax Saving
    Financial Provision for:
                        Spouse/partner/cohabitee
                        Children
                        Grandchildren
                        Nephews/nieces
                        Others
                        Charities

TRUST DEED **TRUSTEES:** (1)	(2)
NAME:	**NAME:**
ADDRESS:	**ADDRESS:**
POSTCODE:	**POSTCODE:**

TEL: Home
    Work
	TEL: Home
	    Work

(3)	
NAME:	
ADDRESS:	
TEL: Home **Work**	
ADDRESS:	
POSTCODE: **TEL: Home** **Work**	
Is Will Held? **Have terms been checked?** **Titles destinations?**	

BENEFICIARIES	
TO: **(1)** **NAME:**	**(2)** **NAME:**
ADDRESS:	**ADDRESS:**
ITEM(S)	**ITEM(S)**
TO: **(3)** **NAME:**	**(4)** **NAME:**
ADDRESS:	**ADDRESS:**
ITEM(S)	**ITEM(S)**
SEND DRAFT	**YES/NO**
SIGNING ARRANGEMENTS?	**HERE or SEND OUT**

FEE QUOTED £	
NEW CLIENTS/EXISTING – IDENTIFICATION	
FINANCIAL ADVICE – referred to: **WILL** **POWER OF ATTORNEY?**	*[Terms of business letter sent]* *[Details]*

A.2 LETTER OF ENGAGEMENT

Date:

Dear

TERMS OF BUSINESS LETTER
Trust deed

We are solicitors in Scotland and as such subscribe to the Law Society of Scotland Guarantee Fund.

We refer to your recent meeting with our Mr Cheatham. We confirm your instructions to prepare a trust deed. The information we require is [. . .].

The Law Society of Scotland has recommended that we set out in writing our terms of business and these are as follows:

1. General

● *Contacting us*

The business will be conducted by our Mr Cheatham and other colleagues. Our office hours are Monday to Friday 9.15 am to 12.30 pm and 1.45 pm to 5 pm. Consultations outwith the office hours are available by arrangement. We are happy to receive information by email, but please note that this is not inspected on a constant basis and while we will attempt to reply as soon as possible immediate replies are not always possible.

● *How long will it take?*

The nature of the work makes it difficult to estimate precisely in many cases how long something will take to complete. Often, however, the speed which we can complete a piece of work is directly affected by the co-operation we receive from other people outwith our control. It is in our interest as much as yours to complete this as quickly and efficiently as possible. If you have not heard recently from the person dealing with your work, then please ring us and ask.

● *Confidentiality*

Information passed to us is kept confidential and will not be disclosed to third parties save as authorised by you or required by law.

● *Financial services*

We only hold an incidental financial business certificate from the Law Society. In effect this does not allow us to give advice but only to pass it on any instructions from clients **where this is incidental to other business conducted by us**.

● *Accounts*

We will issue our Account at the end of the matter. However, we reserve the right to issue an interim fee note after three months.

Mr Cheatham's rate of remuneration for this type of work is of the order of £xxx per hour; to this will be added VAT and necessary outlays.

● *Independent fee assessment*

The Auditor of Court or the Auditor of The Royal Faculty of Procurators in Glasgow is always available to provide a complete independent assessment of a fair fee for a piece of legal work carried out. On occasions, in order to ensure that a file has been correctly charged, we may voluntarily send the file to the Auditor. Unless agreed with you beforehand, we will pay the Auditor's fee. Should you at any time wish to dispute or challenge the amount of a fee charged by us then you are entitled to ask to have the Auditor charge the fee independently. In that case, both sides are bound by the fee as fixed by the Auditor. If the Auditor reduces the amount of the original fee, we will only charge that reduced amount and we will pay the Auditor's costs. If he confirms that our fee is correct or undercharged, then you will be responsible for the Auditor's costs.

● *Client identification/money laundering*

The Law Society Regulations regarding Money Laundering and Client Identification require us to be satisfied as to the identity of our clients.

Before we can proceed to act on your behalf, we require to comply with the regulations. We enclose two lists detailing forms of identification, which are sufficient for this purpose. In this regard, we would be grateful if you could provide **one item** from **each** of the lists below: We confirm that it will be returned to you as soon as possible.

List A	List B
A current signed passport Current UK photocard/driving licence	Telephone Bill Gas Bill Water Bill
Current full UK driving licence	Electricity Bill Credit Card Statement Bank/Building Society Statement Pension Book

● *Restrictions*

We would point out that while IHT saving suggestions may be made by Mr Cheatham, the work carried out may impact on other taxes, e.g. income tax, capital gains tax, pre-owned assets tax and stamp duty. Unless you specifically request it from Mr Cheatham we will assume you will take advice on these from other advisors.

● *Your co-operation*

When we request papers or deeds sent for signature, it goes without saying that it would be helpful to have these back at your earliest convenience.

It may be that there are time limits which have to be met.

Holidays—if you are to be on holiday perhaps you could let us have a note of the dates and a contact number or email address. By the same token if moving house please let us have a note of any time you are incommunicado. This may the time at the date of entry when BT terminates your service at the precise moment we are trying to contact you urgently!

- *Finally*

Our aim is to provide a service, which is satisfactory in every respect. However, if you have any concerns about the manner in which work is being carried out on your behalf, please contact our Client Relations Partner (Mr Smiley) who will be happy to discuss your concerns.

If you have any queries regarding the foregoing letter or otherwise please do not hesitate to contact us.

Yours sincerely

A.3 Deed of Trust

I, MRS ARI DAVIDSON, residing at Twenty two Oberon Street, Glasgow, CONSIDERING that I have recently concluded missives with [*insert details of seller*] to purchase ALL and WHOLE the flatted dwelling-house subjects known as Twenty two Oberon Street, Glasgow and that title thereto has been taken in my name; FURTHER CONSIDERING that FIVE THOUSAND FOUR HUNDRED POUNDS (£5,400) STERLING of the purchase price of ELEVEN THOUSAND FOUR HUNDRED POUNDS (£11,400) STERLING was provided by my son, LEO DAVIDSON, residing at Sixty four Thrade Street, Newton Mearns, THEREFORE I DECLARE that I hold the title to the said flatted dwelling-house subjects at Twenty two Oberon Street, aforesaid in trust for my son the said Leo Davidson and undertake when called upon to do so to grant a Disposition in his favour; And I consent to registration for preservation and execution: IN WITNESS WHEREOF

A.4 BACKLETTER

WE, THOMAS JERICHO and MRS HESTER WALLACE or JERICHO, Spouses, both residing at Nine Bletchley Park, Glasgow CONSIDERING (Primo) that we have purchased our Local Authority dwelling-house at Nine, Bletchley Park, Glasgow, hereinafter referred to as "the said subjects" at a price taking into account the discounting provisions of NINE THOUSAND FOUR HUNDRED AND FIFTY POUNDS (£9,450.00) STERLING, (Secundo) that the said price has been or will be paid and provided by our daughter, MRS CLAIRE JERICHO or ROMILLY, residing at Nine Stuttgart Crescent, Bearsden, Glasgow, (Tertio) that it has been agreed that the title to the property will be taken in our joint names and that both of us will be allowed to remain in the subjects during the whole of our respective lives without payment of rent in respect thereof, (Quarto) that we will, on demand grant and bind our executors and assignees, if required, to convey a clear unencumbered title to the said subjects and without prejudice thereto grant a Disposition of the said subjects in favour of the said Mrs Claire Jericho or Romilly and her executors, assignees and disponees and all necessary Affidavits, Renunciations and others as are required in terms of the Matrimonial Homes (Family Protection) (Scotland) Act 1981 as amended, (Quinto) notwithstanding the foregoing [*insert any other arrangements*]: IN WITNESS WHEREOF

A.5 DEED OF VARIATION

This deed of variation might be suitable for a variation to a deed where there are two grandchildren of full age, one of whom has certain difficulties, which will make it impossible to live at home when his mother passes away.

DEED OF VARIATION relative to the estate of the late **MRS EUPHEMIA WHITE or BLACK** late of 5, Pink Court, Glasgow, ("the said deceased")

by

(FIRST) **MRS MARGARET BLACK or BROWN** residing at 11 Grey Street, Helensburgh, ("Mrs. Brown")

and

(SECOND) **DAVID BEIGE**, Chartered Accountant, residing sometime at 22 Indigo Court, Glasgow, **WILLIAM GREEN**, residing at 7 Blue Street Milngavie, Glasgow, and **MISS FAWN SCARLETT**, Solicitor, Glasgow, the Executors of the said deceased ("the executors")

WHEREAS

(PRIMO) The parties to this deed are as designed above. The said deceased died at Dollar on the Seventh day of June 2001, leaving a Trust Disposition and Settlement dated 1st May 1998 and registered in the Sheriff Court Books of the Commissariot of Tayside Central and Fife in Scotland on 4th September 2001.

(SECUNDO) The executors were appointed in terms of the deceased's Trust Disposition and Settlement conform to Confirmation granted by the Sheriff of Tayside, Central and Fife on 4th September 2001.

(TERTIO) The said deceased was survived by Mrs Brown and by Mrs Brown's children, who are **CAIN BROWN** and **ABEL BROWN**, both residing at 11 Grey Street, aforesaid. Mrs Brown is the only daughter and only child of the said deceased and is the only person who has legal rights against the Estate of the said deceased; she is the Residuary Beneficiary.

(QUARTO) Mrs Brown being of full legal capacity and the only person whose rights are, in terms of the said Trust Disposition and Settlement, being varied, hereby having read the said Trust Disposition and Settlement of the said deceased and being of age and sound mind and having been advised that she is entitled to seek independent legal advice and has elected not to do so and wishes to vary the distribution of the estate laid down by the said Trust Disposition and Settlement by Deed of variation under Section 142 of the IHT Act 1984 and Section 62(7) of the Taxation of Chargeable Gains Act 1992 as follows: NOW THEREFORE THE PARTIES AGREE:

(FIRST) The said Trust Disposition and Settlement of the said deceased is hereby varied by the addition of the following clauses:

"I direct my Trustees and Executors to pay over as soon as convenient to them after my death, free of IHT and any other Government Duties exigible on my death and without interest a legacy of **TWO HUNDRED THOUSAND POUNDS (£200,000) STERLING** to my grandson the said Cain Brown (otherwise designed as "Cain")

and

I direct my Trustees and Executors to pay and assign to my daughter, the said Mrs Margaret Brown, residing at Eleven Grey Street, Helensburgh, the said David Beige, Chartered Accountant residing at 22 Indigo Drive, Glasgow and MISS SKYE BLUE, Solicitor, Dumbarton, and to such other person or persons, body or bodies, as may hereafter be appointed or assumed and to the survivors and survivor of them as my Trustees for the purposes aftermentioned (the major number from time to time resident in the United Kingdom being a *quorum* and the power to act of any Trustee who is an individual being suspended during absence from the United Kingdom) and to the assignees of my Trustees (all hereinafter referred to as "my trustees") the sum of **TWO HUN-DRED THOUSAND POUNDS (£200,000) STERLING** (or property to such value) (which sum or property is referred to as the "Discretionary Fund") for the personal support, maintenance and education or otherwise or for the benefit of the Family Beneficiaries defined below or such one or more of them to the exclusion of the others or other in such manner and, if more than one, in such shares as my trustees from time to time in their absolute discretion think fit.

"Family Beneficiaries" means my children, grandchildren and remoter issue, my nieces and nephews and the spouses, widows or widowers of any such persons.

My trustees shall have the fullest powers of and in regard to retention, realisation, investment, appropriation, transfer of property without real-isation and management of my estate as if they were absolute beneficial owners; and shall have power to do everything they may consider necessary or expedient for administration of the trust; And in particular and without prejudice to these general powers my trustees shall have power to:

(ONE)
(a) to the extent that they deem it appropriate to do so, meet from the Discretionary Fund the funeral expenses (including the cost of a Memorial) of any of the Family Beneficiaries.

(b) invest the whole or any part thereof in the purchase or improvement of any dwelling-house or flat to permit the same to be used as a residence for any of the Family Beneficiaries whether alone or jointly with any other person or persons without being required to insist upon the payment by any person whether or not a joint occupier thereof but my Trustees shall have an absolute discretion as to the terms on which they permit the flat or dwelling-house to be occupied.

(c) exercise the powers of investment without seeking to balance the interest of Family Beneficiaries entitled to capital and income respectively.

(d) invest in corporeal moveables notwithstanding that the value of the Discretionary Fund may become depleted and to permit any one or more of the Family Beneficiaries to have the use and enjoyment of any corporeal moveable in such manner and subject to such conditions as my trustees may consider reasonable without being liable to account for any consequential loss.

(e) to raise capital out of the Discretionary Fund and to lend it on such terms as to interest, security and repayment and otherwise as they think fit to any person to whom or charitable or other body to which they consider that it would be in the interests of the Family Beneficiaries to make a loan without being liable for any consequent loss of capital.

(f) to apply any part or parts of the capital of the Discretionary Fund or towards meeting the cost of:

- Altering or adapting any residence or accommodation in the ownership of any person or body for the more convenient occupation thereof as a whole.
- Purchasing any domestic appliances or procuring domestic assistance for any of the Family Beneficiaries or persons with whom they reside from time to time.
- Purchasing caravans or motor cars appropriate to the needs of any Family Beneficiaries and the person or persons with whom they from time to time reside.
- Holidays for any of the Family Beneficiaries or the expenses incurred by any person or persons to enable them to accompany any beneficiary on holiday or the provision of holidays unaccompanied by them for any person who bears the daily burden of caring for them.
- To accepting the receipt of any person caring or having financial responsibility for any of the Family Beneficiaries as a full and sufficient Discharge for any money intended to be paid to them.

AND

(TWO)

Retention etc. (1)	to retain, sell, purchase, lease or hire the Discretionary Fund or any part thereof;
Investment (2)	to invest the whole or any part of the Discretionary Fund in heritable and leasehold property, investments, securities, insurance policies, deposits and other assets of whatever description, whether producing income or not, whether or not falling within the class of investments authorised for trust funds, whether or not payable to bearer and wherever situated;
Insurance (3)	to effect, maintain and acquire policies of insurance of whatever description; and to insure any property on whatever terms they think fit including on a first loss basis;
Management (of heritage) (4)	to administer and manage any heritable or real property forming part of the Discretionary Fund; to repair, maintain, renew and improve the same and to erect additional buildings and structures to grant, vary and terminate leases and rights of tenancy or occupancy; to plant, thin and cut down timber; to work or let minerals; all as my trustees may think proper and as if they were absolute owners of the Discretionary Fund;
Borrow and lend (5)	to borrow or lend with or without security; and to grant continue any guarantee or indemnity for the benefit of any of the Family Beneficiaries actual or prospective;
Occupation by beneficiaries (6)	to lend or allow to be used the whole or any part of the Discretionary Fund at such rate of interest or rent as they may consider appropriate, or free of interest or rent, to or by any person who is for the time being entitled to payment of a share of the income of the Discretionary Fund or to whom or for whose benefit the income may be paid or applied in the exercise of a discretion then available to my trustees;
Nominees (7)	to allow the Discretionary Fund or any part thereof to be registered in the names of or held or the documents of title to be held by any person, firm, corporation or other body as nominee of my trustees;

Delegation of investment management (8)	revocably to delegate any power or powers of making, managing, realising or otherwise dealing with anyinvestment or deposit comprised in the Discretionary Fund to any person or persons upon such terms as to remuneration or otherwise as my trustees may think fit and no trustee shall be responsible for the default of any such agent if the trustee in question employed him in good faith;
Additions (9)	to accept as an addition to the Discretionary Fund any other property which may be made over to them;
Appropriation (10)	to set apart and appropriate specific property of any description to represent the whole or part of the share, prospective or otherwise, of any beneficiary at such valuation as my trustees shall determine, so that thereafter the particular share or part shall have the full benefit of the appropriated investments or assets;
Settlement (11)	to settle with any beneficiary entitled to any part of the Discretionary Fund by conveying to him or her in satisfaction thereof either specific property or money, or partly one and partly the other, as to my trustees shall seem proper and at such valuation as they shall determine and to compel acceptance accordingly;
Conflict of interest (12)	to enter into any transaction or do any act otherwise authorised by law or by this deed notwithstanding that my trustee is or might be acting *auctor in rem suam* or with a conflict of interest between such trustee and himself as an individual or as trustee of any other trust or any partnership of which a trustee is a partner or any company of which a trustee is a shareholder or director or in relation to any combination of these capacities provided that the trustee or trustees with whom there is or may be any such conflict is or are not sole trustee or trustees;
Participation (13) in discretion	to participate in the exercise of any discretion granted to my trustees notwithstanding that a trustee is or may be a or the sole beneficiary in whose favour the discretion is then exercised provided that there is at least one trustee not so favoured;

Resignation (14)	to resign office notwithstanding any benefit hereunder;
Agents (15)	to appoint one or more of their own number to act as solicitor or agent or any other capacity and to allow him or them the same remuneration to which he or they would have been entitled if not a trustee or trustees;
Non-resident (16) trustees	to appoint any one or more trustees resident out of the United Kingdom and themselves to resign office;
Administration (17) abroad	to carry on the administration of the trust hereby created in some place out of the United Kingdom;
Renunciation (18)	to renounce for themselves and their successors in office the power to exercise any of the foregoing powers in this purpose as if the same were vested in them beneficially and not as trustees;
Immunities (19)	my trustees shall not be liable for depreciation in value of the property in my estate, nor for omissions or errors in judgement, or for neglect in management, nor for insolvency of debtors, nor for the acts, omissions, neglects or defaults of each other or of any agent employed by them.
No apportionment (20)	there shall be no apportionment as between capital or income on any occasion."
(SECOND)	Mrs Brown hereby renounces all legal rights competent to her in respect of legitim or otherwise and accepts the terms set out in the said Trust Disposition and Settlement and in this Deed of variation.
(THIRD)	None of the expenses of these presents shall be paid from the said deceased's estate.
(FOURTH)	The Executors consent to and concur in the provisions hereto which are hereby declared irrevocable.
(FIFTH)	The parties hereto elect and give written notice to the Board of HMRC in terms of Section 142 (2) of the said IHT Act 1984 that Section 142(1) shall retrospectively apply to these presents and the parties hereto do hereby give notice to the Board of HMRC of their intention to have the foregoing variation treated as if it

	had been effected by the said deceased. The parties also give notice in terms of Section 62(7) of the Taxation of Chargeable Gains Act 1992 that Section 62(6) of the said last-mentioned Act shall retrospectively apply to these presents to said Trust Disposition and Settlement of the said deceased.
(SIXTH)	The parties hereto certify that the transfer in respect of which this transaction is made is one which falls within Category L or Category M of the Schedule to the Stamp Duty (Exempt Instruments) Regulations 1987; IN WITNESS WHEREOF these presents are, together with the copy Trust Disposition and Settlement annexed hereto, subscribed as follows: by the said . . .

A.6 DEED OF VARIATION INCORPORATING DISCHARGE OF DESTINATION

This deed of variation incorporates a discharge of a special destination and a discretionary trust, which uses up only that part of the nil rate band which the surviving spouse felt comfortable.

> **DEED OF VARIATION** (incorporating discharge of special destination)relative to estate of the late **FRANKLIN PIERCE** late of Eighteen Alnico Drive, Milngavie 0AZ ("the said deceased")
>
> by
>
> **MRS JEAN JEFFERSON or PIERCE**, widow of the said deceased, residing at Eighteen Alnico Drive, aforesaid, as sole residuary beneficiary ("Mrs Pierce") and as sole Executrix of the said deceased ("the Executrix")
>
> and
>
> **JAMES MADISON MARK PIERCE** residing at Number Eighty three C Bonito Drive, Ducksham G76 0LS, **MRS JOAN LYNN PIERCE or DOWNIE** residing at Flat Three/one Fifteen Prestonpans Avenue, Glasgow G99 99JQ and **CLINTON PAUL PIERCE** residing at Flat One/one, Nine Elbridge Street, Glasgow G88 8BU ("the children of the said deceased.")

WHEREAS
(Primo) The parties to this deed are as designed above. The said deceased died at Glasgow on Seventeenth February in the year Two thousand and five leaving a Trust Disposition and Settlement dated Twenty third October Nineteen hundred and ninety six and registered in the Sheriff Court Books of the Commissariot of North Strathclyde at Paisley on Fourteenth May Two thousand and five ("the Will"). A copy thereof is annexed and signed as relative hereto.

(Secundo) Mrs Pierce was appointed sole executrix in terms of the Will, conform to Confirmation granted by the Sheriff of North Strathclyde at Paisley on 27th May 2005.

(Tertio) The said deceased was survived by Mrs Pierce and by his children; Mrs Pierce is the residuary beneficiary and there are no other legacies.

AND WHEREAS
The Executrix and Mrs Pierce wish to discharge the destination in
Disposition by the said deceased in favour of himself and Mrs Pierce
dated Twenty fifth September and recorded in the Division of the
General Register of Sasines applicable to the County of Renfrew on the
Twenty eighth March both months in the year Two thousand and
CONSIDERING THAT the said deceased and Mrs Pierce were infeft in
ALL and WHOLE the dwelling-house subjects known as Eighteen
Alnico Drive, Ducksham G76 in the Parish of Renfrew and County of
Renfrew being the subjects more particularly described in and disponed
by Feu Charter by Henry Adams Herd in favour of the said deceased
dated Nineteenth and Twenty fourth February and recorded in the
Division of the General Register of Sasines applicable to the County of
Renfrew on fifth March all in the year Nineteen hundred and sixty and
WHEREAS the said last mentioned Disposition contains a survivorship
destination in favour of the survivor of the said deceased and Mrs Pierce
AND CONSIDERING that we, the Executrix in right to said interest of
the said deceased and the said Mrs Pierce **HEREBY AGREE and
CONFIRM** that the said survivorship destination should be evacuated
THEREFORE We HEREBY EVACUATE the aforementioned destination to the effect that the subjects hereinbefore described will be held by
us to the extent of a one-half share by the said deceased, (husband) and
the remaining one-half share by the said Mrs Pierce (wife) and **WE
HEREBY AGREE** and DECLARE that either of us the Executrix or Mrs
Pierce shall be entitled to dispone and convey the respective one-half
share in the subjects by way of *inter vivos* or *mortis causa* Deed; and it is
hereby certified that this instrument falls within Category L in the Stamp
Duty (Exempt Instruments) Regulations 1987.

NOW THEREFORE
Mrs Pierce and James Madison Mark Pearce, Mrs Joan Lynn Pierce or
Downie and Clinton Paul Pierce are all of full legal capacity and are the
only persons whose rights are, in terms of either the Will or by Legal
Rights on succession, being varied herewith. Having read the Will of the
said deceased and being of age and sound mind and having been advised
that they are entitled to seek independent legal advice have either done
so or elected not to do so and wish to vary the distribution of the estate
laid down by the Will by Deed of variation under Section 142 of the
Inheritance Tax Act 1984 and Section 62(7) Taxation of Chargeable
Gains Act 1979 as follows: NOW **THEREFORE THE PARTIES
AGREE**:

(FIRST) the Will is hereby varied by the insertion of the following
clause:

> I direct my Executrix (*Primo*) to make payment of a legacy, free of
> all government duties and taxes and without payment of interest, as
> soon as convenient to my executrix, to my children **JAMES
> MADISON MARK PIERCE** residing at Number Eighty three C
> Bonito Drive, Ducksham G76, **MRS JOAN LYNN PIERCE or
> DOWNIE** residing at Flat Three/one, Fifteen Prestonpans Avenue,
> Glasgow G99 9JQ and **CLINTON PAUL PIERCE** residing at Flat

One/one, Nine Elbridge Street, Glasgow G88 8BU of **NINETEEN THOUSAND FIVE HUNDRED POUNDS (19,500.00) STERLING** equally among them, declaring that issue shall be expressly excluded and (*Secundo*) to make over free of all government duties and taxes and the expenses of delivery, to my children, the said James Madison Mark Pearce, Mrs Joan Lynn Pierce or Downie and Clinton Paul Pierce my motor vehicle Volkswagen 2.SE registration number AE99 equally among them; declaring that issue shall be expressly excluded and (Tertio I appoint my wife, the said Mrs **JEAN JEFFERSON or PIERCE** residing at Eighteen Alnico Drive aforesaid, and my son, the said James Madison Mark Pearce and **HAROLD TRUMAN**, residing at Number Fifty Aaron Gardens, Rutherglen to be my Trustees and I direct my Trustees to hold the following, *videlicet*: **ONE THOUSAND POUNDS (£1,000) STER- LING**, All and Whole a one half share of Eighteen Alnico Drive, Milngavie, 2589 British American Tobacco ordinary shares of 25p, 60 Zurich Financial Services share of CHF6.50, 986 Barclays plc ordinary shares of 25p, 995.87 Marks & Spencer plc UK 100 Companies Fund Accumulation units, 14821.0870 Woolwich UK Stockmarket Fund ACC PEP units , 4414.3550 Woolwich UK Stockmarket Fund ACC ISA units all of which shall be hereafter referred to as "the Discretionary Fund" for such one or more of (One) my wife, the said Mrs Jean Jefferson or Pierce, (Two) my issue, including adopted issue (Three) any person who is or was a spouse of any such issue and (Four) any Trust established by any person for the benefit (whether an income or a capital or a discretionary nature of any one or more of the foregoing persons (all of whom are referred to as "the beneficiaries") and in such share or shares in proportions as my Trustees may by Minute or Minutes at any time or times within two years my wife's death, determine, Declaring:

- that my Trustees may by such minute or minutes grant legacies, shares of residue, interests in income or prospec- tive or contingent interests of any kind in the whole or any part or parts of the Discretionary Fund subject to such provisions as they may determine, including but without prejudice to the foregoing generality provisions as to the accumulation of income, the vesting of capital in any beneficiary, the granting to any beneficiary or any other person of powers to appoint rights to income or capital, and the continuation of their discretionary powers;
- that my Trustees may renounce for themselves and their successors in office the power to exercise any of the foregoing powers as if the same were vested in them beneficially and not as trustees;
- that until the expiry of the period of two years from the date of my wife's death, or until the date or dates when any such determination or determinations take effect or the power to make a determination is renounced by them, my Trustees shall pay and apply the whole of the income of the Discretionary Fund without any apportionment

being made to or for behoof of any or more of the beneficiaries in such shares or proportions and in such manner as they may determine with power during the said period or until the said date or dates to accumulate the income for twenty one years; and

- that in the event of my Trustees having failed to make a determination taking effect in relation to the whole or any part of the residue before the expiry of two years from the date of my wife's death or having renounced the power to make such a determination they shall on and from the expiry of the said period or the date of such renunciation hold the whole or such part of the Discretionary Fund as part of the residue of my estate as if my wife had predeceased me.

My Discretionary Fund Trustees shall have the fullest powers of and in regard to retention, realisation, investment, appropriation, transfer of property without realisation, and management of my estate as if they were absolute beneficial owners; and shall have power to do everything they may consider necessary or expedient for the administration of the trust; and in particular and without prejudice to these general powers my Discretionary Fund Trustees shall have power; and in particular and without prejudice to the foregoing generality the conditions an powers specified and contained in the Schedule annexed and signed as relative hereto shall apply to the administration of my estate and the trusts herein, in so far as not inconsistent with the provisions hereof.

(SECOND) Mrs Pierce, James Madison Mark Pearce, Mrs Joan Lynn Pierce or Downie and Clinton Paul Piece, hereby renounce all legal rights competent to them in respect of *jus relictae legitim*, or otherwise and accept the terms set out in the Will and in this Deed of variation.

(THIRD) None of the expenses of these presents shall be paid from the said deceased's estate.

(FOURTH) The executrix consents to and concurs in the provisions hereof, which are hereby declared irrevocable.

(FIFTH) The parties hereto elect and give written notice to Her Majesty's Revenue & Customs in terms of Section 142(2) of the said Inheritance Tax Act 1984 that Section 142(1) shall retrospectively apply to these presents and the parties hereto do hereby give notice to Her Majesty's Revenue & Customs of their intention to have the foregoing variation treated as if it had been effected by the said deceased. The parties also give notice in terms of Section 62(7) Taxation of Chargeable Gains Act 1992 that Section 62(6) of said last mentioned Act shall retrospectively apply to these presents and the parties hereto do hereby give notice to the Her Majesty's Revenue & Customs of their intention to have the foregoing variation treated as if it had been effected by the said deceased IN WITNESS WHEREOF these presents, consisting of this and the preceding four pages are together with said copy trust disposition and settlement and said schedule both hereto annexed, subscribed as follows, *videlicet*.

A.7 STYLE OF DISPOSITION INCORPORATING SALE OF ONE-HALF SHARE OF
HOUSE BY TRUSTEES TO SURVIVING SPOUSE

DRAFT

DISPOSITION

by

**THE EXECUTOR OF THE LATE FRANKLIN PIERCE and MRS
JEAN JEFFERSON or PIERCE in favour of**

MRS JEAN JEFFERSON or PIERCE

One half *pro indiviso* share of 18 Alnico Drive, Milngavie

Cheatham and Steele, 134 Frederick Street, Glasgow Gx 4xx
FAS: 0000

I, MRS JEAN JEFFERSON or PIERCE residing at Number Eighteen Alnico Drive, Milngavie, Executrix nominate of my husband, the late **FRANKLIN PIERCE** , residing at Number Eighteen Alnico Drive, aforesaid ("the said deceased"), conform to Confirmation granted by the Sheriff of North Strathclyde at Paisley on Twenty seventh May Two thousand and five and as Trustee acting under the Trust Disposition and Settlement of the said deceased, dated Twenty third October Nineteen hundred and ninety six and recorded in the Court Books of the Commissariot of North Strathclyde at paisley on Fourteenth day of May in the year Two thousand and five CONSIDERING (Primo) in terms of his said Trust Disposition and Settlement, the said deceased appointed me his sole Trustee and Executor and his sole beneficiary; (Secundo) that I as an individual am infeft in *inter alia* the subjects hereinafter mentioned by Disposition by the said Franklin Pierce in favour of himself and in my favour dated Twenty fifth September and recorded in the Division of the General Register of Sasines applicable to the County of Rendfew on Twenty seventh day of October both in the year Two thousand; (TERTIO) that by Deed of Variation by me as an individual and as Executrix foresaid and by **JAMES MADISON MARK PIERCE**, residing at Number Eighty three C Bonito Drive, Ducksham, Glasgow G00 0l0, **MRS JOAN LYNN PIERCE or DOWNIE**, residing at Flat Three/one, Number Fifteen Prestonpans Avenue, Glasgow G99 7XX and **CLINTON PAUL PIERCE**, residing at Flat One/one, Number Nine Elbridge Street, Glasgow G88 0BU, dated Eighth and Ninth June and recorded in the Division of the General Register of Sasines applicable to the County of Renfrew for preservation and in the Books of Council and Session for preservation and execution on the eleventh July in the year Two thousand and six, the said survivorship destination was discharged; (Quarto) in said Deed of Variation it was also provided that the subjects hereinafter mentioned should be conveyed in favour of myself, the said Mrs Jean Jefferson or Pierce, the said James Madison Mark Pierce and **HAROLD TRUMAN**, residing at Number Fifty Aaron Gardens, Rutherglen as Discretionary Fund Trustees of the late Franklin Pierce; (Quinto) that the said Trustees have sold the subjects to me IN CONSIDERATION of the price of **ONE HUNDRED THOUSAND POUNDS (£100,000) STERLING** of which they, as evidenced by their signatures hereto, hereby acknowledge receipt and discharge me, **HAVE SOLD** and Do Hereby with the consent and concurrence of me the said, Mrs Jean Jefferson or Pierce as an individual and as Executor foresaid and the said James Madison Mark Pierce, the said Mrs Joan Lynn Pierce or Downie and the said Clinton Paul Pierce, for all right, title and interest in and to the subjects hereby disponed, dispone to and in favour of me, the said Mrs Jean Jefferson or Pierce and to my executors, assignees and disponees, whomsoever heritably and irredeemably ALL and WHOLE a one half *pro indiviso* share in ALL and WHOLE the dwelling-house subjects known as Number Eighteen Alnico Drive, Crowsham, Renfrewshire, in the Parish of Crowsham and County of Renfrew and being the subjects more particularly described in and disponed by Feu Charter by Henry Adams Herd with consent therein mentioned in favour of the late Franklin Pierce dated Nineteenth and Twenty fourth February and recorded in the said Division of the General Register of Sasines on Tenth March all in the year Nineteen hundred and sixty; Together with the dwelling-house and all other erections therein and thereon, the heritable fittings and fixtures therein and thereon, the parts, privileges and pertinents thereof, all necessary rights of access and egress therefrom and thereto and the whole right, title and interest, present and future therein foresaid of me, the said Mrs Jean Jefferson or Pierce as Executrix foresaid and as an individual and the said James Madison Mark Pierce, the said Mrs Joan Lynn Pierce or Downie and the said Clinton Paul Pierce and of the said Trustees, namely, me the said Mrs Jean Jefferson or Pierce, the said James Madison Mark Pierce, and the said Harold Truman; together also with a right of property in common with (First) Henry Adams Herd and his successors as proprietors of the remainder of the whole subjects (of which the subjects hereby disponed form part) in said Parish and County described and disponed in Disposition by John Taylor (Greenock) Limited in favour of the Henry Adams Herd dated Twenty eighth and recorded in the said Division of the General Register of Sasines on Thirtieth both days of October, Nineteen hundred and fifty nine and (Second) Elizabeth Semple and Williamina Semple and their successors as proprietors of the plot of ground extending to One thousand, three hundred and thirty seven square yards and seven ninth parts of a square yard or thereby in said Parish and County, described in Disposition by the said John Taylor (Giffnock) Limited in favour of the said Elizabeth Semple and Williamina Semple dated Twenty ninth May and Sixth June and recorded in the said Division of the General Register of Sasines on Eighth June all in the year Nineteen hundred and fifty nine, to those parts of the carriageway and footpath of Alnico Drive aforesaid shown hatched green on the said plan and also on the plan annexed to the said Disposition in favour of the said Elizabeth Semple and Williamina Semple dated and recorded as aforesaid; But the subjects hereby disponed are so disponed always with and under in so far as still subsisting and applicable thereto, the whole burdens, reservations, reservations of minerals, conditions and others specified in (FIRST) Feu Charter by Margaret Nicol or Sturrock in favour of William Thompson, dated Twenty seventh September and recorded in the said Division of the General Register of Sasines on the Third day of October both Nineteen hundred and thirty three and registered in the Books of Council and Session on the Tenth day of January Nineteen hundred and fifty (SECOND) Disposition by George Leslie Christie as Trustee therein and with consents therein mentioned, in favour of the said John Taylor (Giffnock) Limited dated Eleventh January and subsequent dates and recorded in the said Division of the General Register of Sasines on the Seventh February all in the year Nineteen hundred and fifty and (THIRD) said Feu Charter by Henry Adams Herd with consent therein mentioned in favour of the said Ronald Girvan Pierce dated and recorded as aforesaid; WITH ENTRY as at the last date hereof; Which subjects were last vested in the said the late Franklin Pierce as aforesaid and from whom I as Executrix foresaid acquire right by said Trust Disposition and Settlement and said Confirmation; And I the said, Mrs Jean Jefferson or Pierce as Executrix foresaid, grant warrandice from my own facts and deeds only and bind the estate and in so far as I can competently do so, the beneficiaries interested therein, in absolute warrandice; And we, the said Mrs Jean Jefferson or Pierce, as an

individual and the said James Madison Mark Pierce, the said Mrs
Beverley Lynn Pierce or Downie and the said Gregor Paul Pierce grant
warrandice from my and their own facts and deeds only; And the said
Mrs Jean Jefferson or Pierce, the said James Madison Mark Pierce and
the said Harold Truman as Trustees foresaid grant warrandice in favour
of me, the said Mrs Jean Jefferson or Pierce; And we, the parties hereto,
all hereby confirm and declare that in as much as we remain infeft or
entitled to the subjects hereby disponed, despite the delivery of this
Disposition, we hold the same in trust for the purchaser and her
successors and subject to their directions until registration of the subjects
in the Land Register of Scotland is effected without exclusion of
indemnity; And we hereby certify that the transaction hereby effected
does not form part of a larger transaction or of a series of transactions in
respect of which the amount or value or the aggregate amount or value
of the consideration exceeds **ONE HUNDRED AND FIFTY THOU-
SAND POUNDS (£150,000) STERLING:** IN WITNESS WHEREOF

A1.8 Style of Standard Security Over One-half Pro-indiviso Share
By surviving spouse

I, MRS JEAN JEFFERSON or PIERCE residing at Number Eighteen Alnico Drive, Milngavie **IN**, security of all advances and other sums due and that may become due by me to me the said Mrs Jean Jefferson or Pierce **JAMES MADISON MARK PIERCE**, residing at Number Eighty three C Bonito Drive, Ducksham, Glasgow G00 0l0 and **HAROLD TRUMAN**, residing at Number Fifty Aaron Gardens, Rutherglen as Discretionary Fund Trustees of the late Franklin Pierce; ("the said trustees") acting under his Trust Disposition and Settlement of the said deceased, dated Twenty third October Nineteen hundred and ninety six and recorded in the Court Books of the Commissariot of North Strathclyde at Paisley on Fourteenth day of May in the year Two thousand and five as varied by Deed of Variation by me and others, dated Eighth and Ninth June and recorded in the Division of the General Register of Sasines applicable to the County of Renfrew for preservation and in the Books of Council and Session for preservation and execution on the eleventh July in the year Two thousand and six, in connection with the property belonging to me at Number Eighteen Alnico Drive, Crowsham, Renfrewshire in terms of personal bond by me in favour of the said trustees of even date with these presents (hereinafter called "the Personal Bond") grant a Standard Security in favour of the said trustees over ALL and WHOLE a one half *pro indiviso* share in ALL and WHOLE the dwelling-house subjects known as Number Eighteen Alnico Drive, Crowsham, Renfrewshire, in the Parish of Crowsham and County of Renfrew and being the subjects more particularly described in and disponed by Feu Charter by Henry Adams Herd with consent therein mentioned in favour of the late Franklin Pierce dated Nineteenth and Twenty fourth February and recorded in the said Division of the General Register of Sasines on Tenth March all in the year Nineteen hundred and sixty; the standard conditions specified in Schedule Three to the Conveyancing and Feudal Reform (Scotland) Act 1970 and any lawful variation thereof operative for the time being shall apply; And I agree that the standard conditions shall be varied in accordance with the Personal Bond and I grant warrandice And I consent to registration hereof for preservation and execution: IN WITNESS WHEREOF

A.9 Old Fashioned Trust Disposition and Settlement[1]

I, **ANDREW JOHNSON**, residing at Number Forty Three King Street, Milngavie, for the settlement of the succession to my means and estate after my death do hereby DISPONE and ASSIGN to my wife, **MRS JEAN BROWN or JOHNSON**, and my brother, **FREDERICK THOMAS JOHNSON** residing at Number Two William Street, Milngavie, and the survivors and survivor and the heir of the survivor as my TRUSTEES for the purposes aftermentioned (the major number from time to time acting and resident in Great Britain being a quorum and the power of any Trustee to act being suspended during absence from Great Britain) and to the assignees of my Trustees ALL and SUNDRY the whole means and estate, heritable and moveable, real and personal, of every description and wherever situate, that may belong to me at my death; And further I nominate my Trustees and their quorum foresaid to be my sole EXECUTORS and also to be Tutors and Curators to any beneficiaries who may be in nonage after my death; But these presents are granted IN TRUST for the purposes following, namely: IN THE FIRST PLACE for payment of my just and lawful debts, sickbed and funeral expenses, and the expenses of this Trust; IN THE SECOND PLACE for payment or delivery of such legacies and fulfilment of such instructions as I may leave by any writing under my hand however informal if indicative of my intention and that free of all death duties unless otherwise stipulated; IN THE THIRD PLACE for payment to my wife Mrs Jean Brown or Johnson so soon as convenient to my Trustees after my death of a legacy of Two thousand five hundred pounds and that free of all death duties but without interest; IN THE FOURTH PLACE I direct my Trustees to pay to or for behoof of my said wife if and so long as she shall survive me the free annual income of the residue of my said means and estate and that as a strictly alimentary provision not capable of anticipation nor affectable by her debts or deeds DECLARING that should the foresaid liferent provision be in the opinion of my Trustees insufficient at any time for the comfortable maintenance of my said wife my Trustees shall have full power to pay to or for behoof of my said wife along with the free annual income of the said residue such parts of the capital thereof from time to time as they in their discretion shall consider proper; And with respect to the foregoing liferent provision I direct that (notwithstanding any law or practice to the contrary) my Trustees shall include in the income falling to the liferentrix all dividends interest and other income actually received by my Trustees in respect of the liferented estate during the subsistence of the liferent (including income accrued on estate at my death or when acquired by my Trustees) and shall exclude from the income falling to the liferentrix all other dividends interest and other income (including income comprehended in

---

[1] This style of trust disposition, i.e. will was virtually standard. It had many advantages, mainly flexibility, for drafters but has now been largely abandoned in favour of a will in the indirect form. It is considered that, consisting of virtually one sentence, it is difficult for the lay reader to understand. The modern method is to have paragraphs or numbered headings so that the lay reader can make out the provisions without having to "plough" through the whole deed!

the prices received for liferented estate that may be sold during the liferent and income accrued on the liferented estate at the termination of the liferent) and that in the case of each item of income without apportionment and without reference to the source from which or the period during or in respect of which such item of income may have accrued or may be received; DECLARING that the apportionment or allocations of income that may be made by my Trustees in fulfilment of the foregoing directions shall be final and binding on all concerned; AND IN THE LAST PLACE on the termination or annulment from any cause whatever of the foresaid liferent provision in favour of my said wife should she survive me or on my own death should she predecease me, I direct my Trustees to hold, apply, pay or convey the residue of my said means and estate or the balance thereof then remaining to or for behoof of my children equally among them and the survivors and survivor of them jointly with the lawful issue of any of them who may have predeceased leaving issue (the issue of a predecessor taking equally among themselves the share original and accrescing which would have fallen to their parent if in life); AND TO PREVENT DOUBTS I declare that the share or interest of each beneficiary hereunder or under any Codicils hereto shall vest only when and to the extent that the same may from time to time be set free by the termination or annulment from any cause of any liferent provision affecting the same should the liferentor survive me or in any other case at my own death; And I declare that where any part of my said means and estate shall fall to a minor beneficiary my Trustees shall have full power either to pay or apply the whole or any part of the income or capital falling to such beneficiary for his or her behoof during minority in such way and manner as my Trustees in their discretion may think proper or to retain the same until majority accumulating income with capital; And the provisions herein contained in favour of my said wife shall be in lieu and in full of all terce, *jus relictae* and other legal rights and claims competent to her by and through my death; And to enable my Trustees to carry out the purposes of this Settlement and of any Codicils hereto I confer upon them the FULLEST POWERS including (without prejudice to the foregoing generality) POWER to SELL and REALISE my said means and estate by public roup or private bargain on such terms and conditions as my Trustees may think proper; And I provide that my Trustees shall be entitled to sell to any of the beneficiaries in my said means and estate (notwithstanding that such beneficiary may be a Trustee hereunder) my heritable property known as The Chesters, Truman Road, Milngavie together with the household furniture and plenishing therein and the farm stock and implements and that at the values upon which the estate duty due with reference to my death is settled or on such other terms and conditions as they may think proper; POWER to grant LEASES of the whole or any part of my heritable or real estate for such periods and rents and on such conditions as my Trustees may think proper as also to grant abatements of rent, temporary or permanent, and to accept renunciations of Leases; POWER to BORROW money on the security of my said means and estate or any part thereof to such extent as my Trustees may think proper; POWER to COMPROMISE or settle by arbitration or by the advice of Counsel or in their own discretion all claims competent to or against the Trust, and to take part for the whole or any such claims; POWER to purchase heritage in Scotland; POWER (but without prejudice to the Statutory powers of investment present and future of gratuitous Trustees) in their discretion to continue to hold or to renew, for such time or times as they may think proper or indefinitely, all or any of the INVESTMENTS of any kind or nature and however doubtful and hazardous which may be held by me at my death either at home or abroad (including shares or other investments held by me in Roosevelt and Company Limited) and that whether or not the same be of the nature authorised or permitted by the powers before written or referred to and to INVEST my said means and estate in any such investments and in any other investments and in any other way they may think fit and all as absolutely in the discretion of my Trustees as if they were beneficial owners instead of Trustees, and without my Trustees being in any way liable for any loss to the Trust Estate from depreciation or otherwise which may arise through their so continuing to hold or so making such investments; And POWER to APPOINT any of their own number or any other person to be Factor or Law Agent for the management of the Trust and to allow him or them the usual remuneration for services rendered; And for the encouragement of my Trustees, I declare that they shall be entitled (notwithstanding that they may be also beneficiaries) to the fullest powers, PRIVILEGES and immunities conferred by law on or competent to gratuitous Trustees in Scotland, according to the most liberal interpretation, including power to resign office; and particularly (but without prejudice to the foregoing generality) I declare that it shall not be incumbent on them *qua* Tutors and Curators to give up Inventories; nor shall they be obliged to do any other diligence than to them shall seem proper; nor shall they be liable that the investments made by way of purchase shall yield or realise the sums paid for such investments, nor shall they be liable for the intromissions of any Factor to be appointed by them, nor for the securities on which they may lend out the Trust Funds, provided the said Factor and the said securities were reputed sufficient at the time, nor shall they be liable for omissions nor for one another, but each for his own actual intromissions only; And parties TRANSACTING with my Trustees shall have no concern or right to inquire into the application of the sums paid by them to my Trustees but shall be sufficiently exonerated and discharged by the writs granted by my Trustees; And I REVOKE all former Wills or Settlements made by me; And I RESERVE full power to revoke these presents; And I CONSENT to registration hereof for preservation: IN WITNESS WHEREOF

A.10 DEED OF ASSUMPTION

WE, MRS THOMASINA BLACK or WHITE residing at, Fifty Knave Street, Cardross and JEBADIAH GREEN, residing at Seventeen Kenner Avenue, North Mount Vernon, Glasgow, the original Trustees appointed by and acting under Deed of Trust by me, the said Mrs Thomasina Black or White dated Ninth and registered in the Books of Council and Session on Twenty first both days of January in the year Nineteen hundred and Ninety five ("Mrs Thommie White Charitable Trustees") Do Hereby ASSUME MRS DAVINA INDIGO, Chartered Accountant, residing at Eight Hockeyield Lane, Renfrew to be a Trustee under said Deed of Trust and we DISPONE and CONVEY to ourselves and to the said Mrs Davina Indigo as Trustees under the said Deed of Trust and to the survivors and survivor of us and to the executor of the survivor ALL and SUNDRY the whole Trust Estate and effects, heritable and moveable, real and personal of every description and wherever situated at present belonging to us or under our control as Trustees under the said Deed of Trust; Together with the whole vouchers, title and Instructions thereof; And I, the said Mrs Davina Indigo, hereby accept the office as Trustee foresaid; And we all consent to registration hereof for preservation: And we all hereby certify that this Deed falls within category A in the Schedule to the Stamp Duty (Exempt Instruments) Regulations 1987. IN WITNESS WHEREOF

A.11 Discharge by Beneficiary

I, MRS MARGARET SHERMAN or COOLIDGE, residing at Twenty one White Court, Glasgow CONSIDERING THAT the deceased CHARLES FAIRBANKS who resided at Fifteen Sleet Crescent, Glasgow and who died on First February Nineteen hundred and ninety nine, by his Settlement dated Eighteenth September Nineteen hundred and ninety one as amended, and Codicil dated Ninth December Nineteen hundred and ninety four *inter alia* bequeathed to me his dwelling-house at Fifteen Windhill Crescent aforesaid together with whole furniture and furnishings thereof, the sum of Two thousand pounds and the residue of his means and estate and appointed as his Executors, me, the said Mrs Margaret Sherman or Coolidge, his granddaughter MISS ELEANOR WATSON, residing care of Twenty one White Court aforesaid, later at Three Ping Place, Leith and now at Forty Lexington Crescent, Edinburgh (in which Settlement she is named "Miss Julie Watson") (hereinafter referred to as "the Executors"); FURTHER CONSIDERING THAT the Executors have carried out the purposes of the said Settlement as amended and relative Codicil and that there has been prepared an Account of the Intromissions of the Executors with the funds of the estate showing the legacies and to which I the said Mrs Margaret Sherman or Coolidge am entitled as a beneficiary, a copy of which Account has been examined and approved by me as beneficiary foresaid in the said estate; And now seeing that the Executors have paid or transferred or are about to pay or transfer to me as beneficiary foresaid the said legacy and residue; Now therefore I do hereby ratify, approve and confirm the whole accounts, actings, trans-actions and intromissions of the Executors with the said estate and I do hereby for my own right and interest as beneficiary foresaid herby EXONER, ACQUIT AND SIMPLICITER DISCHARGE the Execu-tors and the respective Executors and representatives whomsoever and Messrs Cheatham & Steele, Solicitors, One Main Street, Glasgow as the Law Agents and Factors employed by the Executors of their whole actings, transactions and management in connection with the said estate including any omissions which may be laid at their charge and I as beneficiary foresaid bind myself to free and relieve the Executors and their foresaids of all claims, if any, which may be made against the said estate and of all expenses incurred in connection therewith but that only up to the values transferred or paid to me as aforesaid; And I grant warrandice: IN WITNESS WHEREOF

A.12 Discretionary Trust

Under this form of discretionary trust, the trustees are given an absolute discretion as to capital and income for a very long period amongst a large class of beneficiaries. The deed also contains powers at any time to appoint part of the whole fund on accumulation and maintenance trust if that is thought appropriate; and in the past this power has frequently been used in trusts to advantage. If the truster is English, the vesting date should not be more than 75 years ahead. For Scottish trusts there is no definite limit but 75 years would seem to be appropriate.

I, [*name and designation of settlor*] (hereinafter termed "the settlor"), CONSIDERING that I desire to make provision for the beneficiaries aftermentioned Do Hereby NOMINATE and APPOINT as trustees for the purposes aftermentioned [*names and designations of trustees*] TOGETHER with such other person or persons who may be hereafter appointed or assumed and the acceptor or acceptors, survivor or survivors of them as such trustees (the trustee or trustees for the time being acting hereunder being hereinafter referred to as "the trustees"); And I DIRECT the trustees to hold and administer all funds, property and assets of whatsoever nature which may hereafter at any time and from time to time be paid, conveyed and made over to the trustees hereunder, (the whole funds, property and assets from time to time held by the trustees and all (if any) accumulated income thereon being hereinafter referred to as "the trust estate") in trust for the following purposes and subject to the following provisions, *videlicet*—

1. Name of trust

This trust shall be known as [*name*].

2. Definitions

In this deed, the following terms, where the context so admits, have the following meanings:

(i) subject to the provisions of clauses 5 and 6 hereof, "beneficiaries" and "beneficiary" mean and include all or any one or more of the following persons, namely:- [*names and designations of beneficiaries*].

(ii) "vesting date" means [*date*].

(iii) the headnotes to each clause or sub-clause are for convenient reference only and shall not affect the terms of this deed.

3. Discretionary trusts

Until the vesting date, the trustees shall hold the trust estate on the following trusts, but with and subject to the discretionary powers herein contained, all which discretionary powers may be exercised from time to time and at any time by the trustees in whole or in part as they in their sole discretion may decide, *videlicet*—

(i) Accumulation of income

To accumulate the income arising from time to time on the trust estate, or on any separate fund as hereinafter provided, for the whole period of 21 years from the last date of execution by the Settlor of these presents, or for such lesser period or several periods within the said period of 21 years as the trustees may decide, or such other period during which income may lawfully be accumulated, all such accumulations of income to be added to and thereafter to form part of the capital of the trust estate.

(ii) Payment of income

To pay or apply the income arising from time to time on the trust estate or any part thereof to or for the benefit of any beneficiary to the exclusion of any other beneficiary or beneficiaries, and that at such time and otherwise in such way and manner as the trustees in their uncontrolled discretion may decide.

(iii) Payment of capital

To pay to, or apply for behoof of, any beneficiary, to the exclusion of any other beneficiary or beneficiaries, part or the whole of the capital of the trust estate, notwithstanding that by so doing they may bring this trust to an end before the vesting date.

(iv) Insurance

To effect in their own name as trustees any policy of insurance upon the life of the settlor or of any beneficiary or upon any other life and to apply income or capital of the trust estate in payment of the premiums thereof, the proceeds of any such policy to be held and applied by the trustees as an accretion to the capital of the trust estate.

(v) Power to appoint

By declaration of trust, executed by the trustees, to appoint part or the whole of the capital of the trust estate, notwithstanding that, by so doing, they may bring this trust to an end before the vesting date, as a separate fund to or for the benefit of any beneficiary or beneficiaries, to the exclusion of any other beneficiary or beneficiaries, such beneficiary or beneficiaries to or for whose benefit such appointment is made being referred to in this clause as "the appointee", and in such declaration of trust to make provision for all or any of the purposes following, *videlicet—*

(a) during and within the said period of 21 years referred to in clause 3(i) hereof, for accumulation of income of the separate fund until a specified date or until the happening of a specified event;

(b) For payment of the income of the separate fund to the appointee either (1) at the discretion of the trustees with the like powers and discretions as are contained in clause 3(ii) hereof; or (2) for life or for any lesser period ending on a specified date or on the happening of a specified event and, whether for life or any lesser period, terminable at the discretion of the trustees;

(c) For payment of the capital of the separate fund, with all accumulations of income, if any, on a specified date or on the happening of a specified event or at the discretion of the trustees to the appointee or to any one or more of the beneficiaries;

(d) For the reverting of the capital of the separate fund (with all accumulations of income if any) to the trust estate at a specified date or on the happening of a specified event or at the discretion of the trustees upon which reversion the purposes of the said declaration of trust shall thereupon forthwith determine and the capital of the separate fund shall revert to and form part of and be held by the trustees as an accretion to the trust estate for the purposes hereof.

(vi) Power to resettle

To make over, by way of resettlement, part or the whole of the capital of the trust estate to the trustees acting under any other settlement, whether created by the settlor or any other person, and whether created in Great Britain or abroad, provided that any one or more of the beneficiaries hereunder is or are amongst the beneficiaries for whose benefit such settlement has been made and that no person other than a beneficiary or beneficiaries hereunder may benefit thereunder but declaring that the rights of the beneficiaries under such settlement may be discretionary or contingent or subject to defeasance at the discretion of the trustees thereunder; And it shall be no objection to the exercise of the power hereby conferred on the trustees that the trustees of such other settlement, or some of them, are resident out of Great Britain, or that the proper law of such other settlement is the law of some country other than Scotland or England provided that under such proper law trusts are recognised and administered as nearly as may be according to rules similar to those which apply to Scottish trusts, and being a proper law under which the other settlement would be recognisable, enforceable, irrevocable and would take effect; and declaring for the avoidance of doubt that the trustees shall not have power to resettle part or the whole of the capital of the trust estate in any manner of way by virtue of which any part of the capital or income which is or has been comprised in the trust estate at any time, nor any property derived there-from, shall be payable to or applicable for the benefit of the settlor, or during the lifetime of the settlor for any spouse of the settlor.

(vii) Expenses of administration

To pay the expenses of the trust hereby created, including all government and other duties which may become exigible during the course of administration.

4. Ultimate destination

Subject to the foregoing purposes, the trustees shall hold the trust estate for such of the individual beneficiaries as are living at the vesting date to whom the trustees were empowered to make any discretionary payment under clause 3 hereof, or failing all such individual beneficiaries then for the executors of the last of such beneficiaries to have previously died, or if no such individual beneficiary was ever in life or if any one or more of them or the said executors cannot be traced then and to that extent for any charitable institution or charitable institutions to be selected at the discretion of the trustees.

5. Power of beneficiary to renounce

If any beneficiary, being of full age and *capax*, shall renounce his or her interest hereunder by deed of renunciation and discharge in favour of and intimated to the trustees, such beneficiary shall, forthwith upon such intimation, cease thereafter to be included in the meaning of the terms "beneficiaries" or "beneficiary" for the purposes hereof.

6. Power to exclude beneficiary

The trustees shall have power, by deed executed by the trustees at any time before the vesting date, to declare that any beneficiary or beneficiaries, either as individuals or as a class, shall, from and after a date to be stated in such deed, cease to be a beneficiary or beneficiaries for all the purposes hereof, whereupon from and after such stated date these presents shall be read and construed as if such beneficiary or beneficiaries were no longer included in the meaning of the term "beneficiary" and "beneficiaries" for all the purposes hereof; but shall not exercise this power in such a way that, following on such exercise, there would be no remaining beneficiary then living who is qualified to benefit hereunder.

7. Administrative powers and indemnities

(i) In addition to the statutory and common law powers and immunities of gratuitous trustees in Scotland, and any special powers herein conferred, the trustees shall have the fullest powers of investment, realisation, administration, management and division of the trust estate or any part thereof as if they were the beneficial owners thereof; and, in particular, without prejudice to that generality, the trustees shall have power:

(a) to invest or apply the trust estate or any part thereof in any way whatsoever in which a man of ordinary prudence would invest or apply his own funds including power to borrow or lend with or without security; and to appoint an investment adviser to advise the trustees in respect of the investment of the trust estate with power for the trustees to delegate to such investment adviser discretion to manage the investment of any part or the whole of the trust estate, and to allow any part of the trust estate or documents of title thereto to be registered in the name of and held by any person, firm, corporation or the like as nominee of and for the trustees;

(b) in the implement of any of the purposes hereof or in the exercise of any of the powers hereby conferred and without prejudice to the foregoing provisions, the trustees are specially empowered to apply part or the whole of the capital of the trust estate in the purchase, development, maintenance and management of any real or heritable property or rights, including shooting rights, fishing rights and sporting rights, mines, quarries, mineral rights, agricultural land, woodlands and commercial and industrial land, with or without buildings on any such property; to employ labour in and enter into partnership for the management and development thereof; to construct buildings, carry out other works and provide suitable services; And generally declaring that, if the trustees exercise this power *in bona fide* for any of the purposes hereinbefore contained, they shall be entitled to act in relation to any such property as freely in all respects as any absolute proprietor thereof and, in particular, the trustees shall not be bound to lay out monies under their charge as trustees with a view to appreciation or to the realisation of profit or the earning of income or revenue; And the trustees shall not be personally liable for any loss incurred by them in so acting nor for diminution or depreciation in the value of the asset or in the capital or income of the trust estate resulting from any such actings;

(c) to settle the entitlement of any beneficiary, in part or in whole, by payment in cash or by the transfer of a specific asset or assets to the beneficiary or to the legal guardian of the beneficiary with power to require the beneficiary or any such guardian to accept such asset or assets at such value or estimate of value as the trustees in their uncontrolled discretion shall deem fair and, subject to any of the foregoing provisions, to set apart and appropriate specific investments or assets to represent the whole or any part or parts of the share or shares, prospective or otherwise, of any beneficiary hereunder at such valuation as the trustees may in their sole discretion determine, so that thereafter the particular share or shares shall have the full benefit and the whole risk of the appropriated investments or assets;

(d) to appoint one or more of their number or any director, secretary or other officer of any corporate trustee, or any firm or company or the like in which such a trustee, director, secretary or other officer is a partner, shareholder, employee or the like, as solicitor or accountant or in any other professional capacity to the trustees, at the usual professional remuneration; but excluding from such an appointment the settlor, or any spouse thereof, declaring that neither the settlor, nor any spouse thereof, should in any way ever benefit under this power;

(e) to appoint any one or more trustees resident out of Great Britain; to change the forum of administration of eat any trust hereby created to some other jurisdiction in any part of the world in which trusts are recognised and administered as nearly as may be according to rules similar to those which apply to Scottish trusts, not being a place or jurisdiction under the law of which any of the trusts, powers and provisions herein declared and contained would not be enforceable or capable of being exercised and so taking effect and that by declaration of trust executed by the trustees to that effect; or to carry on the administration of any trust hereby created in some place out of Great Britain.

(ii) Notwithstanding any rule of law to the contrary, it is hereby expressly provided and declared that the trustees shall be entitled to retain, for so long as they think appropriate, any asset acquired by them from the settlor, including the shares of any private company, any business and any heritable property, notwithstanding that a man of ordinary prudence might deem it prudent to sell the same; And, so long as the trustees act in good faith in so doing, no beneficiary hereunder shall have any claim against any trustee who retains any such asset under this power even although, by so retaining the same, a loss results to the trust estate. Should any beneficiary hereunder seek to claim damages from the trustees for breach of trust because of a loss occurring to the trust estate as a result of the exercise by the trustees of this power in good faith, then any such beneficiary so claiming shall immediately forfeit any benefit which he or she would otherwise take or has already taken under this deed, to the extent required to indemnify the trustees against any such claim; and, if the benefit has already been taken, the same shall be repayable to the trustees to the same extent.

(iii) It is hereby expressly provided and declared that any trustee hereunder, other than a sole trustee, may purchase any asset forming part of the trust estate and that the trustees when more than one, but not a sole trustee, may with funds under their charge purchase or otherwise acquire any asset in which they are authorised to invest trust funds hereunder from any one of their number or any beneficiary hereunder and any trustee so transacting as an individual with the trustees shall not be deemed to be *auctor in rem suam*.

(iv) If any beneficiary is an unincorporated association, the receipt of the treasurer for the time being of that association shall be a sufficient discharge to the trustees.

(v) The trustees may pay any sum due to any beneficiary hereunder who is in minority or *incapax* to his or her parent or parents, or legal guardian or guardians, and the receipt of such payee shall be a full and sufficient discharge to the trustees.

(vi) The trustees may from time to time and at any time by a separate deed or deeds renounce irrevocably for themselves and their successors in office the power to exercise any one or more of the powers conferred on them under this clause as if the same were vested in them beneficially and not as trustees, and to determine that such renunciation shall have effect from the last date of execution of these presents by the settlor or the date of the last exercise of any such power, or the date of the deed, as the trustees in their sole discretion shall determine.

(vii) Every discretion or power conferred on the trustees shall be an absolute and uncontrolled discretion or power and no trustee shall be held liable for any loss or damage occurring as a result of his concurring or refusing or failing to concur in the exercise of any such discretion or power.

(viii) No trustee shall be liable for any loss arising by reason of any improper investment made in good faith, or for the negligence or fraud of any agent employed by the trustees, or by reason of any mistake or omission made in good faith by any trustee or by reason of any act or thing done or omitted to be done in pursuance of any determination of the trustees under these presents notwithstanding that such determination may subsequently be held to have been wrongly made, or by reason of any other matter or thing except wilful and individual fraud or wrongdoing on the part of the trustee who is sought to be made so liable.

8. Exclusion of settlor

It is hereby expressly provided and declared that-no discretion nor power herein conferred on the trustees shall be exercised, and no provision of these presents shall operate, so as to permit or cause any part of the capital or income of the trust estate, nor any property derived therefrom, to become payable to or applicable for the benefit of the settlor, or during the lifetime of the settlor, for any spouse of the settlor.

9. Irrevocability and proper law

These presents and the trusts hereby created shall be irrevocable, and shall be construed, governed by and administered according to the law of Scotland: IN WITNESS WHEREOF

A.13 DEED OF ASSUMPTION AND CONVEYANCE

1. In this deed, the expressions set out below in Column one shall have the meaning and effect respectively set opposite them in Column two, namely—

    Column one   Column two

    (1)   The present trustees:
    (2)   The trust deed:
    (3)   The new trustees:

2. The present trustees as trustees under the trust deed do hereby assume the new trustees as trustees thereunder; and do hereby dispone and convey to the present trustees and the new trustees jointly as trustees foresaid and to the survivors and survivor of them ALL and Sundry the whole trust estate and effects, heritable and moveable, real and personal, of whatever description and wherever situated presently belonging to or under the control of the present trustees as trustees foresaid, together with the whole vouchers, titles and instructions thereof.

3. The new trustees hereby accept office as trustees under the trust deed.

4. The parties hereto hereby certify that this deed falls within Category A in the Schedule to the Stamp Duty (Exempt Instruments) Regulations 1987.

5. In the foregoing deed, where the context so admits, the singular includes the plural and *vice versa*: IN WITNESS WHEREOF

A.14 Deed of Assumption and Conveyance Incorporating Resignation

1. In this deed, the expressions set out below in Column one shall have the meaning and effect respectively set opposite them in Column two, namely—

    Column one   Column two

    (1)   The present trustees

    (2)   The trust deed

    (3)   The new trustees

    (4)   The resigning trustees

2. The present trustees as trustees under the trust deed Do Hereby assume the new trustees as trustees thereunder; and Do Hereby Dispone and Convey to the present trustees and the new trustees jointly as trustees foresaid and to the survivors and survivor of them All and Sundry the whole trust estate and effects, heritable and moveable, real and personal, of whatever description and wherever situated presently belonging to or under the control of the present trustees as trustees foresaid, together with the whole vouchers, titles and instructions thereof.

3. The new trustees hereby accept office as trustees under the trust deed.

4. The resigning trustees hereby resign office as trustees under the trust deed.

5. The remaining trustees accept intimation of the foregoing resignation.

6. The parties hereto hereby certify that this deed falls within category A in the Schedule to the Stamp Duty (Exempt Instruments) Regulations 1987.

7. In the foregoing deed, where the context so admits, the singular includes the plural and vice versa: IN WITNESS WHEREOF

A.15 Style of informal letter to trustees

15 Adlai Street

Drymen

To my trustees
In view of my failing health and since I may not always be available and
wished to set down some matters relating to the trust which may be of
assistance to you. I have set up this trust not because of any wish to
disinherit any one but because I wish to make provision for my wife in
the event of her not having sufficient to live on. I also wished to make
provision for my son Tam who, because of his unfortunate problems with
alcohol, is not really to be trusted with money. I do not believe I am
exaggerating to say that for him to have access to funds without
supervision would be fatal.
I am concerned also about my daughter's forthcoming divorce and am
worried that any funds she receives will find its way into the pockets of
her "ex".

With Kind Regards

Yours ever

. . . .

[*Place*]
[*Date*]

Bibliography

Adler, M. *Clarity for Lawyers—The Use of Plain English in Legal Writing* (The Law Society, 1990).

Barr, A. R., J. M. H. Biggar, A. M. C. Dalgleish and H. J. Stevens *Drafting Wills in Scotland* (Butterworths Ltd, 1994).

Cusine, Professor D. J. *Greens Practice Styles* (W. Green).

Doonan, E. *Drafting* (Cavendish Publishing Ltd, 1995).

Eastway, N., I. Richards and D. Garlick *Tottel's Tax Advisers' Guide to Trusts* (3rd Edn, Tottel, 2005).

Elder, A. H. *Forms of Wills* (W. Green, 1947).

Gowers, Sir E. *The Complete Plain Words* (Her Majesty's Stationery Office, 1986).

Henderson, C. *Candlish Henderson on Vesting.*

Jones, M. and S. Mackintosh *Revenue Law in Scotland* (Butterworths Ltd, 1986).

Kerrigan, J. *Drafting for Succession* (Thomson W. Green, 2004).

Kessler, J. (Q.C.) *Drafting Trusts and Will Trusts—A Modern Approach* (6th Edn, Sweet and Maxwell, London, 2002).

Laidlow, P. *Tolley's Tax Planning for Post-Death Variations* (Tolley, 1993).

Macdonald, D. R. *Succession* (W. Green, 1994).

Meston, Professor M. C., *Scottish Trusts and Succession Service* (W. Green, 2004).

Meston, Professor M. C., *The Succession (Scotland) Act 1964* (W. Green, 1993).

Morley, M. F. *Accounting for Scottish Executries and Trusts* (Law Society of Scotland, 1984).

Munro, M. *Clichés and How to Avoid Them* (Chambers, 2005).

Patrick, H. and A. Ward. *Mental Health (Scotland) Act 1984 and Adults with Incapacity (Scotland) Act 2000* (W. Green, 2001).

Philips, A. *Professional Ethics for Scottish Solicitors* (Butterworths Ltd, 1990).

Reid, K. G. C. and G. L Gretton *Conveyancing* (Avizandum Publishing Ltd, 2006).

Rennie, Professor R., Negligence.

Rennie, R. and D. J. Cusine *The Requirements of Writing* (Butterworths Ltd, 1995).

Scott, C. A. *Trust Accountancy* (Oliver and Boyd, 1950).

Thomson, Prof. J. *Family Law Reform* (W. Green, 2006).

Thurston, J. *Estate Planning for the Middle Income Client* (Tottel, 2005).

University of Glasgow Styles Of Deeds And Practice Notes (The University of Glasgow, 1954).

Ward, A. (with Gordon R Ashton) *Mental Handicap and the Law* (Sweet and Maxwell, 1992).

Ward, A. D. (MBE) *The Power to Act* (Scottish Society for the Mentally Handicapped, 1990).

Wilson, W. A. and A.G.M. Duncan *Trusts, Trustees and Executors* (W. Green, 1995).

Useful Websites

www.journalonline.co.uk
www.bailii.org/
www.lawscot.org.uk/
www.mencap.org.uk
www.nsandi.com
www.hmrc.gov.uk/trusts/
www.plainenglishcampaign.com

Index

Accumulation and discretionary trusts
tax treatment, 3–29
Accumulation and maintenance trusts
beneficiaries, 6–28
changing nature of, 3–32
Finance Act 2006, impact of, 3–06
generally, 6–26A
introduction, 3–30
meaning, 3–31
potentially exempt transfers, 3–09
provisions specific to, 6–29
restrictions on drafting, 4–37—4–43,
    6–26
styles
for grandchildren, 6–31—6–45
with commentary, 6–46—6–60
tax treatment
capital gains tax, 3–37—3–38
income tax, 3–39
inheritance tax, 3–34—3–36
trust funds, 6–30
trustees, 6–27
uses, 3–33
Administration of trusts
deeds of assumption, 7–04
discretionary trusts, 6–21
minutes of meetings, 7–02
running the trust, 7–01
tax issues, 7–03
trustees powers and duties, 5–09, 5–46
Age
uses of trusts, 2–01
Agents, appointment of
trustees powers and duties, 5–09, 5–37
Alimentary liferents
variation of trusts, 8–31
Anti-avoidance legislation
restrictions on drafting, 4–31—4–34
Appearance of deeds
increasing user-friendliness, 4–20
Apportionment
accumulation and maintenance trusts,
    6–42, 6–57
trustees powers and duties, 5–09, 5–30
Appropriation of investments
trustees powers and duties, 5–09, 5–33
Assets
acceptance of additional, 5–09, 5–40
Attorneys
future of trusts, 9–05
setting up trusts, 1–11
Auctor principle
nature of, 4–45
Avoidance of negligence claims *see*
    Negligence

Backletter
style, A.4
Bare trusts
generally, 6–106
income and capital, 6–107
introduction, 6–105
nature of, 3–62
style
basic, 6–108
wealthy truster, 6–109—6–115
tax treatment, 3–62
Beneficiaries
accumulation and maintenance trusts,
    6–28, 6–33, 6–48
discretionary trusts, 6–05, 6–08—6–09,
    6–19—6–20
disablement trusts, 6–97—6–98
introduction, 1–05
liferent trusts, 6–65
payment of income to, 3–25
trustees powers and duties
accommodation for, 5–09, 5–32
loans to, 5–09, 5–31
uses of trusts, 2–01
vested property
restrictions on drafting, 4–30
Bequests
for short periods
anti-avoidance legislation, and, 4–34
redirection of
variation of trusts, 8–22
satisfaction of
trustees powers and duties, 5–09, 5–34
Bereaved minors
trusts for
nature of, 3–64, 6–117
style, 6–118
tax treatment, 3–64
Borrowing
trustees powers and duties, 5–09, 5–22,
    5–24
Business, carrying on of
trustees powers and duties, 5–09, 5–41

Capacity
accumulation and maintenance trusts,
    6–43, 6–58
beneficiaries, 1–05
trustees, 1–03
uses of trusts, 2–01
Capital
accumulation and maintenance trusts,
    6–36, 6–39, 6–41, 6–51, 6–54, 6–56
administration, trusts for, 6–108
bare trusts, and, 6–107
discretionary trusts, 6–17

Capital allowances
liferent trusts, 6–69
Capital gains tax
accumulation and discretionary trusts,
3–29
accumulation and maintenance trusts,
3–37—3–38
bare trusts, 3–62
charitable trusts, 3–58
disabled trusts, 3–55—3–56
discretionary trusts, 3–19—3–21
holdover relief
potentially exempt transfers, 3–09
introduction, 3–07
liferent trusts, 3–46—3–48
offshore trusts, 3–60
variation of trusts, 8–05—8–07, 8–23
Charitable trusts
generally, 6–99
purposes, 6–101
style, 6–102—6–103
tax treatment, 3–58
trustees, 6–100
Charities
alternatives to trusts, 2–09—2–10
Scottish Charity Register, 9–03
trustees investments powers, 9–02
variation of trusts, 8–18
Checklists
avoiding negligence claims, 4–17
style questionnaire, A.1
Child trust fund
nature of, 9–01
Children
trust for bereaved minors
nature of, 3–64, 6–117
style, 6–118
tax treatment, 3–64
trusts for truster's children
anti-avoidance legislation, and, 4–32
Civil partners
legal entitlement of, 4–54
Clients
aims of, 4–28
contact with
avoiding negligence claims, 4–18
Cohabitants
legal entitlement of, 4–54
Companies
family companies
uses of trusts, 2–01
trustees powers and duties, 5–09, 5–27,
5–42
Compromise of claims
trustees powers and duties, 5–09, 5–29
Conflict of interest
trustees powers and duties, 5–09, 5–44
Contingent rights
variation of trusts, 8–32

Debts
administration, trusts for, 6–108

Deed of assumption
style, 7–04, A.10
Deed of trust
style, A.3
Deed of variation *see* **Variation**
Delegation
trustees powers and duties, 5–03, 5–09,
5–35
Destinations *see* **Special destinations**
Disablement trusts
changes to trust tax law, 3–08
generally, 6–95
incapax beneficiaries, 6–97—6–98
tax treatment
capital gains tax, 3–55—3–56
income tax, 3–57
inheritance tax, 3–53—3–54
uses of, 3–52
welfare benefits, 6–96
Discharges
style, A.11
variation of trusts, 8–03, 8–10—8–15,
8–30
Disclaimers
variation of trusts, 8–02, 8–10—8–15,
8–30
Discretion
trustees powers and duties, 5–09, 5–43
Discretionary trusts
beneficiaries, 6–05
family home, 6–03
Finance Act 2006, impact of, 3–06
generally, 6–02
provisions specific to, 6–24
styles
childless truster, 6–06—6–12
long form, 6–14—6–23
truster with children, 6–13
tax treatment
capital gains tax, 3–19—3–21
income tax, 3–22—3–28
inheritance tax, 3–15—3–18
introduction, 3–14
trust funds, 6–25
trustees, 6–04
variation of trusts, 8–20
Dispositions
styles
sale of one half to surviving spouse,
A.7
standard security, A.8
Distributions
discretionary trusts, 3–27
Dividend income
changes to trust tax law, 3–08
Divorce
uses of trusts, 2–01
Domicile
introduction, 1–03
Drafting
Auctor principle, 4–45

Drafting—*cont.*
avoiding claims of negligence
checklists, 4–17
contact with client, 4–18
full particulars, 4–14
introduction, 4–13
letter of engagement, 4–15
reviews, 4–19
styles, 4–17
timescales, 4–16
civil partners, 4–54
clients' aims, 4–28
cohabitants, 4–54
flexibility, 4–53
introduction, 4–01
negligence
avoiding claims, 4–13—4–19
competition, 4–05
duty of care, 4–09
expectations, 4–12
financial services, 4–10
foreign attitudes, effect of, 4–08
introduction, 4–02
Law Society of Scotland, and, 4–06
litigious culture, 4–03
professional indemnity insurance,
4–07
specialisation, 4–04
third parties, 4–11
pre-owned assets tax
calculation of charge, 4–52
excluded transactions, 4–48
exemptions from, 4–49—4–51
intangible property, 4–47
nature of, 4–46
restrictions
accumulations, 4–37—4–43
anti-avoidance legislation, 4–31—4–34
illegal purposes, 4–36
liferents, 4–44
perpetuities, 4–35
vesting in beneficiaries, 4–30
spouses, 4–54
trustees, selection of, 4–29
user-friendliness
appearance, 4–20
plain English, 4–21—4–27
Duty of care
negligent drafting, 4–09

Engagement, letter of
avoiding negligence claims, 4–15
English, use of plain
increasing user-friendliness, 4–21—4–27
Entry tax charge
and see **Taxation of trusts**
introduction of, 3–06
Exit tax charge
and see **Taxation of trusts**
introduction of, 3–06
Expectation
negligent drafting, 4–12

Expenses
accumulation and maintenance trusts,
6–32, 6–47
administration, trusts for, 6–108
discretionary trusts, 6–17
liferent trusts, 3–50, 6–69
trustees powers and duties, 5–09, 5–38

Family home
discretionary trusts, 6–03
Financial services
negligent drafting, 4–10
Flexibility
need for in drafting, 4–53
Forms of deeds
see also Styles
variation of trusts, 8–27—8–28
Full particulars
avoiding negligence claims, 4–14

Gifts
alternatives to trusts, 2–03
gifts with reservations
Finance Act 2006, impact of, 3–06
variation of trusts, 8–17
Grandchildren
liferent trusts, 6–75
style accumulation and maintenance
trust, 6–31—6–45
Guardians, payments to
alternatives to trusts, 2–04

Heritable property
joint property
incapax spouse, 3–70
legacy evacuating special destination,
3–71
special destinations, 3–67—3–69
management of
trustees powers and duties, 5–09, 5–26
High net-worth individuals
discretionary trusts, 3–15
style bare trust, 6–109—6–115
uses of trusts, 2–01
HMRC
notice to
variation of trusts, 8–29
Holdover relief
potentially exempt transfers, 3–09

Illegality
restrictions on drafting, 4–36
Immunities
administration, trusts for, 6–108
bare trusts, 6–115
liferent trusts, 6–79
Incapax beneficiaries
disablement trusts, 6–97—6–98
liferent trusts, 6–69—6–70

Income
  accumulation and maintenance trusts,
     6–34, 6–39, 6–40, 6–50, 654—655
  bare trusts, and, 6–107
  discretionary trusts, 6–17
Income tax
  accumulation and discretionary trusts,
    3–29
  accumulation and maintenance trusts,
    3–39
  administration, trusts for, 6–108
  bare trusts, 3–62
  charitable trusts, 3–58
  disabled trusts, 3–57
  discretionary trusts, 3–22—3–28
  liferent trusts, 3–49
  offshore trusts, 3–61
  variation of trusts, 8–08, 8–24
Indemnities
  to trustees, 5–09, 5–14
Indemnity insurance
  negligent drafting, 4–07
Inheritance tax
  accumulation and maintenance trusts,
    3–34—3–36
  bare trusts, 3–62
  Budget 2006, impact of, 3–05—3–06
  charitable trusts, 3–58
  disabled trusts, 3–53—3–54
  discretionary trusts, 3–15—3–18
  exemptions from POAT charges, and,
    4–50—4–51
  gifts, 3–04
  introduction, 3–03
  liferent trusts, 3–41—3–45
  nil-rate band, 8–11
  pilot trusts, 3–63
  variation of trusts, 8–04, 8–11
Insurance
  discretionary trusts, 6–17
Insurance products
  alternatives to trusts, 2–08
  uses of trusts, 2–01
Intangible property
  pre-owned asset tax, 4–47, 4–52
Investments
  trustees powers and duties, 5–03, 5–09,
    5–20, 5–33
Irrevocability
  discretionary trusts, 6–23
  trusts, of, 5–49

Joint property
  heritable property, 3–67—3–69
  incapax spouse, 3–70
  introduction, 3–66
  legacy evacuating special destination,
    3–71
  moveable property, 3–72

Law Society of Scotland
  negligent drafting, 4–06

Learning disabilities
  alternatives to trusts, 2–10
Legal rights
  variation of trusts, 8–33
Lending
  trustees powers and duties, 5–09,
    5–21—5–22
Letter of engagement
  avoiding negligence claims, 4–14
  style, A.2
Liferent trusts
  beneficiaries, 6–65
  cautionary note, 6–62
  Finance Act 2006, impact of, 3–06
  description of property, 6–63
  generally, 6–61
  potentially exempt transfers, 3–09
  provisions specific to, 6–66
  restrictions on drafting, 4–44
  social security benefits, 3–51
  specific asset, 6–68
  style
    liferent to second wife, 6–81—6–94
    son imprudent with money,
      6–71—6–80
    son who is incapax, 6–69—6–70
  surviving spouses, 3–11
  tax treatment
    capital gains tax, 3–46—3–48
    expenses, 3–50
    income tax, 3–49
    inheritance tax, 3–41—3–45
  termination, 6–74, 6–90
  trustees, 6–64
  uses, 3–40
  vesting, 6–67
Liferents
  alimentary liferents
    variation of trusts, 8–31
Lifetime transfers
  Finance Act 2006, impact of, 3–06

Minors
  trust for bereaved
    nature of, 3–64, 6–117
    style, 6–118
    tax treatment, 3–64
Minutes
  trustees meetings, 7–02
Moveable property
  joint property, 3–72

National Savings
  alternatives to trusts, 2–05
Negligence
  avoiding claims
    checklists, 4–17
    contact with client, 4–18
    full particulars, 4–14
    introduction, 4–13
    letter of engagement, 4–15

Negligence—*cont.*
avoiding claims—*cont.*
reviews, 4–19
styles, 4–17
timescales, 4–16
competition, 4–05
duty of care, 4–09
expectations, 4–12
financial services, 4–10
foreign attitudes, effect of, 4–08
introduction, 4–02
Law Society of Scotland, and, 4–06
litigious culture, 4–03
professional indemnity insurance, 4–07
specialisation, 4–04
third parties, 4–11
Negotiorum gestor
alternatives to trusts, 2–11
Nominees
alternatives to trusts, 2–07
trustees powers and duties, 5–03, 5–09,
5–23
Non-resident trustees
trustees powers and duties, 5–09, 5–45
Notarial execution
requirements, 1–07

Offshore trusts
advantages of, 3–59
deed of variation, 8–07
scope of, 6–104
tax treatment
capital gains tax, 3–60
income tax, 3–61

Parents, payments to
alternatives to trusts, 2–04
Pension schemes
uses of trusts, 2–01
Periodic tax charge
and see **Taxation of trusts**
introduction of, 3–06
Perpetuities
restrictions on drafting, 4–4–35
Personal injury
uses of trusts, 2–01
Pilot trusts
generally, 6–116
tax treatment, 3–63
Plain English, use of
increasing user-friendliness, 4–21—4–27
Policies of assurance
trustees powers and duties, 5–09, 5–25
Post-death interests
liferent trusts, 3–43
Post-death planning *see* **Deeds of variation**
Potentially exempt transfers
changes to tax treatment of, 3–09
Power of attorney
alternatives to trusts, 2–06

Pre-owned assets tax
calculation of charge, 4–52
excluded transactions, 4–48
exemptions from, 4–49—4–51
intangible property, 4–47
nature of, 4–46
Private residence relief
changes to trust tax law, 3–08
Professional indemnity insurance
negligent drafting, 4–07
Proxies
trustees powers and duties, 5–09, 5–28
Public funds
uses of trusts, 2–01
Purchase of estate
discretionary trusts, 6–17
trustees powers and duties, 5–09, 5–18

Quorum of trustees
establishment of, 5–09, 5–12
Quoted shares
revaluation relief
variation of trusts, 8–32

Renunciation
trustees powers and duties, 5–09, 5–48
Requirements of writing
generally, 1–06
notarial execution, 1–07
Resignation
trustees powers and duties, 5–09, 5–36
Retained interests
anti-avoidance legislation, and, 4–33
Revaluation relief
quoted shared
variation of trusts, 8–19
Reviews
avoiding negligence claims, 4–19
Revocable settlements
anti-avoidance legislation, and, 4–33

Sale of estate
discretionary trusts, 6–17
trustees powers and duties, 5–09, 5–17
Scottish law Commission
future of trusts, 9–04
Setting up trusts
attorney, 1–11
generally, 1–10
Short period bequests
anti-avoidance legislation, and, 4–34
Social security benefits
liferent trusts, 3–51
Special destinations
legacies evacuating, 3–71
post-death variation, 8–16
use of, 3–67—3–69
variation of trusts, 8–16
Special powers
trustees powers and duties, 5–51

Spouses
incapax spouse
joint property, 3–70
legal entitlement on death, 4–54
liferent trusts, 3–11
surviving, sale of one half to, A.7
uses of trusts, 2–01
Stamp duty
liability to, 3–65
variation of trusts, 8–09, 8–26
Stamp duty land tax
liability to, 3–65
variation of trusts, 8–09
Standard security
style deed, A.8
Statutory powers
trustees powers and duties
Trustee Act 2000, 5–06
Trustee Investments Act 1961, 5–05
Trusts (Scotland) Act 1921,
5–02—5–03
Trusts (Scotland) Act 1961, 5–04
Styles
accumulation and maintenance trusts
for grandchildren, 6–31—6–45
with commentary, 6–46—6–60
avoiding negligence claims, 4–17
backletter, A.4
bare trusts
administration, 6–108
wealthy truster, 6–109—6–115
bereaved minors, 6–118
charitable trusts, 6–102—6–103
checklist, A.1
deed of assumption, 7–04, A.10
deed of trust, A.3
deed of variation, A.5, A.6
discharge, A.11
discretionary trusts
childless truster, 6–06—6–12
long form, 6–14—6–23
truster with children, 6–13
disposition
sale of one half to surviving spouse,
A.7
standard security, A.8
informal letter to trustees, A.13
letter of engagement, A.2
liferent trusts
liferent to second wife, 6–81—6–94
son imprudent with money,
6–71—6–80
son who is incapax, 6–69—6–70
trust disposition and settlement, A.9

Tax credits
dividend income
changes to trust tax law, 3–08
Tax pools
discretionary trusts, 3–08, 3–26
Tax rate
changes to trust tax law, 3–08

Taxation of trusts
capital gains tax
accumulation and discretionary trusts,
3–29
accumulation and maintenance trusts,
3–37—3–38
bare trusts, 3–62
charitable trusts, 3–58
disabled trusts, 3–55—3–56
discretionary trusts, 3–19—3–21
introduction, 3–07
liferent trusts, 3–46—3–48
offshore trusts, 3–60
common aspects, 3–13
forms to be completed, 7–03
income tax
accumulation and discretionary trusts,
3–29
accumulation and maintenance trusts,
3–39
bare trusts, 3–62
charitable trusts, 3–58
disabled trusts, 3–57
discretionary trusts, 3–22—3–28
liferent trusts, 3–49
offshore trusts, 3–61
inheritance tax
accumulation and maintenance trusts,
3–34—3–36
bare trusts, 3–62
Budget 2006, impact of, 3–05—3–06
charitable trusts, 3–58
disabled trusts, 3–53—3–54
discretionary trusts, 3–15—3–18
gifts, 3–04
introduction, 3–03
liferent trusts, 3–41—3–45
pilot trusts, 3–63
introduction, 3–01—3–02
new trusts, 3–10—3–12
pre-owned assets tax
calculation of charge, 4–52
excluded transactions, 4–48
exemptions from, 4–49—4–51
intangible property, 4–47
nature of, 4–46
potentially exempt transfers, 3–09
recent reforms, 3–08
stamp duty, 3–65
Third parties
negligent drafting, 4–11
Timescales
avoiding negligence claims, 4–16
Trust deeds
format of, 5–52
Trust disposition and settlement
style, A.9
Trust funds
accumulation and maintenance trusts,
6–30
discretionary trusts, 6–25
liferent trusts, 6–69

Trustees
accumulation and maintenance trusts, 6–27
capacity of, 1–03
charitable trusts, 6–100
discharge of, 5–09, 5–15
discretionary trusts, 6–04
firms as, 1–04
indemnity to, 5–09, 5–14
informal letter to, A.13
liferent trusts, 6–64
quorum of, 5–09, 5–12
selection of, 4–29
vesting of interests, 5–09, 5–13
Trustees powers and duties
additional powers, 5–51
administration, trusts for, 6–108
discretionary trusts, 6–12, 6–17
exclusion of benefit, 5–51
general powers
additional assets, acceptance of, 5–09, 5–40
administration, 5–09, 5–46
agents, appointment of, 5–09, 5–37
all-inclusive power, 5–09, 5–39
allocation of, 5–09, 5–16
apportionment, 5–09, 5–30
appropriation of investments, 5–09, 5–33
beneficiaries, accommodation for, 5–09, 5–32
beneficiaries, loans to, 5–09, 5–31
bequests, satisfaction of, 5–09, 5–34
borrowing, 5–09, 5–22, 5–24
business, carrying on of, 5–09, 5–41
change of proper law, 5–09, 5–47
companies, 5–09, 5–27, 5–42
compromise of claims, 5–09, 5–29
conflict of interest, 5–09, 5–44
definitions relating to, 5–10
delegation, 5–03, 5–09, 5–35
discretion, exercise of, 5–09, 5–43
expenses, payment of, 5–09, 5–38
heritable property, management of, 5–09, 5–26
introduction, 5–08
investments, 5–03, 5–09, 5–20
lending, 5–09, 5–21—5–22
nominees, 5–03, 5–09, 5–23
non-resident trustees, 5–09, 5–45
policies of assurance, 5–09, 5–25
proxies, 5–09, 5–28
purchase of trust estate, 5–09, 5–18
renunciation of, 5–09, 5–48
resignation, 5–09, 5–36
retention of estate, 5–09, 5–19
sale of trust estate, 5–09, 5–17
schedule of, 5–09
introduction, 5–01
liferent trusts, 6–78
policy statement, 5–07

Trustees powers and duties—*cont.*
special powers, 5–51
statutory powers under
Trustee Act 2000, 5–06
Trustee Investments Act 1961, 5–05
Trusts (Scotland) Act 1921, 5–02—5–03
Trusts (Scotland) Act 1961, 5–04
Trusts
alternatives to
charities, 2–09—2–10
guardians, payments to, 2–04
insurance products, 2–08
introduction, 2–02
National Savings, 2–05
negotiorum gestor, 2–11
nominees, 2–07
outright gifts, 2–03
powers of attorney, 2–06
beneficiaries *see* **Beneficiaries**
classification of, 1–08
constitution of, 1–09
definitions, 1–02
domicile, 1–03
introduction, 1–01
irrevocability, 5–49
legal requirements, 1–06
notarial execution, 1–07
Scottish law, application of, 5–50
setting up, 1–10—1–11
taxation of *see* **Taxation of trusts**
trustees *see* **Trustees**
types of
and see under individual headings
accumulation and maintenance trusts, 6–26—6–60
bare trusts, 6–105—6–115
bereaved minors, 6–117—6–118
charitable trusts, 6–99—6–103
choosing the correct type, 6–01
disablement trusts, 6–95—6–98
discretionary trusts, 6–02—6–25
liferent trusts, 6–61—6–94
offshore trusts, 6–104
pilot trusts, 6–116
uses, 2–01

User-friendliness
appearance, 4–20
plain English, 4–21—4–27

Variation
alimentary liferents, 8–31
capital gains tax, 8–05—8–07
charities, 8–18
clarification of wills and trusts
capital gains tax, 8–23
effect in practice, 8–25
generally, 8–21
income tax, 8–24
redirection of bequest, 8–22

Variation—*cont.*
contingent rights, 8–32
destinations, 8–16
discharges, and, 8–03
discretionary trusts, 8–20
form of deeds, 8–27—8–28
generally, 8–02
gifts with reservation, 8–17
HMRC, notice to, 8–29
income tax, 8–08
inheritance tax, 8–04
introduction, 8–01
legal rights, 8–33
postponed vesting, 8–32
revaluation relief for quoted shares,
    8–19

Variation—*cont.*
stamp duty, 8–09, 8–26
stamp duty land tax, 8–09
style deed, A.5, A.6
uses of, 8–10—8–15
Vesting
liferent trusts, 6–67
restrictions on drafting, 4–30
trustees powers, 5–09, 5–13
variation of trusts, 8–32
Vulnerability
uses of trusts, 2–01
Welfare benefits
disablement trusts, 6–96U

INSTRUCTION FOR USE OF THE COMPANION CD
Introduction
These notes are provided for guidance only. They should be read and interpreted in the context of your own computer system and operational procedures. It is assumed that you have a basic knowledge of WINDOWS. However, if there is any problem please contact our help line on 020 7393 7266 and they will be happy to help you.

CD Format and Contents
To run this CD you need at least:
IBM compatible PC
CD-ROM drive
Microsoft Word 6.0/95

The CD contains selected files from the appendix of *Styles* in this book. It does not contain software or commentary.

Installation
The following instructions make the assumption that you will copy the data files to a single directory on your hard disk (e.g. C:\Scottish Trusts—Styles).
Open your CD Rom drive, select and double click on setup.exe and follow the instructions. The files will be unzipped to your C drive and you will be able to open them from the new C:\Scottish Trusts—Styles.

LICENCE AGREEMENT
Definitions
1. The following terms will have the following meanings:
"The PUBLISHERS" means W GREEN & SON incorporated in Scotland under the Companies Acts (Registered No. 8894) whose registered office is 21 Alva Street, Edinburgh EH2 4HS, (which expression shall, where the context admits, include the PUBLISHERS' assigns or successors in business as the case may be) of the other part (on behalf of Thomson Legal & Regulatory Europe Limited incorporated in England & Wales under the Companies Acts (Registered No. 1679046) whose registered office is 100 Avenue Road, London NW3 3PF).].
"The LICENSEE' means the purchaser of the work containing the Licensed Material.
"Licensed Material" means the data included on the disk;
"Licence" means a single user licence;
"Computer" means an IBM-PC compatible computer.

Grant of Licence; Back-up Copies
2.(1) The PUBLISHERS hereby grant to the LICENSEE, a non-exclusive, non-transferable licence to use the Licensed Material in accordance with those terms and conditions.
((2) The LICENSEE may install the Licensed Material for use on one computer only at any one time.
(3) The LICENSEE may make one back-up copy of the Licensed Material only, to be kept in the LICENSEE's control and possession.

Proprietary Rights
3.(1) All rights not expressly granted herein are reserved.
(2) The Licensed Material is not sold to the LICENSEE who shall not acquire any right, sale or interest in the Licensed Material or in the media upon which the Licensed Material is supplied.
(3) The LICENSEE, shall not erase, remove, deface or cover any trademark, copyright notice, guarantee or other statement on any media containing the Licensed Material.
(4) The LICENSEE shall only use the Licensed Material in the normal course of its business and shall not use the Licensed Material for the purpose of operating a bureau or similar service or any online service whatsoever.
(5) Permission is hereby granted to LICENSEES who are members of the legal profession (which expression does not include individuals or organisations engaged in the supply of services to the legal profession) to reproduce, transmit and store small quantities of text for the purpose of enabling them to provide legal advice to or to draft documents or conduct proceedings on behalf of their clients.
(6) The LICENSEE shall not sublicense the Licensed Material to others and this Licence Agreement may not be transferred, sublicensed, assigned or otherwise disposed of in whole or in part.
(7) The LICENSEE shall inform the PUBLISHERS on becoming aware of any unauthorised use of the Licensed Material.

Warranties
4.(1) The PUBLISHERS warrant that they have obtained all necessary rights to grant this licence.
(2) Whilst reasonable care is taken to ensure the accuracy and completeness of the Licensed Material supplied, the PUBLISHERS make no representations or warranties, express or implied, that the Licensed Material is free from errors or omissions.
(3) The Licensed Material is supplied to the LICENSEE on an "as is" basis and has not been supplied to meet the LICENSEE's individual requirements. It is the sole responsibility of the LICENSEE to satisfy itself prior to entering this Licence Agreement that the Licensed Material will meet the LICENSEE's requirements and be compatible with the LICENSEE's hardware/software configuration. No failure of any part of the Licensed Material to be suitable for the LICENSEE's requirements will give rise to any claim against the PUBLISHERS.
(4) In the event of any material inherent defects in the physical media on which the licensed material may be supplied, other than caused by accident abuse or misuse by the LICENSEE, the PUBLISHERS will replace the defective original media free of charge provided it is returned to the place of purchase within 90 days of the purchase date. The PUBLISHERS' entire liability and the LICENSEE's exclusive remedy shall be the replacement of such defective media.
(5) Whilst all reasonable care has been taken to exclude computer viruses, no warranty is made that the Licensed Material is virus free. The LICENSEE shall be responsible to ensure that no virus is introduced to any computer or network and shall not hold the PUBLISHERS responsible.
(6) The warranties set out herein are exclusive of and in lieu of all other conditions and warranties, either express or implied, statutory or otherwise.

(7) All other conditions and warranties, either express or implied, statutory or otherwise, which relate in the condition and fitness for any purpose of the Licensed Material are hereby excluded and the PUBLISHERS shall not be liable in contract, delict or in tort for any loss of any kind suffered by reason of any defect in the Licensed Material (whether or not caused by the negligence of the PUBLISHERS).

Limitation of Liability and Indemnity

5.(1) The LICENSEE shall accept sole responsibility for and the PUBLISHERS shall not be liable for the use of the Licensed Material by the LICENSEE, its agents and employees and the LICENSEE shall hold the PUBLISHERS harmless and fully indemnified against any claims, costs, damages, loss and liabilities arising out of any such use.

(2) The PUBLISHERS shall not be liable for any indirect or consequential loss suffered by the LICENSEE (including without limitation loss of profits, goodwill or data) in connection with the Licensed Material howsoever arising.

(3) The PUBLISHERS will have no liability whatsoever for any liability of the LICENSEE to any third party which might arise.

(4) The LICENSEE hereby agrees that

(a)the LICENSEE is best placed to foresee and evaluate any loss that might be suffered in connection with this Licence Agreement,

(b)that the cost of supply of the Licensed Material has been calculated on the basis of the limitations and exclusions contained herein; and

(c)the LICENSEE will effect such insurance as is suitable having regard to the LICENSEE's circumstances.

(5) The aggregate maximum liability of the PUBLISHERS in respect of any direct loss or any other loss (to the extent that such loss is not excluded by this Licence Agreement or otherwise) whether such a claim arises in contract or tort shall not exceed a sum equal to that paid at the price for the title containing the Licensed Material.

Termination

6.(1) In the event of any breach of this Agreement including any violation of any copyright in the Licensed Material, whether held by the PUBLISHERS or others in the Licensed Material, the Licence Agreement shall automatically terminate immediately, without notice and without prejudice to any claim which the PUBLISHERS may have either for moneys due and/or damages and/or otherwise.

(2) Clauses 3 to 5 shall survive the termination for whatsoever reason of this Licence Agreement.

(3) In the event of termination of this Licence Agreement the LICENSEE will remove the Licensed Material.

Miscellaneous

7.(1) Any delay or forbearance by the PUBLISHERS in enforcing any provisions of this License Agreement shall not be construed as a waiver of such provision or an agreement thereafter not to enforce the said provision.

(2) This Licence Agreement shall be governed by the laws of England and Wales. If any difference shall arise between the Parties touching the meaning of this Licence Agreement or the rights and liabilities of the parties thereto, the same shall be referred to arbitration in accordance with the provisions of the Arbitration Act 1996, or any amending or substituting statute for the time being in force.